GAME OF MY LIFE

NEW YORK

YANKEES

GAME OF MY LIFE

NEW YORK

YANKEES

MEMORABLE STORIES OF YANKEES BASEBALL

DAVE BUSCEMA

SPORTS
PUBLISHING

Sports Publishing books may be purchased in bulk at special discounts for sales promotion, corporate gifts, fund-raising, or educational purposes. Special editions can also be created to specifications. For details, contact the Special Sales Department, Sports Publishing, 307 West 36th Street, 11th Floor, New York, NY 10018 or sportspubbooks@skyhorsepublishing.com.

Sports Publishing® is a registered trademark of Skyhorse Publishing, Inc.®, a Delaware corporation.

Visit our website at www.sportspubbooks.com

10 9 8 7 6 5 4 3 2 1

Library of Congress Cataloging-in-Publication Data is available on file.

ISBN: 978-1-61321-206-6

Printed in the United States of America

To my mother, for being stronger than anyone knows.

To my nonnas, for loving me more than I know.

To my father, for teaching me to laugh, work and believe.

*And in memory of my grandfather and Uncle Joe
for endless hours in the backyard and in front of
the television playing and watching games.*

I love baseball because it reminds me of all of you.

Contents

Acknowledgments

Thanks especially to my family and friends across the country for their support, especially Thomas Buscema, whose late-night Internet pep talks helped.

To Gordie Jones, one of the best columnists in Pennsylvania, who provided many valuable late-night feedback sessions via e-mail. To Wayne Lockwood, who can make any writer's copy better and give him a great design to boot. To Wallace Matthews, a tenacious reporter, talented writer and fantastic friend. To Mike Vaccaro, the *New York Post* columnist who proves you can be among the country's best, but not forget the papers you've come from.

To Tracy Vogel, a trusted friend and a writer too humble to recognize her own talent. Ditto Tom Joyce.

To Luis Bravo, my best friend and a constant sounding board, for picking me up during stalled spots. To Manny Bravo, for his enthusiasm and encouragement. To Mike Flick for pushing me to write stronger and inspiring me with his own creativity.

To Patrick Verdi, whose dad, Ron, taught him the game and who taught me to remember the people for whom I'm writing. A part of this book is in honor of his memory, Pat.

To Raymond "Flip" Johnson, who keeps me honest even when he doesn't know it.

To my godmother, Irma Rossi, and Jeannie Murphy for endless support.

Thanks for a great edit to Bob Quinn, one of the best editors I've had because he has the confidence to let me go and the cockiness to rein me in.

To Herb Gluck, who first inspired me through his work on *The Mick: An American Hero*, then became the best mentor a pain in the neck could have. I owe you more than I can express here. but thanks for pushing me so hard. To Jeff Gilbert and Paul Vigna, former bosses who still inspire me.

To Ed Lucas, one of the most inspiring people around the ballpark, a talented writer, an endless resource for baseball knowledge and a wonderful friend. To John Pennisi, the talented sports cartoonist who makes anyone who can call him a friend fortunate and can always make me laugh.

To the Hall of Fame's Jeff Idelson and Bill Francis, whose research produced huge assistance with perspective-filled newspaper reports.

To the Yankees' public relations staff, Jason Zillo, Monica Yurman, Ben Tubelitz and especially Rick Cerrone, for his cooperation and patience in whatever request I made. Thanks to Dave Kaplan at the Yogi Berra Museum, Tom McEwen and Andrew Levy for putting me in touch with players and, for that matter, all the players and managers who gave their time. Special thanks to Kathy Jacobson for her extra effort.

To the Yankees beat writers who provided information and support, specifically Dom Amore, who will be shocked to discover the book is completed.

To Bob Herzog at *Newsday*, one of the business' nice guys, an extremely talented writer, trusted editor and valuable baseball historian.

To Mike Pearson at Sports Publishing for bringing me on board, Scott Rauguth for helping me adjust projects on the fly and Dave Brauer for patience, poise and a great job overall that greatly improved this book.

To Julie Ganz, for her fine editing, support, feedback and understanding in helping ensure the final edition was the best it could be.

To John W. McCarthy, Peter Zellen and Marc Lucas for some last-minute assistance.

And most of all, thanks to Jesus. For everything.

Introduction

After I hugged the best friend who had finally returned to New York, outside of Yankee Stadium, we took the subway ride back home to Queens, to the bar where I knew I'd find the friend I became close to when I made my return to the city three years before.

This was the kind of night the Yankees had given New York once again in October 2003, holding off the Red Sox, making the part of the city that loves them show off its unending energy and passion.

My friend, Lou, was finally getting a taste of what it meant to be back after adopting the L.A. lifestyle he still clung to even after making the decision to return. We hugged not because the Yankees had won, but because he had finally gotten a glimpse of just what made him come home.

The Broadway Station bar in Astoria was still as packed as I expected it to be, every Yankee fan in the place drunk off the Yankees' comeback against Boston, Aaron Boone's home run sending them back to the World Series.

"Let's hear it again," Brendan, the bartender, said and he'd flip the jukebox on the same kind of endless loop of Sinatra's "New York, New York" that played on at the stadium.

People had been dancing on the bar, hugging strangers, united by the Yankees the way they would whenever I'd come home from work after another exciting game, trying to unwind after filing my story.

Now, amid the buzz, a non-stop parade of passion and noise, my friend Pat—who helped me find an apartment when I came back to Queens in 2000, who helped me rediscover *my* New York, the New York full of characters, not mannequins, and more compassion than anyone thinks—pulled me aside.

He slipped his arm around my shoulder, talked into my ear so I could hear him above the noise.

"Dave, you know my father's dying," he said. "You know that's why I'm going to California next month. Today, I said a little prayer.

"Just let them just get back there one more time for him."

This is what baseball can be at its absolute best—distraction, inspiration. A bond between father and son, between friends.

Something so pure it can yank you out of whatever fog you're in and provide the clarity of childhood, just ready to root your heart out for something good to happen. Ready to believe it can.

Of course, baseball is far from the pastoral purity of all those old Norman Rockwell paintings. There's tons of flaws from steroids to superstar egos so removed from why you love the game they think those cheers are all for them.

And, sure, in many ways they are.

But not really.

Most times when you're sitting there screaming your heart out for another comeback, it's not for them; you are rooting for yourself too, aren't you?

You've had a tough day. Worked your butt off. Just got dumped.

Enter baseball.

You root for you and the people close to you; the memories the present can spark.

I understood Pat's prayer even though I turned in my cheers when I picked up my sports writer credential. I still remembered sitting in the back-yard with my grandfather listening to Phil Rizzuto "holy cow" his way through the summer.

Or playing ball with my 60-year-old grandfather, carpet strips for bases, a well-placed wild pitch into the bushes sending me searching for it while he'd scurry his tired body into the house laughing, leaving early the way Rizzuto would rush over the bridge before the end of a broadcast.

I'd remember my Uncle Joe, his knees caving on him after supporting the family with endless hours of construction work, turning on the TV and relaxing with a game.

They were gone now, but the Yankees weren't and each glimpse of Rizzuto or Yogi throwing out a first pitch was a chance to remember them.

Just like each story I'd tell of a father and son was a way for me to think of my dad, who now lives across the country in Las Vegas. He coached my baseball team because he was working so hard, he didn't get to spend enough time with me; now the game keeps me so busy I probably don't call enough. But there's endless times at work when I'm flashing back to the batting cage he kept taking me to, the catches we'd have, the talks about the game, always as eager to laugh at a goofy play as we were to celebrate a great one.

It was just fun.

Baseball provided an escape all those nights my grandmother was in the hospital the last few years, the Parkinson's Disease stealing her expressions and turning her face to a mask at times before she died in 2006.

We'd watch a ballgame on the hospital TV the way we used to in the house and she would act as urgent as ever, worried about whether the Yankees would win because she thought I still wanted them to. Of course, by that time the rooting interest was gone and the only thing I cheered for was her ability to make me laugh again, the way she could by speaking from her gut without a filter, her thick Italian accent making it even better.

"Nonna," I told her once, "I'm going to Phil Rizzuto's house to interview him. I'm going to bring cannoli."

Excited about this ode to our past, when the family that had now shrunk was still full around the table, she said ...

"How mucha you gonna bring? Don't bringa too much!"

Rizzuto laughed when I told him the story because he understood it as much as anyone. Baseball is an escape to remind you of the people you care about; not something to be put above them.

So the escape baseball provides has allowed me to be out covering games, where I can pretend I'm still a boy, my grandmother's still here and her biggest concern is making me happy. Still, I'll ramble on about the stress of work to my mother, who took care of my grandmother and had no such stress. Or dis-traction. She was there every day, no escape from the reality that comes from aging and disease. But she'll perk up over a game or a story and we'll laugh like the old times.

So, the stories in here are about the memories ballplayers have provided for you to share with the people you idolize, not tales of heroes who should replace the role models in your own lives. Many of them thrived in their biggest moment for the same reason you have in yours—the people who cared about them drove them along the way.

You'll read about some of the most exciting games in Yankees history, but not necessarily the best. You'll read about some of their greatest triumphs, but not all of them come from the greatest players or, even, the games you'd expect them to pick.

So Dave Righetti opts for a game pitched in front of his father rather than the no-hitter he threw in Yankee Stadium. Mel Stottlemyre talks about beating phenom Vida Blue in a meaningless regular-season game because "my boys didn't think I could do it."

Derek Jeter refuses to pick his famous "flip" play because the Yankees didn't win the World Series that year. He stuck with that philosophy in 2012 for the updated version, passing on the chance to include the individual honor of his 3,000th hit, which, of course, went for a homer at Yankee Stadium as part of his famed 5-for-5 day.

Much has changed since this book was written in 2004, including a trip across the street from the old Yankee Stadium to the new place, which was christened by the 2009 World Series champions.

The Yankees have bid farewell to players such as Jorge Posada through retirement and felt a much stronger impact from the real loss of so many treasured members of the organization.

The hit was especially hard in 2010, when, in the same week, the Yankees lost their Boss, George Steinbrenner, and their voice, Bob Sheppard.

There have been new faces, lured by one more spending spree by Steinbrenner's son, Hal, after the 2008 season, when CC Sabathia, Mark Teixeira, A.J. Burnett and Nick Swisher joined the Yankees and, along with Alex Rodriguez, helped them win one more ring for the Boss.

We'll take a look at those 2009 champions here now, too, through the thoughtful eyes of ace CC Sabathia, who took his place in Yankees lore by recognizing he was brought here to help the Yankees win a championship, and whose high expectations matched those of his new city and team.

Sabathia acknowledged he had something to prove when he came here—and does every time he takes the ball. But the test he must pass is for himself and the ability to do so comes with help from the people who supported him along the way.

Like most of his successful Yankees predecessors, he sought those pressure-filled challenges he was able to meet.

As the 2009 Yankees showed like the champions who came before them, there's no place to hide in the big moments.

That's what you root for; the place that takes you back to the purity of just wondering whether you can do something and proving you can.

The place that makes you think of the people who encouraged you to do all that you could, whether it was in a backyard, batting cage or anywhere else.

That's what makes the games great. That's what makes you love them.

Prologue

The Babe

"Sons of bitches," Babe Ruth muttered to the reporters. "Gets you to the World Series and they're too cheap to give him a share."

The Sultan of Swat, rumored to forget his teammates' faces at times, sure knew all about his old Murderers' Row mate, Mark Koenig.

So when the Yankees took on the Cubs in the 1932 World Series, the Babe let everyone know he wasn't happy with the cheapskates in Chicago.

Koenig had joined the Cubs late and contributed key hits on the way to the Series. But the players didn't vote him a full share, and the Bambino blasted them in defense of his old teammate.

Hey, the Babe had never failed to speak his mind before. Why start now?

Whether it was telling Yankees owner Colonel Ruppert off or manager Miller Huggins, or boasting to the boys from the papers about having a big-

Sporting News/Getty Images.

ger salary than the president—"Hey, I had a better year than he did"—the Babe was the biggest thing the game had seen.

His boastful ways were even part of the rumored reason the Boston Red Sox sold him to the Yankees for a song—literally. At least that's the legend—one that's been disputed through the years—that Red Sox management needed the cash to back the musical "No, No Nanette."

Either way, Ruth went to the Yankees in 1920, giving birth to the Yankees as they are now known, as well as the "Curse of the Bambino" that hangs over Boston's head.

Ruth didn't just build the house that is Yankee Stadium; he laid the foundation for a tradition unmatched in sports.

The Ruth Yankees was the first team to leave the rest of the league crying over a lack of competition, the '27 Yankees slashing through the league like Ruth crashed parties across the country.

"I used to play bridge with Bill Dickey and with Ruth and Gehrig on all the train rides," said Bill Werber, a Yankees shortstop in the '20s and '30s. He carried a bottle of Seagrams and he'd call for the porter and he'd get the glass and he'd pour, I judged, about eight ounces of Seagram's in that glass. Between Chicago and St. Louis, he'd sit there and sip on that whiskey."

He is one of the first American icons, a mythical figure hard to imagine in real life. He loved kids, or "keeeds" as he called him in that husky, welcoming voice.

He was the first example of why those keeds can only follow a ballplayer's habits so far, known for chuggin' beer and chasin' skirts, a never-ending search for a night so raucous even today's hedonistic players would, no doubt, bow in submission.

The old films show him darting around the bases, a bowling ball running on pins, but the younger Babe could sprint after the ball in right as easily as he could swat it out of sight.

He was the opposite of Lou Gehrig, who brought his mother to events when his wife couldn't attend.

The rivalry foreshadowed Yankee lore of Mantle and Maris, but the players never had trouble following each other's deeds on the field.

"They avoided each other principally," Werber said. "If you asked Ruth how he liked Gehrig, he'd say, 'I put up with him.' If you ask Gehrig he'd say 'He's all right.'

"They weren't friends. They were very much alike when the ballgame started. They were competitors, and you'd better be a damn competitor too, because they'd warn you—I won't say they liked each other, but they respected each other and they pulled for each other."

That's been the mark of every Yankee dynasty from Murderer's Row to the M & M boys to the Bronx Zoo and the more peaceful Torre story of the late '90s. The Bronx Bombers have always battered opponents not just with a home run but with the kind of teamwork often overlooked due to their extravagant payroll and stadium's worth of superstars—even when they didn't like each other.

The Yankees have always followed one simple formula.

Their guys come through more when the pressure demands someone does.

Even when the pressure is self-inflicted.

So when Ruth arrived in Chicago for the '32 Series, he had no problem sticking up for one of his former mates.

And when the Cubs jeered him from the dugout as he stepped to the plate, Ruth cackled as confidently as ever.

Here's where the stories split, myth and reality traveling separate roads through the years.

Did Ruth really call his shot?

Did he point to center field and predict a home run?

In the next day's papers, several newspaper reports state Ruth pointed to center field before hitting a home run there.

The other story goes that Ruth merely held up a finger after his second strike, telling the Cubs he had a strike left.

Either way, Ruth certainly made an, uh, Ruthian boast of some sort.

So when he sent the ball soaring over the wall in center, he couldn't have been more pleased.

That's the way to stick it to those sons of bitches.

Which is why, 62 years later, when she approached the elevator at Yankee Stadium, Julia Ruth Stevens had no problem remembering her father's favorite game.

She had just presented the Babe Ruth award to Yankees third baseman Alex Rodriguez, the 2003 home run champ. The Stadium crowd cheered on a sunny, late spring day, and Ruth Stevens, along with some other family members, prepared to take in the game.

Ruth Stevens chuckled remembering her father's favorite game, and his recollection of whatever boast he made.

"The thing he said was, 'I would have been a real chump if I struck out, huh?'" she said. She smiled. "But he never did. He always rose to the occasion."

CHAPTER 1

Tommy Henrich:
Sultan of a Strikeout

October 5, 1941, World Series Game 4

at Brooklyn
Yankees 7, Dodgers 4

The stats: AB R H
4   1 0

Author's note: The interview with Tommy Heinrich took place in 2004 and the chapter was written shortly after, five years before his death in 2009, with Heinrich gracefully challenging the aging process as strongly as he could, his charm, will and loving bond with his wife all coming through.

The 90-year-old voice spoke softly ... slowly ... the words struggling to exit Tommy Henrich's mouth though they raced inside his brain.

"I'm awfully sorry, but I don't think I can do this," he said over the telephone from his California home.

Is it your memory, he was asked.

"*No*," he said, his voice finding force.

The muscles around Henrich's mouth betrayed his mind, still sharp enough to detail everything from meeting Lou Gehrig to playing with Joe DiMaggio.

"I ought to be able to say this better," he said repeatedly.

In the background his wife, Eileen, chided him playfully.

"She says I shouldn't make you think I'm that old," Henrich said with a chuckle.

You could picture her holding his hand, steadying it. Eventually, she would ask her husband, "Haven't you been on long enough?"—a polite form of protection.

Henrich laughed when it was suggested she keeps him in line.

"She's nodding very nicely," he said.

"Jiminys, everything happened," Yankees outfielder Tommy Henrich said of the 1941 World Series rally he started by running to first on a dropped third strike. After the ball eluded Brooklyn catcher Mickey Owen, the Yankees went on to win a game they seemingly had ended with a strikeout. *AP/WWP.*

They've been together 64 years, and the former Yankee known as "Old Reliable" knows he couldn't rely on anyone more.

But she's still not his first love.

That came at 7.

It came over telegraph lines and through newspaper print, all the way from New York to Massillon, Ohio.

Henrich can tell you how the Yankees tradition began, a baton passed from generation to generation, the best players of each New York Yankees era doggone determined to live up to the last.

They come charging in as sons of the bustling city or tiptoeing stepchildren from small towns, longing to match reality with their imagination. Either way, those who thrive on the biggest stage in the biggest city often find a link to their pinstriped predecessors.

It all began with seven-year-olds like Henrich, who couldn't wait to get the telegraph reports from New York. Today, they dial up or DSL their way to the 'net or flip on the 50th cable channel to watch a Derek Jeter highlight.

If you want a straight line to where the Yankees tradition began, listen to the shaky voice.

"Doggone, I don't know," Henrich said when asked what it meant to be a Yankee. "But I had that dream in 1920."

His voice grew strong, his first love steadying him as effectively as his wife's hand had.

"I'm sure of that now," Henrich said, laughing. "Because that's the year the Yankees got Babe Ruth.

"And I fell in love with the Babe and it never left me."

*** *** ***

It was the biggest day of his life, but Henrich couldn't have felt smaller.

Yankee Stadium.

The Yankees.

Boy, oh, boy.

He arrived in the dugout in 1937, which only 10 years earlier had been manned by "Murderers' Row," the fearsome foursome of sluggers that changed the game.

Henrich's spikes clanged down the runway, into the dugout his hero had inhabited; he poked his head out for that first glimpse of a field bigger than any he'd played on.

And here came the guys. The Babe was retired, a broadcaster, advising Henrich to "cash his check."

But, jiminys, this was still something else.

Bill Dickey. Joe DiMaggio. Tony Lazzeri.

And the great Lou Gehrig.

How was Henrich ever gonna fit in here?

"The regulars came into the dugout and they met me," Henrich said. "They were very, very cordial.

"And when I met Lou, he was just the same as the rest of them."

Life in the big leagues began.

So did the humbling moments.

Those big league pitchers, boy, they could throw.

Like Johnny Allen, the ex-Yankee who manager Joe McCarthy hated almost as much as Gehrig, who thought the pitcher was a head-hunter.

All Henrich knew about him was he couldn't hit his breaking ball.

"Jiminys," Henrich said after a strikeout, "he's got good stuff."

McCarthy darted his head up.

"The guy's got *nothing*," he barked.

Henrich gulped.

"That's the best nothing I ever saw," he thought.

A year later, Henrich faced Allen at the Stadium. The Yankees trailed, but rallied for four runs in the ninth—thanks in large part to Henrich's double.

The screams and catcalls of a clubhouse celebration echoed across the room and Henrich was smack dab in the middle of it.

When he thought he had a moment alone, Henrich reflected on this rite of passage, pleasing his manager and learning to hit a guy he couldn't have pictured touching the previous year.

"I'm the happiest guy in this clubhouse," Henrich muttered to himself.

A few feet away, sitting on a bench and letting a cigarette crease his contented smile, Gehrig overheard Henrich. He nodded his head.

"Tom, come over here," Gehrig said. Henrich complied.

"You're not the happiest guy in this clubhouse," Gehrig whispered. "I am."

By the next season, Henrich would discover the happiest guy in the clubhouse also considered himself the luckiest man on the face of the earth.

*** *** ***

Gehrig didn't want to speak.
The microphone waited along with the crowd on July 4, 1939, but the Yankees Iron Horse didn't want to make this speech.

The Yankees had held a day for him and Gehrig, his body ravaged by the disease that would be named for him, was scheduled to speak.

He tried to opt out.

He had been an intensely private man, and this was as private a time as he could have.

He was dying.

He knew it.

Hardly anyone else did.

But they pushed, and Gehrig nudged himself nervously to the microphone for his famous speech.

The riveting words, enhanced by their echo over the speakers throughout Yankee Stadium, have been imitated in tribute countless times by Yankee fans, players and entertainers.

Fans, for the past two weeks you have been reading about a bad break. Yet today I consider myself the luckiest man on the face of the earth ...

But Henrich was there for the real thing. The real man.

A man Henrich considered himself lucky to be close to.

So when Henrich thinks of the day his fiercely private friend addressed all of Yankee Stadium, he has no words to offer, no echo to emulate.

"What a man," Henrich said. "Jiminys, I don't know what to say. That took a lot of guts to reveal himself like that.

"Oh, what a guy."

*** *** ***

ALS claimed Gehrig's life in June 1941. Henrich was shipped off to fight in World War II the next year, eight months after the bombing of Pearl Harbor.

That was baseball then, when seasons were stopped, careers lost.

In 2002, with the country facing a war in Iraq a year after the September 11 terrorist attacks, the question was whether players would stop playing.

Because they considered a strike.

Sixty years earlier, after Pearl Harbor had been bombed, many players had no choice but to stop playing. So Henrich served his duty and sacrificed his career, losing three years.

The "day of infamy" on December 7, 1941 changed the country as September 11 would eventually. But just two months before the bombing— and 10 months before Henrich would suit up for the coast guard instead of his beloved team—the Yankees were finishing one of the most incredible seasons a team could have.

Shortly after their old captain's death, the 1941 Yankees won 41 of 47 games, a streak that counted only as second best that year.

Right behind DiMaggio's legendary 56-game hitting streak.

Henrich not only witnessed the streak, he ensured it would continue.

The streak was at 38 when DiMaggio waited on deck in the ninth against Detroit.

The Yankees had one out and one on in a game they led. Henrich was up, DiMaggio, who had gone hitless, next.

A paralyzing thought struck Henrich.

If he grounded into a game-ending double-play, DiMag's hitting streak would be over, and Henrich wouldn't forgive himself.

He had an idea.

"Is it all right if I bunt?" Henrich asked McCarthy, still his manager.

McCarthy winced. Thought.

"Yeah," McCarthy said, "that'll be all right."

It worked.

Henrich sacrificed the man to second and DiMaggio was guaranteed another at-bat. He smacked a basehit to extend the streak.

Many years later, Henrich was talking to Elden Auker, who had been pitching that day for the Tigers.

"Did it surprise ya that I did that?" Henrich asked.

Tommy Henrich (center) dreamt of playing for the Yankees after following telegraph reports of Babe Ruth as a boy in Ohio. He became a Yankees mainstay playing along legends like Lou Gehrig and Joe DiMaggio (second from right). *AP/WWP.*

"Surprise me?" Auker said. "I was *glad* that you did it. Because you hit me better than Joe."

Henrich laughed.

"I did," he said.

So, did the great DiMaggio offer a pat on the bat or a thank you for keeping his streak alive?

Henrich laughed as he remembered the man history has shown to be a loner.

"No," Henrich said, the idea too absurd to consider, "he wouldn't come out and say anything."

There was one more game for Henrich to remember that year in 1941. It is one of the most famous World Series games of all time and the one Henrich chose to label the game of his life.

This child of the Babe, the right fielder who roamed Ruth's ground, hit a game-winning home run in the ninth inning of a World Series game once.

But that wasn't the game.

That home run came in 1949, when Henrich's shot off Don Newcombe gave Allie Reynolds a 1-0 win. Great memory.

But not the one.

"No, no," Henrich said. "It was 1941 ... Mickey Owen."

The dropped third strike.

Brooklyn Dodgers catcher Mickey Owen dropped what would have been a game-ending strikeout of Henrich. The Yankees rallied for four runs and a 7-4 win in Game 5.

They would go on to win the next game and their first Subway Series triumph over their Brooklyn rivals.

The Bums' cry of Wait 'til Next Year was typified here, with a ball rolling past Owen's glove and the Yankees running away with a game.

And here's the first reminder that for all of the Yankees' bombast and cold, hard cash, there is a lot more to their best games than mammoth home runs.

A strikeout.

The favorite moment of a man who grew up salivating over Babe Ruth's home runs is a strikeout.

*** *** ***

In between playing with legends, Henrich built an All-Star career for himself. He hit .320 in 67 games as a rookie, drove in 100 runs with 25 homers as a vet in '48 and earned the nickname "Old Reliable" for his ability to come through in the clutch.

He especially warmed to the October spotlight when he returned from war, hitting .323 with a homer and five RBI in the Yankees' Series victory over Brooklyn in 1947.

He also smacked that game-winner the next year to help the Yankees again beat the Dodgers.

In the 1941 Fall Classic against 'dem Bums, Henrich didn't fare as well. He batted .167, struggling throughout the Series.

The Yankees were up two games to one as they prepared to play Game 4 at Ebbets Field.

The Yankees trailed 4-3 when Henrich came up with two outs and no one on in the ninth, his day as hopeless as that of his team.

He had gone 0-for-3 and the 33,813 fans at Ebbets Field were rising, ready to watch the Dodgers tie the Series. All set for a nice, peaceful night where a Brooklyn fella could have taken his lady for a stroll and let bandleader Glenn Miller offer her a "Moonlight Serenade" in celebration.

Then, all of a sudden, it wasn't so calm.

Hugh Casey zipped through the first two batters, before running the count to 3-2 on Henrich.

Then he threw a curve that dropped so abruptly Henrich knew he shouldn't have swung as he was still swinging.

Too late.

Except it wasn't.

The pitch bounced away from Owen.

The cops, preparing to protect the field from the delirious Brooklyn fans, bounded toward the plate.

Turned out there was nothing to protect. Except the Dodgers' lead.

The game wasn't over yet.

Henrich hustled to first, safe on the dropped third strike.

"That was incredible," said Phil Rizzuto, then the Yankees shortstop. "People were running out on the field. We were gonna run into the clubhouse and we see Tommy running."

What happened next left the fans in Brooklyn muttering their familiar lament of "only in Brooklyn."

Joe DiMaggio followed with a single. Charlie Keller doubled. The Yankees rallied for four runs and Brooklyn was dumbfounded by a 7-4 loss.

"It was the fault of them ... cops," disgusted Dodgers manager Leo Durocher told reporters, claiming interference as Owen tried to get the ball. "There was one stupid sergeant standing at home plate, and Mickey never had a chance to get the ball."

In another portion of the complaining clubhouse, Dixie Walker sounded like so many defeated Yankee opponents would for decades.

"I tell you, those fellows have got all the luck on their side," Walker told reporters. "Never saw a team get so many breaks as they have."

In the Yankees clubhouse, the room had the feel of a man who had torn his pants bending down, but picked up a winning lottery ticket on the way up.

"Well," DiMaggio said with a grin, "they say everything happens in Brooklyn."

Happened by design, Lefty Gomez and Red Ruffing said through snickers.

"It was just the way we planned it," the pair told the press. "We've been working on that play for months—on the quiet, you understand, and we didn't have it perfected until today."

Didn't feel so perfect for losing pitcher Casey.

"I've lost a lot of ball games in some funny ways," Casey told reporters, "but that is the first I've lost by striking out a man."

Game of My Life
Tommy Henrich

"Jiminy, everything happened. Well, it was the ninth inning, the count was 3-2 and Casey threw it and I swung at the ball. He threw me a curve ball and I started to swing and I thought it broke so much, I said to myself, 'Jiminys, I didn't touch the ball.'

"I said, 'Boy oh boy, that's the doggone best curve Hugh Casey ever threw.' And it went right down. And I said, 'Maybe Mickey's having trouble too.'

"And he had the trouble, the ball went into the dirt and went all the way back to the backstop. I turned around, faced him and saw the ball rolling. And I started for first base. And I made first base. Holy Jiminys!

"And DiMaggio is the next batter and he singled to left-center, a real vicious drive and I got to second base. The next batter (Charlie Keller) hit a softball off the right-field wall. And I'm on second base and I had no problem scoring.

"But Joe DiMaggio roared around second and into third and (third-base coach) Art Fletcher signalled 'Go on home' and he ran home, and I'm picking myself up and then Joe came in and he slid and doggone—DiMaggio hit home plate with such force that his body went through home plate about 10 feet—that's how much speed DiMaggio had.

"I think that run put us ahead, and we scored at least three or four runs. And Johnny Murphy was put in to pitch and he got 'em out 1-2-3 and the game's over."

*** *** ***

The Yankees won the next game and the Series—this time helped by a Henrich homer.

He laughed when asked if anyone had given him credit for hustling to first instead of sulking back to the dugout.

"Nobody said 'nice going,'" he said. "That was what I was supposed to do."

It's not always what's done these days, but Henrich knows a lot of great things still are by his old team. That Paul O'Neill, Henrich said, was a heck-uva ballplayer.

But the time for talking was done. Eileen was at his sleeve, tapping him to go.

There was just one question left.

What does it mean to be a Yankee? What makes the men who preceded and followed him come through in the clutch like Old Reliable so often did?

"Now that so many more games have been played, the image is so great that everybody knows about it," he said. "And when I got there they started to be because of the Babe and so forth.

"It was known to an ordinary guy that, this is something. 'You've gotta be aware where you are now. You'd better do something now.'"

CHAPTER 2

Phil Rizzuto:
Holy Cow, What a Bunt

September 17, 1951

vs. Cleveland
Yankees 2, Indians 1

The stats: AB   R   H   RBI
                4   0   3   2

Author's note: The interview with Phil Rizzuto took place at his New Jersey home in 2004 and the chapter was written shortly after, three years before his death in August 2007. The Scooter was as gracious as ever, no surprise for a man who was beloved for his down-to-earth nature and ability to connect with fans. A few years after this interview, even after Rizzuto had moved into a retirement home, he found the strength to inspire smiles, once rising out of bed after being unable to earlier, because a visitor wanted to see him. As his good friend John Pennisi recalled, the Scooter combed his hair and made his way to the hallway, gaining the strength to make his fan feel special. "Holy cow!" he told the visitor, who had been disappointed when turned away. "You look beautiful!"

Cora's upstairs and the cannolis are in the fridge so—*andiamo*—"Let's go." "Somebody else is coming," Phil Rizzuto said, still getting endless interview requests at 87. He sighed, good naturedly. "It's getting unbearable."

But he opened the door with the same welcoming grin that greeted viewers when he broadcast Yankee games.

He's thinner now, frail. His voice is as sweet as ever, but not as sharp, his "hoooly cows" more whispers than exclamations.

He led the way through the hall of his Hillside, N.J., home, the one he spent all those years rushing over the George Washington Bridge to reach— often before game's end.

"The picture came out; it was so great, too ... in the on-deck circle was Mickey Mantle, *jumping* up in the air," Phil Rizzuto said about his suicide squeeze play on September 17, 1951. Here's the picture. Mantle, then 19, leaps after Rizzuto fended off a head-high pitch from Cleveland's Bob Lemon to send Joe DiMaggio home with the winning run. *AP/WWP.*

He wore a light blue shirt with a picture of a halo-topped cow—much like the huckleberry that knocked him over on Phil Rizzuto day when the Yankees retired his number.

He settled in the den, his baseball trophies modestly lining the wall along with a picture of Rizzuto as a cut, young athlete, an Italian-American from the bushy, dark hair to the rugged nose.

But the Rizzuto most fans picture now is the gray-haired grandfather who made them laugh their way through summer.

He was in your backyard for 40 of them, his New Yawk accent offering a nasal contrast to the smooth, southern sound of Mel Allen when Rizzuto first broke in. Other legendary broadcasters like Vin Scully offered a regally cadenced invitation to "pull up a chair and spend part of your Saturday with us."

Rizzuto?

He came to you.

And brought blunt, Brooklyn-born birthday wishes with him.

Or get-well greetings. Or pastry previews from your favorite bakery— and whichever one earned a plug by fulfilling his quest for cannolis.

"Ohhh, I loved to do that," Rizzuto said. "But a lot of the writers didn't like that. They wanted the old school, 'ball one, ball two'. ... And the people loved it. Because I'd mention their uncle, their aunt, everybody in the neighborhood, and I got a big kick out of it."

Rizzuto joined your neighborhood whether you were standing on a corner in Brooklyn like he used to as a boy or out on the Hamptons beach, where he reconnected you with the city.

Not that you could expect one thought to connect to the next, because with the Scooter, the thoughts always come out as scattered ...

"Ooooh, the Hamptons," Rizzuto said. "Geez, I tell ya, we were there *once* in our lives. It's such a looong trip. Holy cow. Almost three hours."

... as the topics of a Sunday barbecue with your relatives laughing and talking over each other.

This is the gift Rizzuto gave Yankee fans for 40 years, a generation recognizing him as the grandfatherly figure who chuckled at the huckleberries and offered "Hoooly cows" for the latest Yankee star to get a big hit.

He'd be calling a pop-up to second a home run one minute, interrupting the action to wish a "Happy birthday to Mary D'Angelo!" the next.

And all along, Rizzuto enjoyed laughing right along with you, slipping in perfectly intoned inflections for dramatic parts of the game.

All of it was a far cry from who he had been before the Yankees forced him off the roster and into the broadcast booth in '56—the shortstop Red Sox slugger Ted Williams said was *the* difference for the World Series-winning Yankees every year.

Rizzuto the broadcaster made baseball a part of summer, but remembered its place. It was no more important than the breeze hitting you on the deck, day slowly switching shifts with night. He loved the Yankees enough to be a fan, loved the fans enough to stall his way back to the booth and head to the upper deck to talk to them.

And he loved a Yankees win as much as they did.

But he still loved leaving early because what awaited on the other side of the bridge was the only thing more important to him than the Yankees.

His wife, Cora. The kids. The grandkids.

Look, it's the *people* that make the game so great.

"The best thing about baseball," Rizzuto said, "people might be down and out.

They can go to a ballgame and forget about it."

The people in the stands who would command Rizzuto's attention when the game didn't, when he'd talk baseball then return to mark a couple of "WWs"—"Wasn't Watchings"—in his scorecard for plays he'd missed and endure the teasing of partner Bill White.

The people at home watching from their living rooms or hospital beds or wherever they gathered to get away from the rest of the world for a few minutes.

They were worth all the dirty looks Rizzuto would get from the purists who didn't want birthday greetings or calls for cannoli mixed in with their play-by-play.

And the people on the other side of the bridge were worth going home to early.

Especially if you could miss the traffic, right, White?

Ohhh, I tell ya, heh, heh, sitting in that traffic, boy ...

His affection for people started Rizzuto's career in baseball, back in Brooklyn and then Richmond Hill High School in Queens. He played everything, but loved baseball, the teamwork aspect trumping the other sports.

That's why, if you ask Rizzuto for his favorite game, he'll pick the time he brought Joe DiMaggio home on a suicide squeeze play, bunting a head-high pitch from Cleveland's Bob Lemon.

That's the highlight of his Hall of Fame career—a bunt.

"That would have to be it," Rizzuto said with a chuckle. "I didn't hit a lot of home runs."

No, but he did have a 200-hit season in 1950 to win the MVP award. He did prompt teammate Vic Raschi to say, "My best pitch is anything the hitter grounds, lines or pops in the direction of Rizzuto."

And he could bunt. Boy, could he bunt. Even when the ball was aimed straight for his head as it was when Lemon threw it on September 17, 1951.

Heh, Lem was soooo mad when he got that bunt down.

Almost as mad as Rizzuto was the day he vowed to make it in the big leagues.

He was 19 when he showed up for a tryout at Ebbets Field, where Casey Stengel managed the Dodgers at the time. His Uncle Mike, who turned him into a Dodgers fan as a kid, tagged along.

Rizzuto was ready to make his dream come true in the spot it had been born.

He knew he'd prove he belonged once he got on that field and ...

"Listen, kid," Stengel told Rizzuto, picking out his five-foot-six body from the line of potential players. "The only way you're gonna make a living is with a shoeshine box."

The Rizzuto who went home that day was nothing like the grandfather figure who would guide countless Yankee fans through their summers.

He was as focused as his scattershot thoughts were not during his broadcast career.

And the humility that would prompt him to say he'd be a "ballboy if they need one in Heaven," was not yet present.

He was a ballplayer. Not a ballboy.

Definitely not a shoeshine boy.

And he was going to prove it regardless of what Stengel said.

"If I was dejected I wouldn't have gone any place," Rizzuto said. "I was mad. I mean, I really was *ohhh*."

*** *** ***

He started playing with the big guys when he was 10 years old, trying to tag along with the 20-year-olds from down the block.

"I was too dumb to give up on it," he said.

They'd play stickball in the street, where Rizzuto's mother quickly remedied a neighborhood problem of broken windows.

"One of the best things we had," Rizzuto said. "My mother, she got a baseball, took it apart, stuffed it with stuff from pillows and—me!—you could really throw it and curves and hit it and it didn't go hard enough to break the pane of glass.

"That was a great idea. On the corner is where we lived; four corners and four poles. We played everything; racquetball, touch football. All day long, I'd be outside."

Uncle Mike would take him to the Dodgers games, Phil growing up a Brooklyn fan regardless of how many championships Muderers' Row racked up.

He could wait 'til next year along with the Dodgers, because he was just as much of an underdog.

That's why his coach at Richmond Hill High pulled Rizzuto aside and taught him to bunt, because he knew there was no way this short a shortstop would make it without some extra tricks.

But Stengel didn't even give Rizzuto a chance to show off what he'd learned. Just took one look and told him to forget it. So Uncle Mike dragged Rizzuto to a tryout with the Giants.

Nothing doing.

Rizzuto felt as welcomed as he did when he was running home from a game, the bigger kids trying to bully him.

"They'd throw rocks at us 'til we got to the subway," he said, laughing.

But after the dash home, the Scooter felt as safe as ever. There's safety in numbers.

And the Rizzuto family had as many as you could count.

The Italian family was as close-knit as could be and in those days there was little choice.

"We had a house in Brooklyn in an alley," he said. "Two ... four ... six ... eight ... all the relatives. Uncles, aunts. They'd come out with the mandolins and ohhhh ..."

The sauce. The fresh dough. *Madon,* was it good!

So he kept playing, ducking the rocks and forgetting all the people he vowed to make foolish after they told him he couldn't cut it.

Finally, the Yankees gave him a shot. A real shot. A week-long tryout where Rizzuto could show off his speed and bunting and fielding ...

They signed him.

Seventy-five bucks a month. No bonus.

"I'd go for nothing," Rizzuto said.

One request. Could he start off at the minor-league team in Virginia, where it was nice and warm? You know, I can't take the cold and ... so it was.

He started off in Bassett, Virginia, 512 miles and a world away from his Brooklyn upbringing.

Sure, the house was filled with people, just like back home. But down here in a town seemingly smaller than the busy Brooklyn block Rizzuto lived on, everything moved slower.

Plus, they had that "honey talk" and "how y'all doin" and all that.

"You couldn't understand them, they couldn't understand us," Rizzuto said.

And when the food came out, no one was pushing Rizzuto to *mangia, mangia* like they would back home. Instead, they were pushing him away from the table.

"The house where we stayed, everybody, all the players, they put their food out," Rizzuto said. "I couldn't uh ... I couldn't get it. No, they were big guys. Luckily, there were two or three other kids from Brooklyn who helped out."

Not that Rizzuto was in a rush to get to all the food. He told you that much back in 1994 during the most infamously uproarious Hall of Fame induction speech ever made.

"Hey, White," Rizzuto called out, looking for his old broadcast partner in the middle of his speech. "What's that stuff that looks like oatmeal? Grits! Grits. I didn't know what it was. I put 'em in my pocket."

It's down in Virginia that Rizzuto earned his "Scooter" nickname, a teammate telling everyone "this guy doesn't run, he scoots." As usual, Rizzuto let them say what they wanted, his easygoing nature making him a prime target for pranks throughout his career.

"We used to keep our gloves out on the field," former Yankees second baseman Bobby Richardson said. "One of the reasons we stopped that is, the other team would put bugs in Phil's glove when he went in."

And a bum leg almost kept Rizzuto from even worrying about bugs, lightning or any of his other famous phobias.

He stepped in a pockmarked part of the infield and his leg gave out. Next thing he knew, he was in the hospital.

The words blurred.

"Call your mother ... gotta operate ... right away."

Holy cow.

"Gangrene had set in," he said. "I was in the hospital for over a month. I wanted to get back so bad. The doctor said you can never play baseball again. I said, 'Doctor, I can't; that's my life.' He says, 'I tell you what. You go down there about 20, 30 yards and run as hard as you can. And if it stays there and doesn't split up or anything, then you'll be all right.'

"I got my rosary beads out and I ran ..."

It didn't split up or anything.

He was OK.

He got his first call to the majors in '41. By now Rizzuto was a cocksure kid, ready to take on anything. He was so sure of himself his first time at the plate ...

"I almost wet my pants," he said. "Dutch Traynor was pitching. I think I might have hit it on one bounce. I was never so happy."

The veterans weren't happy to have him. For one thing, he was ready to take over for respected Yankee Frank Crosetti. For another, he was a rookie.

The vets didn't have a lot of use for rookies other than to see what they could do to them when they weren't looking.

"They'd nail my spikes to the floor," Rizzuto said. "The ballplayers of that era, they couldn't stand rookies."

Finally, more out of practicality than kindness, Joe DiMaggio cleared a path for Rizzuto to practice.

"If this kid's going to be on the ballclub," the Yankee Clipper said, "we oughta see if he can hit."

He could.

He hit .307 in 133 games in '41, put together a nice, double-digit hitting streak dwarfed by DiMaggio's 56-game mark.

DiMaggio.

Rizzuto's small size inspired future Yankees manager Casey Stengel to send him home from a Brooklyn Dodgers tryout in the 1930s. Two decades later, Rizzuto won the MVP award for Stengel's Yankees on his way to a Hall of Fame career as a shortstop. *Photo File/Getty Images.*

Rizzuto had to stop his heart from beating louder whenever he looked over his shoulder and saw the legend out in center field. So his heart was broken along with DiMaggio's hitting streak when third baseman Ken Keltner robbed the Yankee Clipper of a shot at a 57th straight game in Cleveland.

The rest of the team had finished dressing and Rizzuto was about to do the same when DiMaggio called over from his locker-room stool.

"Wait," he said, grimly.

DiMaggio, the loner, didn't want to be alone. Nor did he want company.

He didn't know what he wanted.

Other than the hits that were gone in Keltner's glove at third.

But he asked Rizzuto to walk out of the ballpark with him and down to a local bar.

As they approached the entrance, DiMaggio searched his pants and discovered he had left his money in his locker. He asked Rizzuto if he had any money on him.

Rizzuto handed over the $18 that was supposed to last him the rest of the two-week road trip.

"You go home," DiMaggio said.

So Rizzuto did. Even if he wasn't sure how he'd get around after that.

"I couldn't wire home for money," he said. "They didn't have any."

*** *** ***

"Cora, I'm coming home."

"Cora and I ..."

"Cora was saying ..."

Without ever seeing her, Yankee fans listening to Rizzuto's broadcasts were introduced and reintroduced to the Scooter's wife.

Sometimes with more information than necessary.

"She didn't need a girdle, I'll tell you that," Rizzuto said during his rambling Hall of Fame speech. "She's pretty well built."

He met her in 1942 and fell in love at first sight.

She was tall and blonde, he was short, but rugged, and her practicality complemented his child-like innocence.

Everyone has a trap door in their mind to catch the things they say before they say them, she told her husband. But your trap door doesn't work.

Good thing hers did.

Rizzuto headed off for war in '42 when athletes were called overseas following the Pearl Harbor attack. For Rizzuto, the real war was with the waves that shook up his boat when he joined the navy.

Thirty days on the ship. Thirty days, he was seasick.

They wanted him on deck. He said, sure, long as you keep a bucket strapped under my chin.

He was set to go AWOL, but Cora talked him out of it.

Just like she talked him out of joining a Mexican League when he got back from the war in '46.

"She saved me twice," Rizzuto said. "In the war, I said, 'I'm gonna go home.' Cora said, 'Don't you dare.'

"The other one was with Mexico. (The scouts) walk around with guns in their hand. They wanted us to go to Mexico that night."

Rizzuto was upset because the Yankees hadn't given him a raise from the year before. Plus, he wasn't hitting too good and figured this was a good deal. Cora all but yanked Rizzuto by his ear and into the Yankee manager's office.

"No," Cora insisted, "we've gotta tell Joe McCarthy."

So he avoided the court marshals. And stayed with the Yankees.

Good thing, too.

While he was busy trying to learn Spanish in Mexico, he would have missed one of the Yankees' greatest dynasties.

From 1949 to '53, the Yankees won five straight championships and Rizzuto was right at the top of the list of the "October Twelve"—the 12 players in pinstripes for all five years as well as the title for Rizzuto's first book.

He also would have missed a reunion with a manager who suddenly saw he was fit for more than shining shoes.

McCarthy was gone after the '48 season and Rizzuto was less than thrilled to see his replacement.

In came Stengel, 13 years after telling Rizzuto to beat it and six years after his last managerial job, with Boston.

At this point, Rizzuto and any of the other Yankees might have wondered if Stengel was the one in need of another profession.

In nine years of managing Brooklyn and the Boston Braves, he had topped the .500 mark just once. His best finish? Fifth.

Rizzuto, meanwhile, had become one of the Yankees' most valuable players, stealing hits at short and setting up runs as the league's best bunter.

A look at the Scooter's stats now would provoke a shrug.

Today's shortstop is a tall, athletic player who can send balls out with a flick, race around the bases and cover as much ground as a wall-to-wall carpet. It started when Cal Ripken became a shortstop in the '80s and redefined the position. Players like Derek Jeter, Alex Rodriguez and Nomar Garciaparra followed the Iron Man's lead.

Before then, shortstops were to asked to field first, second, third, fourth and ... OK, can you hit now?

So Stengel had to begrudgingly admit he was wrong about Rizzuto when he arrived. The manager would soon do more than that.

While Rizzuto made life easy for pitchers like Raschi with his darting defense at short, he also started making life tougher for the ones on the other side.

In '49, he motivated Stengel to move him up in the order from the eighth spot to lead off, showing he could spark many a Yankees rally. Combined with his fielding, his .275 average and 110 runs scored placed him second in the MVP voting—behind Boston's Ted Williams, who just missed a triple crown.

By 1950, he had developed enough of a stroke to go with his ability to bunt any ball thrown near him. He choked way up on the bat and slapped hits to whatever field the ball would take them.

In his best year—the one that gave him a statistical argument to help him finally win entry into the Hall of Fame in 1994—Rizzuto captured the MVP award.

He started the season in a hitless slump, before a teammate suggested he try a different bat and choke up. He got a hit.

Then he barely made an out.

He finished the season with a .324 average, 200 hits, 125 runs scored and 66 RBIs. It was his best season and ... it didn't ensure anything the next year.

Rizzuto knew nothing was guaranteed back then. Heck, DiMag had wanted a mere $10,000 raise after his 56-game streak in '41 and they didn't give it to him—even after he sat out a month.

Besides, he might have learned to play for Stengel, but he couldn't exactly trust him. Especially with all this hubbub about some hotshot shortstop in the minors who could do everything. Run. Hit. Hit with power.

Some Oklahoma kid named Mickey Mantle.

Rizzuto thought he was done.

What kind of shortstop could do all that and field, too?

None yet, it turned out.

Mantle was horrible at short.

Horrible enough to have fans in spring training search for armor if they were seated behind first base.

Rizzuto's position was safe. DiMaggio's job, it turns out, was not.

Mantle moved to center where he would take over for the Yankee Clipper the next season.

But not yet.

*** *** ***

The Indians took the field at Yankee Stadium tied for the division lead on September 17, 1951, determined to finally put a dent in the Yankees' World Championship run.

They had reason to feel good about their chances. Seventeen-game winner Bob Lemon, a future Hall of Famer and Yankees manager, was on the mound trying to even a two-game series.

By this point, Mantle was in the leadoff spot, taking Rizzuto's position in the batting order, if not the field. The Scooter was back down to eighth and DiMaggio had dropped to sixth, one notch below catcher Yogi Berra.

Nineteen-game winner Eddie Lopat pitched for the Yankees and the hurlers threw zeroes at each other for the first four innings. The Yankees didn't record their first hit until there were two out in the fourth. The Indians waited until the fifth.

The game, *New York Times* scribe Frank Finch wrote, "was tighter than my rich uncle."

But in the bottom of the fifth, the Yankees broke through. Third baseman Bobby Brown doubled to right.

Rizzuto lined a single to right, and the Yankees were up, 1-0.

But the ever-reliable Rizzuto committed a gaffe the next inning. His throw to first was low and catcher Jim Hegan was safe. Two batters later, the game was tied when Hegan scored on a single to center by Bob Avila.

It stayed that way until the ninth.

DiMaggio contributed a one-out single and the 42,072 fans stirred, ready for a game-winning rally.

They jumped out of their seats when Gene Woodling followed with a single, sending DiMaggio to third.

Inexplicably, the Indians opted to walk Brown and load the bases for Rizzuto, who had two of the Yankees' six hits against Lemon.

Waiting in the on-deck circle, along with Lopat, stood the 19-year-old rookie, Mantle. This was more excitement than any game back in Commerce, Oklahoma, that was for sure.

Standing at third, DiMaggio suddenly had the feeling Rizzuto would bunt.

Soon, he'd be sure of it.

Rizzuto had worked out a signal system with the Yankee Clipper. So, when the Scooter took the first pitch for a strike, he was thrilled.

It gave him the opportunity to employ his strategy.

He turned to argue the call with the ump, lifting his bat horizontally across his chest—the sign for a suicide squeeze.

DiMaggio was to take off on the next pitch, Rizzuto would bunt and the Yankees would score before Lemon could do anything about it.

Except, for one problem.

Lemon saw DiMaggio leave early. He was onto them.

And he sent the pitch where that squirt, Rizzuto, couldn't possibly bunt it.

Right in his ear.

*** *** ***

Game of My Life
Phil Rizzuto

"Well, it'd have to be the game when I bunted on the suicide squeeze play because I didn't hit a lot of home runs. (Chuckles.) Though I did hit two home runs in one game once. But it would be the game with the bunt. Ohhh yeah, that'd be it.

"Well, because they tried to throw at me and everything. 'Cause I could bunt, jump up in the air, do everything to get out of the way and still bunt the ball. And Joe and I had this signal between us. It was hardly ever needed. We were playing against the Cleveland Indians. Joe was on third with one out.

"On deck, the picture came out, it was so great, too. If you ever saw it ... In the on-deck circle was Mickey Mantle, *jumping* up in the air.

"Thing was, that Bob Lemon was pitching. Joe left a little early from third. So he threw it right at my head. *Right* at my head. And I jumped up

Hoooly cow, the Scooter was often a Yankee Stadium favorite, as revered for his warm birthday wishes in between pitches as a former broadcaster as he was for the five straight World Series titles he helped win from 1949-'53. *Al Bello/Getty Images.*

and I bunted the ball. And Lemon was so mad, he picked the ball up, and the glove, threw it up in the screen.

"And I made a mistake when he came in to manage (in 1978). I said, 'Hey, Lem, you remember that ...' Oh my. ... He got mad. They would have been in the World Series."

*** *** ***

Rizzuto chuckles.

Then he turns, nice and polite.

"Hey, how much longer?" he asks. "Not too much, huh?"

Cora's waiting upstairs. Somebody else is coming. It's getting unbearable, but he bears it.

He's one of the most beloved Yankees, because you don't have to look up to him to admire him.

Ruth, DiMaggio, Mantle.

They're up *there*, where you crane your neck to see.

Rizzuto?

He's right *here*, eye level or less, always ready to laugh at himself.

Today, the ballplayers wouldn't appreciate a bunt as much, the home run era, literally, driving it into oblivion. Today, Rizzuto still stays up to watch the games, rooting for Jeter, who for all his more impressive assets, still demonstrates his greatest value in ways not measured by stats. Still bunts. Still wins.

Just like Rizzuto.

He'll stay up to watch the games now, fretting and fussing over each one. The announcers don't wish happy birthdays, just call balls and strikes and try to come up with signature calls

Rizzuto just took pride in trying to capture the game for the people listening at home. Tried to give them a few minutes to escape whatever worries they had.

The biggest joke always seemed to be on him and he laughed right along with it.

"Oh, I do all the time," he said of laughing at himself. "Cora says 'Oh, there he goes again, he's always making these stories longer and longer.'

"I want to kick her in the shins."

He chuckled again, as harmlessly as ever. But it was time to go.

The Scooter was ready to shuffle you out of the house as quickly as he used to dart over the bridge.

He had a lot to do.

One thing he never had to do, though.

Pick up a shoeshine box.

CHAPTER 3

Don Larsen:
Perfect for a Game

October 8, 1956, World Series Game 5

vs. Brooklyn
Yankees 2, Dodgers 0

The stats: IP H R ER BB SO
        9   0   0   0   0   7

A few hours before Game 5 of the 1956 World Series, Yankees coach Frank Crosetti placed a baseball in Don Larsen's shoe.

When he spotted it, Larsen gulped.

He was pitching.

"Don't mess this game up like you messed the second game up," he told himself.

He would not.

Twenty-seven up, twenty-seven down.

On another night, the figures could have referred to Larsen's bar tab.

Not this one.

Strike three! A no-hitter! A perfect game for Don Larsen!

And underneath the broadcast booth where Bob Wolff made his call for NBC, bedlam broke out.

The 64,519 fans in Yankee Stadium screamed themselves hoarse long after catcher Yogi Berra leaped into the stunned Larsen's arms, reverse piggyback style. It was a lot of screaming over nothing.

More nothing than anyone had ever seen in a World Series game.

"If you work hard enough, I believe everybody's entitled to one good day," Don Larsen said. Larsen's came on October 8, 1956, when for 27 batters, Larsen was perfect, a World Series feat unmatched and worthy of Yogi Berra's famous bear-hug. *AP/WWP.*

When he reached the clubhouse, Larsen's eyes were as wide and clear as they were often rumored to be bloodshot. His teammates, usually mannequin-like in celebrating the victories they produced on an assembly line, hooped and hollered, even Mickey Mantle letting out a rare public cheer.

Larsen accepted an unending round of congratulatory pats on the back. They came from the most unexpected of sources.

"Would you sign this for me?" Dodgers president Walter O'Malley said, passing Larsen a ball in front of the press.

Larsen smiled continuously, but that shouldn't have been a surprise. He usually did, whether the news was good or bad. The previous spring, Larsen shrugged off a 5 a.m. car accident in which he hit a tree.

His life was a wink and a smile, even if he creased old man Casey Stengel's lips into a confounded frown.

"Larsen can be one of baseball's great pitchers any time he puts his mind to it," the Yankees manager had said once.

Larsen put his mind to it in Game 5, permanently etching his spot in a game that would humble him often.

"Imagine," he told the United Press after, "something like a perfect game happening to me? It can't be true. Any minute now, I expect the alarm clock to ring and someone to say, 'Okay, Larsen, it's time to get up.'"

In the umpire's room, home-plate ump Babe Pinelli slowly peeled off his equipment, knowing he would never call a game behind the plate again. It was the end of a 22-year career, and Pinelli punctuated it with a jabbing right-hand strike call on pinch-hitter Dale Mitchell for the final out.

"I'd never seen anything like this before," Pinelli said after the game.

Neither had anyone else.

In the stands, Larsen was converting Yankee-haters all over the Stadium, including the 16-year-old kid sitting in left-center. "I was rooting for the Dodgers until the fifth inning," future Yankees manager Joe Torre remembered years later.

A few thousand miles away, back home in San Diego, Larsen's mother couldn't contain her pride—for herself.

"I make it a rule never to watch Don when he pitches," Charlotte Larsen told the Associated Press. "Seems like every time I watch him, he loses. So, I just don't do it. I didn't today, and see what happened?"

Not to be outdone, over in Berkeley, California, Larsen's father claimed credit with some outside help.

"I didn't realize I had prayed that hard," James Larsen told the *Los Angeles Times*. "I got down on my knees last night and prayed for Don. No, I didn't pray for a no-hitter. I just asked God to help Don beat those Bums."

In Santa Monica, California, Judge Mervyn Aggeler decided justice could wait for this man.

Aggeler adjourned court in the ninth, passing along a play by play of each pitch to the courtroom. When Larsen struck out Mitchell, everyone from prosecutors to defendants momentarily forgot their differences and rose to cheer together.

And back in New York, Vivian Larsen rooted hard for Larsen, too.

To pay up.

A few hours before the game, about the time Larsen gulped at the sight of a ball in his shoe, Larsen's estranged wife, Vivian, entered the State Supreme Court.

She contended her husband had abandoned her and their 14-month-old daughter three months after their April 1955 marriage.

She wanted child support.

So along with all the awe-filled shakes of the head, hugs and handshakes, Larsen had something else waiting for him in the postgame clubhouse. A bill for $420 delivered from the nearby Bronx courthouse.

He paid it.

Two days later, Larsen would tell his side of the story to the court, explaining he dated the woman a few times in Baltimore and married her "only to do a decent thing as far as the child is concerned." He explained, as covered in *The Washington Post*, "at no time in our marriage have we spent the night under the same roof" and that it was expected they would be divorced.

By that time, the newspaper accounts from across the country detailing every angle of Larsen's perfect game were a day old. But one has lived forever in New York press boxes, the first sentence written by the *Daily News'* Joe Trimble aptly capturing the historic event of October 8, 1956.

"The imperfect man," Trimble wrote, "pitched a perfect game yesterday."

*** *** ***

He arrived in New York as part of that convoluted 18-player deal with Baltimore in 1955. Yankee fans wished he had remained player No. 19.

Larsen went 3-21 in '54, but two of the wins had come against the Yankees. They saw something in the kid.

Heck, he had darned near no-hit them in one of the games.

Started out all right, too, turning things around in '55 by going 11-2 and making the ole' Perfessor, Stengel, look good.

If you won, the old man might look the other way if you weren't keeping your business square outside the lines—within reason. Stengel had enough of a job chasing after Mickey Mantle, Whitey Ford and Billy Martin all the time, the trio always ready to tie one on.

So when Stengel addressed reporters about Larsen's 5 a.m. car crash in spring '56, he simply quipped of the pitcher's late-night activity, "He was mailing a letter."

Larsen followed up his '55 campaign with a decent year in '56, taking a 7-5 record deep in the season. But he kept walking people and getting behind in the count, so he approached his pitching coach with a proposition.

"Well, I was having a few problems with control," Larsen said. "I asked Jim Turner, 'You mind if I try something different?'"

Larsen chuckled.

"He said, 'I don't care what you do, long as you win.'"

So Larsen did.

Both.

He started tinkering with a no-windup delivery and somehow it worked. All these years later, he's still not sure how he came up with it.

"I don't know how I thought about it," he said. "Big deliveries didn't help. You've got to be comfortable. Some guys have tried it since, said, 'I didn't have any luck with it.'"

But Larsen had plenty.

He finished the season with four straight wins for an 11-5 record and a 3.26 ERA. More importantly, he rode into the World Series on a hot streak as the Yankees prepared for a rematch with the Dodgers.

In '55, the Brooklyn Bums were first-class citizens, beating the Yankees for their first Series win over them.

The news reel style Major League Baseball video of the '56 World Series will tell you that president Dwight D. Eisenhower personally asked to shake the hands of the men on both teams before Game 1.

Narrator Lew Fonseca, his voice that of a gangster reporting to his boss, noted "For a few hours, at least, he was able to leave behind the cares of state. Just as millions of other fans during the season escaped the stress and strain of their own lives by the relaxation of watching a ballgame."

For the Yankees, it hadn't been so relaxing. Sal "The Barber" Maglie shut them down for a 6-3 Dodgers win.

Larsen's stress and strain would come in Game 2.

Staked to a 6-0 lead in the second, he seemed set to help the Yankees cruise toward a tied Series.

But he gave up a single, watched another hitter reach on an error, yielded a sacrifice fly and walked another man and that was enough for Stengel.

A few batters later, relievers Johnny Kucks and Tommy Byrne blew the Yankees' lead and Brooklyn was on its way to a Game 2 win.

The Yankees won the next two games to even the Series, leaving Game 5 as the pivotal one. The Yankees needed to win or face the not-so-promising prospect of taking two at Ebbets Field.

If Stengel had decided on a starter for Game 5, he hadn't told many people.

Arthur Richman, now a Yankees official and then a newspaper writer, was close friends and drinking buddies with Larsen. He remembers the two sharing many a nightcap. The night before Game 5, Richman recalls acting on a tip from Stengel that Larsen would draw the start and got the pitcher to bed early without any booze.

But Larsen tells a different story, saying he had a few drinks and didn't know he was pitching until he saw the ball in the shoe.

A few other people were busy the night before Game 5.

Larsen's father knelt, saying his prayers in case his son should get the start.

And third baseman Andy Carey's father seemed to be pretty sure Larsen would get the ball, too.

According to Larsen's autobiography, *The Perfect Yankee*, Carey's father purchased a pair of mock newspaper headlines, including one that said Larsen would pitch a perfect game.

But Larsen, apparently, showed no such premonition.

When he arrived at the park and saw the signal of a ball in his shoe, he all but swallowed his tongue.

Locker mates Hank Bauer and Moose Skowron laughed.

"You're always a little nervous and stuff," Larsen said.

*** *** ***

L arsen stood on the mound, all eyes and ears at 27, his short hair fitting snugly under his cap.

He chewed a wad of gum so hard he might as well have bit through it and into his tongue.

In the second inning, Jackie Robinson lined a shot to third. The ball ricocheted off Andy Carey ... and straight to shortstop Gil McDougald, who recorded the out. In fetching the ball, McDougald looked like a man bounding toward another's discarded trash.

Only later would Larsen recognize the irony of the liner hit to Carey.

In '54, Larsen nearly threw a no-hitter against the Yankees, but Carey broke it up with a single.

Now, Carey saved a perfect game along with some help from McDougald in what would become one of the game's most famous plays. But in the second inning, Carey and McDougald had saved the life of an infant without knowing it would grow into a genius.

"You didn't start thinking about any of that yet," Larsen said.

And if you did, you were more likely to think about a no-hitter on the other side.

Not only had Sal "The Barber" Maglie won Game 1 of the Series, but he was just 13 days removed from pitching a no-hitter for the Dodgers. Then he retired the first 11 Yankees.

But Mantle ended Maglie's bid and saved Larsen's—all in an inning's worth of ball.

Mantle roped a home run into the right-field seats, the ball landing snugly inside the foul pole.

In the Brooklyn fifth, Gil Hodges lined a shot into the left-center gap.

Well, it's either one or two, Larsen thought, picturing a single or double.

It would be neither.

The old Yankee Stadium outfield was so wide players all but lobbied for a rest stop between left and center. But pausing to catch his breath was the last thing on Mantle's mind as he raced to his right.

Starting in front of the monuments and flag pole still in the field of play at the Stadium, Mantle sprinted.

Seemingly forever.

The play was as smooth as it was sweaty, Mantle, no doubt, grunting while he appeared to be gliding.

He finally thrust his glove down in a last-gasp backhanded attempt that thwarted the ball's bid to hit grass.

It was, Mantle would say after he retired, the best catch he ever made.

Or, at least, the most important.

At the time, Mantle merely guarded a 1-0 lead, not yet knowing he had protected Larsen's perfection.

The next hitter, Sandy Amoros, appeared to smack both into oblivion.

The ball shot out to the right-field corner like Mantle's had in the fourth.

Gone. A home run.

If it stayed fair.

It did not.

Missed by inches. Twenty-four of them.

Umpire Ed Runge would later say the ball landed foul by "two feet," leaving Larsen with a leg to stand on in his bid for immortality.

In the bottom of the sixth, Larsen needed to block out any thoughts of a no-no. He arrived at the plate to see Carey standing on first, a rare baserunner against the Barber.

The sign came in from the dugout, though everyone knew what it would be.

Bunt.

Larsen did, a good one that advanced Carey to second. Hank Bauer followed with a single and the Yankees had as much breathing room as they'd get—a 2-0 lead.

The buzz started going through the Stadium, fans whispering and wondering if Larsen could really stay perfect.

In the dugout, the professional Yankees—a team of bankers routinely depositing hits and wins—remained eerily silent.

Larsen, like a care-free child, had already broken the rule of no talking about a no-no in the seventh.

"Hey, Mickey," he said to Mantle, "wouldn't it be something? Two more innings to go."

"Shut the hell up," Mantle said.

Larsen didn't feel the nerves yet. Maybe because he wasn't fully aware of what was going on. He didn't realize he had a perfect game until the thing was over, anyway. Just knew he was throwing a no-hitter.

In the eighth, Robinson grounded weakly back to Larsen.

Five outs to go.

Gil Hodges lined out to Carey at third.

Four outs.

Amoros sent a fly to Mantle in center.

Three outs from history.

"My stomach was jumpin' and my head felt like it was going to bust wide open," Larsen wrote in *The Perfect Yankee* of taking the mound for the ninth.

"Let's all take a deep breath as we go to the most dramatic ninth inning in the history of baseball," broadcaster Vin Scully said.

And everyone did.

James Larsen, over in Berkeley, California, who had prayed for his son to win, but hadn't dreamt of him doing it this way.

Judge Aggeler in Santa Monica, who thought the tension too much to take and canceled the court's work.

The fans remained trapped between applause and silence, desperately wanting to cheer, terrified to do anything that might cost them their shot at history.

In the Yankees dugout, Stengel warded off all the well-meaning "coaches" who clamored to help him rearrange the outfield.

"I had more managers around me on the bench than any pilot ever had before," Stengel said afterwards. "The boys were helping me place the outfielders."

Second baseman Billy Martin, according to Larsen's book, gathered the infielders around and vowed *nothing gets through.*

In center field, Mantle, the Triple Crown wonderboy ... tried to keep his knees from shaking.

And out from behind the plate, catcher Yogi Berra shared the thoughts of an old teammate nine years and a couple of thousand miles removed.

"I just wanted to win the game," Berra said. "It was only 2-0. Remember, I had caught Bevens's game."

Nine years earlier, Floyd "Bill" Bevens stood in just about the same spot Larsen did. He had been one out from pitching the Series' first no-hitter, though he had hardly been perfect, scattering several walks.

It all went away in the ninth when pinch-hitter Cookie Lavagetto smacked a double and Bevens ended up losing the no-hitter and the game, 3-2.

From his home in Salem, Oregon, Bevens watched Larsen try to avoid a similar fate.

A while later, he would tell the Associated Press happily, "Larsen pitched a lot better game than I did."

Back on the mound, Larsen tried to calm his nerves.

He turned toward center field and appealed to the same power his father had the previous night.

"Get me through this," he prayed.

Carl Furillo came to the plate.

He took a strike. Fouled a pitch off.

Ball high.

Foul ball.

Foul ball.

Agony of an at-bat.

Fly ball to right.

Two outs to go.

Roy Campanella up next.

He lined a shot down the left-field line ... foul.

The fans got their breath back, followed by their cheers. Then they got something else.

Causing enough tension with one swing, Campanella ended it on the next, grounding weakly to Martin at second base.

Nothing got through.

One out to go.

The fans took their fingernails from their teeth long enough to let out a relieved roar.

Through the stadium, stunned, anxious and eager all at once, fan after fan turned to each other and wondered "Is this really happening?"

At the public address microphone, the man in charge of announcing the next batter—the one hitter standing between Larsen and perfection—could barely breathe.

Bob Sheppard had been working for the Yankees the past five years, his greatest joy offering that regal intonation of "Number 7, center fielder, Mickey *Man*-tle. Number 7." It just rolled off the tongue.

But Sheppard could barely get his mouth open when he saw who he was announcing now.

"Batting for Maglie, Number 8, Dale Mitchell," Sheppard announced when he finally regained his breath. "Number 8."

(Nearly 50 years later, the legendary PA announcer—dubbed the "voice of God" by Reggie Jackson and asked by Alex Rodriguez to recount introductions of famous players—still said no game had surpassed Larsen's gem for excitement at the Stadium. "After about 4,000 or 5,000 games, you want me to pick out one?" Sheppard said, sounding incredulous. "It's easy. Don Larsen.")

Mitchell made his way to the plate, the crowd suddenly silent.

It was the final season of his 10-year career and Mitchell was what had been known as a "professional hitter," finishing with a lifetime average of .312.

In 19 games for the Dodgers, after coming over from Cleveland, he had batted .292.

"Dale Mitchell was a pesky hitter, I had remembered him from the American League," Sheppard said. "I thought if anybody in the world could spoil this perfect game, it would be this chunky left-hander."

He had faced Larsen in Game 2, popping up weakly to third.

This is it, Larsen thought. Just throw what you've got as hard as you can and live with it.

So he did, all through that no wind-up delivery that made him appear to do no more than play catch.

The first pitch was a ball.

Boos.

Sickened, disgusted, how-the-heck-can-you-rob-this-guy boos.

Pinelli's last game behind the plate as an ump after 22 years and this is what he gets—an invitation to a heart attack and a potential date with a lynch mob.

Next pitch.

Strike.

Cheers. That's-better-and-keep-it-up-if-you-know-what's-good-for-you cheers.

The next pitch was low, but Mitchell swung.

Strike two.

Neverending noise.

Larsen just wanted some quiet somewhere in the middle of it all.

He reached down and touched the rosin bag. Removed his cap, brushing away the sweat with his forearm.

And he would get his quiet. Suddenly everyone in the stadium was too busy sucking air to cheer.

One strike from a perfect game.

C'mon, get me through this Larsen thought.

In the broadcast booth, Bob Wolff made his call.

Two strikes and a ball … Mitchell waiting, stands deep, feet close together. Larsen is ready, gets the sign. Two strikes, ball one. Here comes the pitch …

Mitchell tried to swing. Then he tried to stop.

Neither worked.

Pinelli's right arm jabbed the sky.

"Strike three!" Wolff announced. "A no-hitter! A perfect game for Don Larsen!"

*** *** ***

Game of My Life
Don Larsen

"I didn't know I was gonna start the fifth game 'til I came to the ballpark. Frank Crosetti put the ball in my shoe. I took a gulp and said, 'Don't mess this game up like you messed the second game up.' You're always a little nervous and stuff. Have to prepare yourself mentally rather than physically because it's the World Series.

"I never had no routines anyway. You might have a routine, but you didn't know it.

"Jackie Robinson led off the second inning, hit it to Andy Carey and it deflected to Gil McDougald. You didn't start thinking about any of that yet.

"(On Gil Hodges' ball in the fifth inning): The park was a lot bigger then too. Mickey could run like a deer. I said, 'Sayonara.' I was glad.

"(On Sandy Amoros's near-homer that was called foul in the fifth): "I talked to Ed Runge after. Ed told me that the ball was only foul two feet.

All over the country, fans, relatives and friends were riveted by each pitch of Larsen's perfect-game bid. Even decades later, Larsen said his accomplishment "hasn't yet" sunk in. *AP/WWP.*

"After the seventh inning, I bumped Mickey. I told him, 'Wouldn't it be something? Two more innings to go.' When I said that, everybody got real quiet.

"Sure, I was nervous. Maglie was pitching a helluva ballgame. On the bench, I was joking, having fun. On the field, there was lots of confetti and stuff.

"In the ninth, I was happy on the mound. I knew I had a no-hitter, but I didn't know it was a perfect game until after the game was over. You go out and do your best. Only thing that got me was when I had 26 in a row. Dale Mitchell comes out. Dale was a fine hitter. Very fine hitter. One of the hardest guys to strike out. When he took the third strike, Dale sorta half-swung at the ball.

"(Did it sink in after the game?) No. It probably hasn't yet."

*** *** ***

The Yankees would go on to win the Series, thanks to Larsen's catcher Berra, who smacked two homers in Game 7. Yogi would continue his Hall of Fame career.

Larsen would return to mediocrity, winning no more than 10 games in a season.

But before he did, he lived as large as any celebrity in the '50s for one night.

After the game, his buddy Richman called the exclusive Copacabana for a table.

"We're booked," he was told.

"Hey, I've got Don Larsen here," Richman replied.

"Hey, if you bring Larsen, we'll get you a table right up front."

And so it went. Comedian Joe E. Lewis announced Larsen, and the people in the club gave him a hearty cheer.

Not so cheery was Richman when the Copa handed him a bill for $500.

"After all the publicity we gave them," Richman muttered.

It wouldn't be a problem. Lewis picked up the tab.

Larsen picked up a few endorsement offers in the off season, but nothing like his perfect game successors, David Wells and David Cone would four decades later.

But he did get to stand on that stage in a suit and Yankees cap, peering into the camera wondering who he was about to face ... before doing a double take and exclaiming "That's a hitter?" when a familiar face came into view.

"Doing the Bob Hope show," Larsen said. "That was great. I was nervous as the devil. I had seen him on TV. ... We just did a little skit together. Course he loved baseball anyway."

He pitched another three years for the Yankees before getting sent off to Kansas City as part of a trade for a right fielder.

Roger Maris.

The lifetime record contains more losses than wins, an 81-91 mark showing that while Larsen might have been one of the greats when he put his mind to it, he was not able to do it consistently.

He'll always be revered as a Yankee, though, taking his place in the stadium's history with his perfect game.

Forty-three years later, the Yankees chose Larsen to throw out the ceremonial first pitch when they finally welcomed Yogi Berra back to the Bronx after a spat.

Larsen threw out the pitch, and Yogi caught it. Then the pair watched along with the rest of the stunned crowd as David Cone threw a perfect game of his own.

There isn't a lot of other excitement for Larsen these days as he leads a mostly sedate life out in California.

What's he doing now?

"Nothing," he said with a laugh, in 2004. "Doing some fishing. Doing some card shows, doing a few appearances."

He knows he will forever be known for one day, one game. He knows he could have been known for a lot more.

But it's OK. He's learned to accept what he has.

"Well, everybody thinks about that game and nobody thinks about the boo-boos I made," he said. "If you work hard enough, I believe everybody's entitled to one good day. Whether it's marriage, having a child. Some have more than others.

"I happened to have a good day that day."

CHAPTER 4

Yogi Berra:
It Ain't Over ... with One Homer

October 10, 1956, World Series Games 7

at Brooklyn
Yankees 9, Dodgers 0

The stats: AB R H RBI HR
 3   3   2   4   2

Author's note: The interviews for this chapter were conducted in 2004, shortly before the chapter was written. Yogi was a frequent visitor to Yankee Stadium during that time. While his visits have been limited as he's gotten older, he received a loud roar at Old-Timer's Day in 2012, befitting his place as a beloved icon.

Yogi Berra's mouth opened to reveal the grin that's all teeth and heart at once.

The one that makes him America's grandpa as well as its mascot.

It's the one he's flashed from the time he was a Hall of Fame ballplayer—defying the unathletic perception his tree stump of a body created—to the 2002 commercial when he reminded everyone he was Yo-*gi*. Yo-*gi*.

Ask him about the Yogisms and the title of his old book, *I Really Didn't Say Everything I Said* and he gives you that grin.

"Most of them I *did* say, though," he said.

OK, so start it up, Yog.

It ain't over 'til it's over.

Nobody goes there any more. It's too crowded.

It gets late early out there.

When you come to a fork in the road, take it.

Thing is, they make sense.

"The fork in the road is where I live," he said. "You got Highland Avenue and we got a fork. Going up to the fork in the road, take either one, you're on Highland Avenue."

Yogi Berra's two home runs in Game 7 and 10 RBIs for the 1956 World Series earned him a handshake from manager Casey Stengel, but no Most Valuable Player prize. "Larsen pitched the no-hitter, beat me out of the car," Berra said. *AP/WWP.*

He laughed.

"It just comes out; my kids always catch me," he said. "They write it down. They might want to write another book. They say, 'Dad, you said another one.' I don't even know what the hell I said. There are too many of them."

The same could be said of his career highlights, which sometimes get obscured by the cuddly personality that inspired a cartoon character to be named for him.

Thing is, he wasn't so embraceable—or humble—when it came to opposing pitchers.

"I always knew I could hit," Berra said with the same kind of confidence his young buddy, Derek Jeter, shows.

They compare rings now, Berra taunting Jeter about how far he has to go to catch him. Jeter thought he had a shot with four out of five World Series championships at the start of his career, but then he was kept at bay.

Berra, the Yankees' ringleader, has 10.

And after he watched Jeter's Yankees fall to Arizona in their bid for a fourth straight title in 2001, Berra playfully protected his mark of five straight back in 1949-'53.

"Now," he told Jeter, "you have to start all over."

When you have that many highlights, it's hard to pick one. So Yogi picked two—both in the 1956 World Series.

Catching Don Larsen's perfect game was his signature moment, when Berra bear-hugged Larsen at the end.

But push him to pick one and Berra decides to go for Game 7 of the '56 World Series. He smacked two home runs to help the Yankees beat the Dodgers, 9-0, and seal the title.

Even his son was surprised at the choice.

"I thought he would pick the Larsen game," Larry Berra said. "I thought that would be it. But I guess the one he performed in, the one he hit the two home runs off of (Don) Newcombe."

Yep, it was a great hitting performance for the kid out of St. Louis who used to practice with a broomstick and bottle caps. But, it turns out, there was more to the choice than the hitting.

It took a newspaper clipping to reveal exactly why the game was so special.

Berra's mother, Paulina, had been hospitalized during the World Series. She was diabetic. The doctors told her they'd have to amputate.

Told her she'd have to lose a leg.

But, as she did from the time she cooked those Italian feasts for "Lawdie"—her limited English kept her from pronouncing his given name of Larry—and his friends, she tried to keep a happy face.

So, after her son called to tell her about catching a perfect game in Game 5, she had a request to make her feel better.

Hit a home run for me, she said.

Forty-eight years later and a couple of months after first talking about his favorite game, Berra was approached again.

"Hey, you left something out," he was told.

Yogi grinned.

"Oh, you found out about that, huh?" he said.

*** *** ***

He first started playing baseball in St. Louis, where he was born in 1925. Back then they called him Larry or, following his mother's lead, Lawdie. But coming home from the movies one day, a friend noticed Berra walked like a character in the show, a yogi.

Not many people have called him Larry since.

They didn't have a lot of money, so Yogi would help out.

And in between doing what he could to help, Yogi would play softball, football and soccer with the neighborhood kids. On a good day, his older brothers would let him play, too.

They made do with what they could. Especially when there weren't enough kids around to make up a team.

"We used to play with bottle caps, you know; you use a broomstick, try to hit with bottle caps," Berra said. "We always played, you know, usually we'd need nine guys on each side to play. That game, bottle caps, we used to play it two on each side, pitching and catching. Foul ball, you're out."

He was 17 when Branch Rickey approached him from the hometown Cardinals.

Rickey had signed fellow catcher Joe Garagiola for $500, but offered Berra just $250.

Hey, Yogi wasn't going to take half if Rickey was paying the other guy double.

"I wanted the same thing Garagiola got—$500," Berra said.

The Yankees stepped in, paid the $500 and Berra was on his way to New York.

He drove in 23 runs in a doubleheader for Class B Norfolk. This is the game that showed Berra he could be something special. The game that made him realize just how good he could be.

The game that proved ...

Nothing.

"I always knew I could hit," he said with a sly grin.

But he wouldn't get the chance for a while. He joined the navy in 1944 and went off to fight in World War II. When the troops stormed Normandy on D-Day, Yogi was among them.

Years later, Berra never could understand why he kept getting the cold shoulder from fellow vet, Indians Hall of Famer, Bob Feller.

Finally, Feller fessed up.

"You're a draft dodger," Feller told him.

"Whattaya talking about?" Berra replied. "I was at Omaha Beach on D-Day."

Feller apologized and a friendship was born.

Berra's career finally got started when he returned from the service in 1945. He went to Triple-A Newark the next year and was up with the Yankees later that season.

What's he remember from his call-up?

"Well, he said, "I hit a home run."

There would be 357 more of those by the time Berra completed a Hall of Fame career. His compact swing contained the movement of a jab and the power of an uppercut.

"He'd just flick it," his son, Larry said, motioning with his wrists. "Flick."

He'd chase balls pitchers wanted him to chase, then make them realize they didn't want him to chase them.

"He was the best bad-ball hitter I've ever seen," has been the quote of many a player through the years.

Yep, he was one of the best offensive weapons the Yankees had seen, even if it came in a surprising package.

Compact and disproportionate, Yogi's body seemed more suited for providing children a short hop of a piggy back ride rather than a Hall of Fame baseball career.

But he could hit.

And he'd learn to catch.

"They thought I had a bad arm and everything, but I did have a good arm," Yogi said. "I just didn't know where it was going."

Coach Bill Dickey, the Yankees' legendary catcher who played with Babe Ruth and Lou Gehrig, worked with Berra. He told him if he wanted to be a better catcher, he'd have to pretend he wasn't one.

"He helped me a lot," Berra said. "He told me how to step into the throw just like an infielder. Went after the ball like an infielder. ... The breaking ball always goes one way to righties, like Dickey taught me, you can cheat like hell."

So Berra started blocking balls better. Started throwing out more runners.

And he finally started learning how to call a game, studying batters' tendencies and predicting the perfect pitch.

You can't call any mistakes if they don't get any hits and Berra did that enough in his career. Twice with Allie Reynolds. And Larsen, who he led into immortality in '56.

Of course, Berra barely escaped infamy on one of Reynolds' no-hitters, dropping a pop-up ... with two outs in the ninth ... hit by Ted Williams.

With the stadium hushed and thousands of people ready to twist Berra into a yogi-shaped pretzel ... Williams popped it up again. Right to Berra, who made the play.

"Yogi," Reynolds said after, "I hope the good Lord gives me a second chance like he did for you."

Not that Berra was so willing to give Williams a second chance after a disagreement.

See, Yogi liked to talk.

And talk.

And talk.

So Berra bantered with the only people he could—the hitters.

They dug into the batter's box and Berra switched on his chatterbox.

"What are you doing tonight?"

"Seen any good movies?"

"Where you having dinner?"

Williams, the Splendid Splinter who vowed as a teen to become the greatest hitter who ever lived, didn't want to waste precious seconds summing up his day.

"Shut up," he told Berra one day.

"Fine," Yogi said. "If you don't talk to me, I'll never talk to you again."

*** *** ***

Soon, Yogi became one of the biggest Yankees icons ever, up there with Ruth, DiMaggio, Mantle.

Someone for the current ones, such as Yankees captain Derek Jeter, to chase.

As Yogi reminds Jeter often, he has a long way to go to catch him.

Ten rings. Fifteen All-Star appearances. Three MVP awards.

"I always knew I could hit," Yogi said. But it was more important than ever in the '56 World Series. Berra's mother lost a leg
to diabetes as doctors were forced to amputate. She told her
son to hit a home run to make her feel better. He hit two.
Hulton Archive/Getty Images.

Yogi started amid the first dynasty by moving from the outfield to catcher and finished the next by moving from behind the plate to the outfield.

He drove in 90 or more runs nine times and hit .290 or better six times.

And come October, he was a monster, smacking 12 home runs and driving in 39 RBIs in 75 games.

Combined with his Yankees managing career and "It ain't over 'til it's
over" rally cry with the '73 pennant-winning Mets, Yogi became one of the
nation's icons. Actually, he had reached that status back in his playing days.

But an icon in the 1950s had a different lifestyle than the ones today,
when players like Jeter and Alex Rodriguez live in lush penthouses where they
can peer down on the rest of the city.

"Well, back then it was different," Yogi's son, Larry, said. "You were a
part of the community. You didn't have to hide. I mean he made a little more
money than other people, but still he had to work. He did a lot of things in
the winter time. He did a lot of banquets.

"They all hoped to win the World Series or win an MVP or a batting title because then they got to go on a banquet tour and they got $100 a night for talking or something like that and make a couple extra bucks."

Except Berra wouldn't accept all that extra cash in the off season. He'd make some bucks in his joint business venture with Phil Rizzuto—the pair opened a bowling alley.

But he wanted to stay close to home in the winter since he couldn't in the summer.

Every Sunday, they'd gather 'round for the raviolis. The spaghetti and meatballs. It was all like living back on the Hill in St. Louis, Yogi and his wife, Carmen, enjoying the Sunday family dinners the way his folks had when he was a kid.

Or when he'd go back to St. Louis as a Yankee and bring his teammates home to eat his mom's cooking. They'd go back to the hotel and Yogi would stay put—Mama's orders.

"She would've been hurt if I hadn't slept in my old bed," he said.

And he'd be hurt if he didn't have some time to spend with his own kids.

"I mean, the winter time, my mother always said he could have been a millionaire many-times over," Larry Berra said. "He didn't want to go. He didn't get to see us in the summer so he wanted to be home. He didn't want to travel. He wanted to stay around us.

"He used to come and watch us play basketball games, soccer games, the football games. Baseball, he couldn't see us. Never got to see us.

"If (a speaking engagement) was local, he would take me. I used to love to go to them. But every Saturday and Sunday, if he was home, and there was something on at Madison Square Garden, we were there. We used to go see the hockey games, the basketball games, the fights."

It was quite the life Yogi was creating for his kids, a star-studded spectacle a world away from the scrapping-to-make-a-buck background he had grown up with in St. Louis.

They could tune in to the TV and see their dad pop up in strange places, as he and several Yankees did on *The Phil Silvers Show* one year. They walked in, each trying to pitch a southern "prospect" on playing for New York.

"Thanks, you-all," Yogi said in a punch line punctuated by his Italian accent.

The Berra kids would pal around with legends like Mickey Mantle and Whitey Ford. They'd hang out in the clubhouses and get all the extra baseball cards. Then they'd stay up all night, witnessing the kind of celebrity feasts New Yorkers in the '50s would have dreamed about.

Thing is, it wasn't so different than the way Yogi grew up as a kid. The Berra boys just learned to play with the Mick and Whitey the way Yogi had all the kids who'd play with bottle caps and broomsticks.

"The best part about it was, the team I grew up with, they were all family," Larry Berra said. "Every Saturday afternoon after a day game, we'd have barbecues. (Gil) McDougald, Bill Skowron and Mickey. And my brothers and I and all the kids and we'd be barbecuing. So everybody knew everybody. It wasn't that you made 10 million, you didn't deal with this (guy).

"And then we would go to Toots Shor's after the games and I'm talking seven, eight, nine, 10, 11 years old, and I'd be sitting having dinner with

gihing to do. And that was it, I'd
sit there and have dinner with these people and go, 'Dad, let's go home.'"

Only after he'd grown up and had his own kids did Larry Berra realize
how special a role his father had played in Yankees history. Only then did he
understand what it was like to have his dad become such an integral part of
the Yankees.

And to watch it all get taken away.

*** *** ***

The rift lasted 14 years.

His fierce pride prohibited Berra from returning to Yankee Stadium after
owner George Steinbrenner fired him 14 games into the 1985 season. It was-
n't just the firing.

George didn't call him personally.

It was an insult.

And Berra wouldn't return.

But even though he wouldn't go back to the Yankees, he never left.

"He loves it," Larry said of his father's affection for baseball. "He watches it constantly. Even when he had the rift with George, he still watched the
Yankees on television. You know, he's been doing it for 60 years now."

Still, he couldn't go back.

Until Steinbrenner finally apologized.

He had strict orders.

The Yankee Clipper, Joe DiMaggio, had long enjoyed his role as "the
greatest living Yankee," savoring his status as the last man announced on old-
timer's day. But as he grew ill, DiMaggio pointed his finger Steinbrenner and
gave the Boss an order shortly before his death.

"You've got to get him back," he said.

Berra's children had been pushing him hard to end it, too. Dale Berra
played briefly for his father as a Yankee and saw firsthand just what it meant
to see an older Yogi in pinstripes.

But he was afraid of some other important people not getting to see the
same thing.

"You know," Dale told his dad once, "your grandkids have never seen
Yankee Stadium; they really don't know what you mean to the Yankees."

So, when Berra finally returned to the stadium, "it was mainly for the
kids," Larry Berra said.

In 1999, broadcaster Suzyn Waldman helped arrange a meeting at the
Yogi Berra museum in Montclair, N.J. With cameras following, Steinbrenner
actually looked nervous.

Not that it should be a surprise. For all his hard-hearted antics,
Steinbrenner has always shown a soft spot for those who have served the
Yankees well.

And, on the rare occasion, such as his spat with Berra or his decision to
let Reggie Jackson get away, he'll even admit some fault.

So on this day, as Steinbrenner started an awkward reconciliation with
one of the Yankees' favorite icons, it was up to Yogi to ease the tension.

"You're late," Yogi told him.

He smiled. The men laughed.

The rift was over.

Yogi threw out the first pitch at the Yankees' home opener in 1999. He helped raise the championship banner of the '98 Yankees. And, three months later, on July 18, they held a Yogi Berra day to welcome him back.

Yogi was paraded around and feted like the prodigal son, his grandkids finally getting to see all the ways their grandfather had contributed to Yankee lore.

Then they'd see something else.

With Don Larsen throwing out the first pitch and Yogi catching it with then-Yankees catcher Joe Girardi's mitt, one of those Yankees' magical moments was set.

Girardi would catch David Cone's perfect game, forty-three years after Larson's gem.

No one in the building could believe the latest example of the Yankees' mystique.

Of course, as Yogi would say, to get here, you had to go there first.

*** *** ***

The Yankees had lost to the Dodgers for the first time in World Series history in 1955.

So, as the Yankees entered the '56 Series, Yogi and his mates wanted revenge.

But Yogi had bigger things on his mind. He had completed another All-Star season, hitting .298 with 30 homers and 105 RBIs.

But as the World Series went on, Berra's mother was hospitalized.

The diabetes had taken over and forced doctors to amputate her leg.

She was a proud, tough woman who didn't want any pity.

Yogi did his best not to worry, but how could he avoid it? She had done everything for him.

Heck, he never would have made it to the World Series without her. Or the big leagues. When he was struggling to get by with barely enough to eat in the minors, she was the one who sent him money. And did it as secretly as she could lest her husband find out and decide he was right about this no-good game of baseball.

"Don't let your father find out or you'll have to come home and quit," she'd tell Yogi after sending money.

So he called her after Game 5. Wanted to tell her about the game. Wanted to know how she was.

She told him she was OK. You want to make me feel better? Hit a home run.

So, when Yogi arrived at the ballpark for the World Series, he was able to block out any concerns for his mother.

"Once you got on the field, you forgot about it," he said.

The euphoria from Larsen's perfect game was erased when Brooklyn came back to win Game 6 at Ebbets Field. For all the fanfare of Larsen's his-

toric game, it would be reduced to a side story in favor of the Dodgers' second straight World Series title if the Yankees couldn't take Game 7.

Johnny Kucks took the mound for the Yanks against Newcombe.

The Dodgers pitcher won at least 20 games three times and added a 19-
win season another year. But Brooklynites never forgave him for failing to
come through when they needed him most.

He had a reputation for giving up the big game and he was looking to
change that in Game 7.

Berra wouldn't give him a chance.

In his first two at-bats, Berra used that smooth swing of his—flick—to
pop the ball over the fence in right, the second out of the park and sending
kids screaming toward a car dealership to claim the ball.

Another homer by Moose Skowron and a shutout by Yankees starter
Johnny Kucks and the Yankees had a 9-0 win.

Berra had fulfilled a promise to his mother.

"That's for you, mom," Yogi thought as he rounded the bases after the
first shot, according to his 1961 autobiography.

After the game, he called to let her know he had come through.

"Very good," she told him proudly.

Very good, indeed. For the Series, Berra drove in 10 runs. Smacked three
homers. And he led Larsen through a perfect game that ultimately left Yogi
feeling robbed when the pitcher picked up the MVP prize.

"I had a good series," Berra said. "Larsen pitched the no-hitter, beat me
out of the car."

*** *** ***

Game of My Life
Yogi Berra

"The one who got the pressure was Johnny Kucks. He didn't know he was
pitching until the ball was in his shoe.

"I didn't take that much batting practice. I felt good, like I always did.

"Johnny Kucks pitching. He pitched a heckuva game, 9-0. I tell ya, he
pitched a four-hitter or something like that. And Larsen, naturally, a big one
too, no-hitter in the '56 World Series.

"I didn't get nervous (during the perfect game). Because I had caught
Reynolds. He got it. It's just one of them things. You worry about winning
more than the no-hitter. When it comes to that time ...

"(When do you start thinking about it?) The eighth. The seventh is still
a little too early. Everyone asked me what was the best part of the game. I said
the last strike.

"(The home runs in Game 7:) They were the first two times up. If I
swung hard to hit a ball, I missed it. Then the big one when Moose hit the
home run. Won, 9-0. Kucks had good stuff that day. Real good."

From his Yogisms to the warm welcome he offers fans and friends, Yogi Berra has become an American icon.
Doug Pensinger/Getty Images.

*** *** ***

These days, you can find Yogi back home at Yankee Stadium often. Every few homestands, he'll shuffle through the clubhouse, veterans bounding over to greet him.

He'll give them the grin and a pat on the back.

"How you doing, kid?" he says.

He's glad to be back. So glad, the running joke around the stadium is a poor man's Yogism.

They couldn't get him back, now they can't get rid of him.

Not that anyone would ever want to let go of a man who still serves as an inspiration.

In 2001, when the Yankees were down 0-2 in a best-of-five playoff series against Oakland—and faced two road games—Torre looked to Yogi for inspiration.

He approached the press conference podium with a hat that read "It ain't over 'til it's over."

And it wasn't.

The Yankees rallied to win three straight games and eventually advanced to the World Series.

Then they lost to Arizona and Yogi could tell Jeter that if he wanted to finish that run toward his rings, he'd have to start first.

Of course, Berra wouldn't really mind if Jeter ever caught up to his championship ring record.

The Yankees current captain might just receive a telegram, like the one Reds Hall of Fame catcher Johnny Bench did when he broke Berra's record for home runs by a catcher.

"Johnny—congratulations," the telegram read. "I always knew my record would stand until it's broken."

CHAPTER 5

Bobby Richardson:
Making the Yankees Proud

August 5, 1955

vs. Detroit
Yankees 3, Tigers 0

The stats: AB   R   H   BB
3   1   1   1

The Yankees trailed by four in the bottom of the ninth, but the bases were loaded and Mickey Mantle loomed on deck.

Not a bad situation for the home team, long as second baseman Bobby Richardson could reach base.

Except for one problem.

"I don't feel so good," Mantle told Richardson in the on-deck circle. "Why don't you hit a grand slam?"

Pretty funny, Mick.

Richardson was a table setter, just looking to get on so Mantle and Roger Maris could send him trotting home with another round-tripper. He averaged three homers a season.

And yet ...

He hit the game-tying grand slam upon request.

As the crowd roared in shocked delight, Mantle rushed to receive Richardson at the plate.

"I didn't think you could do it," Mantle said, laughing.

Mantle should have known better. The pair of unlikely friends would surprise people throughout their lives.

"We were closer than people think," Richardson said.

When they first met, behind a batting cage, Mantle calmed 17-year-old Bobby Richardson's nerves.

When they last met, 42 years later, Richardson did the comforting.

The Mick lay dying, a ravaged liver ready to claim his life. The sight of his old friend and teammate perked him up, though he so often avoided him in the past.

"I'm drinking so much," Mantle would tell Richardson, embarrassed, "I don't want you to see me."

After their final meetings, Mantle was ready for the world to see him.

But not as the Mick, the intoxicating image that could prompt grown men to ignore his flaws and remember only how he made them feel forever young.

He didn't want people to see only the picture they had of the hero perfectly cast for 1950s and '60s America—broad-shouldered, blonde hair, perfect country grin packed with just enough mischief to make it say more than "aw shucks."

No, the Mantle the world saw at the end was the one Richardson had known all along. This was a human Mantle, made not to be worshipped, but admired for athletic talent and teamwork. One full of the flaws he would admit to as his life neared its end.

"I would like to say to the kids out there—take a good look," Mantle said, his face gaunt, his guilt great after a life of alcoholism and adultery. "You talk about a role model. This is a role model—don't be like me."

Richardson's voice softened as he thought of one of his friend's final speeches. He knows he helped Mantle reach that point by sharing his faith with him. He knows Mantle had responded to his requests to read the Bible with less reluctance than he had as a player when Richardson would nudge him toward the team chapel.

But most of all, Richardson knows this:

"He was the most courageous person in that interview," Richardson said. "On national television—he had on that cap I'd given him from the All-Star Game—'I'm no hero. I'm no role model.' That was the best part of his life."

This might be Richardson's best moment as a teammate, the one he's said passes up any baseball memory.

He is best remembered for his role as the vacuum cleaner of a second baseman who also batted in front of the M & M boys in the '60s. While Mantle and Maris were battling for the home run crowns, Richardson was slapping base hits and taking them away.

He was also spending his free time in the clubhouse reading the Bible while on the other end, the Mick or Whitey Ford offered recaps of the latest round over at Toots Shoor's.

In the Yankees locker room you watched your tongue around Richardson, the normal clubhouse conversations not seen as fit for such a devout Christian.

His career started as a wide-eyed kid from the south, eager to join the Yankees after staring, riveted, at a movie screen depicting them.

The Pride of the Yankees painted a portrait of Lou Gehrig's Yankees as fun-loving fellas, but mostly it showed Gehrig's class and grace even as disease stole his career, then life.

Bobby Richardson had the series of his life in the 1960 World Series, driving in 12 RBIs, including a grand slam in Game 3 ... but it still wasn't his favorite game. "We lost the Series," he said. Instead he opted for his first game as a Yankee.
Art Rickerby/Time Life Pictures/Getty Images.

Richardson wanted to be a part of an organization like that, so when 12 out of the 16 teams chased him, he knew there was only one he'd accept.

He would bide his time, stuck on the bench in Casey Stengel's platoon situation, sometimes sent out of the game so early for a pinch hitter, he'd threaten to leave.

When Ralph Houk inherited Stengel's job in 1961, Richardson claimed the second base position for himself.

Houk told Richardson he'd be his second baseman no matter what he hit—which helped Richardson hit as well as ever.

Except, of course, for that '60 World Series when he stunned Stengel and everyone else with a grand slam and six RBIs in Game 3. He became the Series MVP, outhitting Mantle, Maris and Yogi Berra, compiling 12 RBIs.

And this would be the game Richardson chose above all others if it wasn't for one small detail.

"Nope, can't be that one," he said. "We lost the Series."

The trait connects the best Yankee teams through the years, the desire to win clouding every other highlight. It's why Richardson also declined to pick his game-tying grand slam with the Mick on deck.

The Yankees lost that one in extra innings.

So Richardson went back to the beginning.

The day he was called up at 19, the same age at which his friend, Mantle had made his debut four years earlier.

It had been two years since his first workout, when Mantle first embraced him.

Now Richardson was batting second, right in front of Mickey and behind Hank Bauer. Berra batted cleanup.

Richardson drew a walk, stole second and scored on Yogi's homer. He later picked up his first hit in a 3-0 win amid a pennant race.

This was the game.

Richardson will never forget becoming a Yankee, the organization that first drew him in as he sat in a movie theater.

He would soon discover the clubhouse wasn't always as clean-cut as the movie depicting Gehrig's old team. But while he wasn't big in social circles with his teammates then who were more apt to reach for a martini than the "milkshakes" they jokingly said Richardson and shortstop Tony Kubek would drink, his teammates would gravitate to him later.

He read the eulogy at Maris's funeral.

And at Mickey's.

All those years after falling in love with an image he watched on the big screen, Richardson provided some pride of his own for the Yankees.

*** *** ***

He grew up in Sumter, South Carolina, along with all of about 24,999 other folks.

Sun up, sun down, he played ball. Loved it. Loved the Yankees.

A scout named Mel Smith saw Richardson play and told him his dream would come true.

"When you graduate high school," Smith said, "I'll see to it you have a chance to sign with the Yankees."

He was 17 years old and about to enter Yankee Stadium for the first time. They wanted to work him out after signing him to a $4,000 contract.

It was a long way from Sumter.

And the players weren't exactly ready to offer any southern hospitality.

Veterans still guarded the batting cage with a sneer or a smirk, protecting their playing time by hording the practice time.

But not Mantle.

Mantle had been snubbed as a rookie, ducking for cover after dropping a pop up.

"Stop messing around with our money!" Bauer growled then.

So as he adjusted to big-league life and grew older, Mantle offered the welcomes he never received.

Richardson hung out hesitantly by the batting cage, afraid to blink the wrong way.

"Hey, kid," Mantle said, wrapping his arm around Richardson's shoulder, "you can go hit. No problem."

A friendship was born.

*** *** ***

Eight years later, Richardson would receive more comforting news.
He had been so tired of Stengel's platoon system. Don't get him wrong,
Casey was a good manager.

It's just that Richardson didn't care for Stengel's motivational methods.

Maybe because Stengel would say things like this about Richardson:

"He don't drink, don't smoke and he still can't hit .250."

"I don't want to say this the wrong way ... Ralph Houk was heads above
motivating," Richardson said. "Casey would make you mad ..."

And Houk would settle everyone down.

"First thing he said, 'You're my second baseman, whether you hit .200
or 300,'" Richardson said.

The Yankees were about to have one of their most legendary seasons,
sparking debate over whether the '61 Yanks had topped the Murderer's Row
of '27.

Mantle and Maris would take on Ruth and Gehrig in the kind of on-
field, off-the-field rumors of rivalries started in both time periods.

But before they could get to the glory of the '61 season, they had to overcome the pain of 1960.

Richardson can still see it.

No, not the grand slam he smacked in Game 3, half-expecting Stengel
to pinch hit for him on his way to the plate.

No, not any of the 12 RBIs he drove in during the Series, earning a rare
MVP nod on a losing side.

Pirates second baseman Bill Mazeroski's home run to end the Series.

This one hurt, the players covering their faces in the clubhouse, trying
to hide tears.

But ...

"In '61, we came right back," Richardson said.

And the M & M boys were born.

The most dramatic home run chase of all time has been chronicled in
everything from newspapers to books and movies.

It was an easy script to follow.

Mantle, the homegrown star, the player who bore the pressure of replacing DiMaggio and survived the city's scorn vs. ... well, that intruder from
Kansas City.

The fans rooted for Mantle.

The media pushed Mantle.

And guess who else?

"We were all pulling for Mantle, of course," Richardson said matter-of-
factly, about the players. "Roger was an outsider."

He chuckled.

"I don't know if Roger was even pulling for (Mantle) too," Richardson
said. "Roger was unique. He didn't care for publicity at all."

Not that Mantle loved it. He had come up at 19 and felt the burden of
expectation from a press corps that stopped comparing him to DiMaggio only
when it thought Ruth was the better match-up.

It had taken him five full years to show what everyone expected, when he won over the fans with a triple crown season in 1956.

But late in the '61 season, Mantle was stopped by the shot heard 'round the room—an errant flu shot that sidelined him and cost him a shot to chase the record.

Maris would do it, finally, in the season's last game, setting a new mark with 61 homers.

And unprecedented stress levels.

"He did lose his hair," Richardson remembered. "Every reporter wanted to have that personal interview. He was shy; he wasn't arrogant. He was probably one of my closest friends."

Ironically, two of Richardson's closest friends on the team would help connect him to his original dream.

The success of Mantle and Maris caused some clubhouse remodeling, their picture going up, another coming down. Pete Sheehy, the legendary clubhouse man who would sit around telling stories of Babe Ruth and had a knack for assigning a low number to a great player, knew who should get the original.

"I think," Sheehy told Richardson, handing him the picture of Ruth and Gehrig, "this is something you would like to have.'"

*** *** ***

So many memories. So many games.

Richardson, a career .266 hitter in the regular season, was like most revered Yankees.

He saved his best for October.

He hit .305 in 36 World Series games. Made a sure-handed snag of Willie McCovey's liner to clinch the '62 World Series title against the Giants.

And he provided his teammates with an alternative to their usual rabble-rousing, much like Gehrig had amid the antics of the Babe.

But while the quiet, family lifestyle of Gehrig kept him from connecting with the Bambino's party-a-night mentality, that wasn't the case for Richardson and the Mick.

They were small town guys who both reached New York and all its pressures at a young age. And, as much as Mantle might have hit the bottle, Richardson said he was also ready to hit the Bible.

"We'd pick out a room; Elston Howard would get the team together," Richardson said of the Yankees' former catcher. "I said, 'I'll call Mickey.'

"I'd tell him, 'Tomorrow, we're gonna have a devotion.' He'd say, 'We'll see. Call me in the morning.' Then I'd call and he'd say, 'I don't want to come to that thing.' Fifteen minutes later, he'd walk in the door."

And when Richardson's kids ran into the clubhouse, they'd sprint right past him and over to Mickey's locker.

"A lot of people don't know, in the mid-60s, we had a little place together—Grandfather Mountain," Richardson said of the vacation spot in Carolina. "Tennis resort, skiing. Mickey and I were both ski marshals. He couldn't ski and I couldn't ski, but we got the pictures posed so it looked like we knew what we were doing."

Richardson laughed.

"Mickey ... he did something for me that I don't think he'd do for any-body. He retired in '69. In '70, I built a fundraising drive for the YMCA. I asked him, 'Will you give a batting exhibition?'"

"For *you*, I will," Mantle replied.

The memories started making Richardson chuckle again, mischeviously.

"Kubek came in to throw to Mickey," he said. "Tony changed the pitch up on him and Mickey swung and missed. He was so upset. He signed 500 bats. The kids came over from the dugout. Just a great night."

Lot of great days on the field for Richardson to choose from.

But the best personal games ended up as losses, and any Yankee from Gehrig to Mantle wouldn't accept that.

No, the only one that made sense was to pick the game that started it all. The one when Richardson first became a Yankee, with no way of knowing just how much of an impact he would have on his teammates.

*** *** ***

Game of My Life

Bobby Richardson

"I was called up in August. I was 19 years old. The Yankees were battling for the pennant. Gil McDougald was hit by a line drive. (Minor-league coach) Johnny Pesky's wife was on the plane and I sat by her. I kept asking about life in the big leagues. She, of course ... she mentioned Yankee Stadium.

"There's pressure involved playing in a city like New York. I could feel that pressure. I didn't sleep much on the plane. I talked the whole way. She was very nice to stay up with me and was nice enough to talk to me.

"It was a late-night arrival. Stayed at the Concourse Plaza Hotel. Walked down to Yankee Stadium. Didn't know exactly how to get in. I'd try to get into ballparks and they'd look at me and say, 'Hey, kid, you can't go in there.' One time I went with Bobby Shantz. I said, 'Bobby, tell him who I am.' Bobby said, 'I never saw you before.'

"So, yeah, they were tough on rookies.

"Jim Bunning was a rookie and he was starting and he was working on a shutout and I walked. Don Larsen was pitching for the Yankees. He had been called up. Yogi was catching, of course. I stole second base. Then Mantle walked too, and Yogi hit a three-run home run. I was batting second behind Hank Bauer, Mantle was batting third. It was a great lineup.

"I called my father after the game. My dad was always a quiet person. Only saw me play one game in the major leagues live but watched it on tele-vision. Well, I got my first hit in the seventh. Somebody made me a plaque with a ticket stub and the write-up. I have my first game and my last game like that. I keep it in my office."

Richardson (center) and Mickey Mantle were "closer than people think," Richardson said. The lifetime bond began when Mantle embraced Richardson as a nervous rookie and endured until Mantle's last days when he was strengthened by Richardson's presence. *Art Rickerby/Time Life Pictures/Getty Images.*

*** *** ***

The last game came in '66, Richardson retiring after 11 years in the big leagues.

The Yankees would have a day for him, which made him feel good since the dream had started when he watched the film version of Gehrig's famous day.

"I got to tell them how lucky I was," Richardson said.

He started coaching college ball back in Carolina. Kept in touch with his old mates. Had no choice with some of them. He started coaching their kids.

Thirty-eight years after his last game, post-Yankees life was good for Richardson in Carolina. Richardson's still married to his high school sweetheart, Betsy. Still attends church every Sunday, where he's especially glad to see the man preaching.

"My son's my pastor," he said.

He'll never forget his time as a Yankee, from admiring one icon from afar and becoming friends with another up close.

He'll never forget, either, that scene in Mickey's hospital room, when his old teammate told him all his preaching had worked.

Before he died, Mantle said he shared Richardson's faith in Jesus, that he felt his soul had been saved.

"I'm at peace," Mantle told Richardson.

Richardson's wife, Betsy, asked Mickey what he would say if the Lord asked why he should be admitted to heaven. All those Bible studies Richardson believed in, the ones Mantle sometimes grudgingly attended, stuck deeply in the end.

In answering Betsy, Mantle quoted a Bible verse: "'For God so loved the world that he gave his only begotten Son, that whosoever believeth in him, should not perish, but have everlasting life.'"

Richardson read the eulogy at Mantle's funeral, including the same poem he had read for Maris, "God's Hall of Fame." It talked about different degrees of success, how fame might not always be what it's cracked up to be.

All those years later, after his teammates were more likely to search for a martini than a milkshake, they solemnly nodded their heads.

Richardson had made the Yankees proud.

CHAPTER 6

Mel Stottlemyre:
For the Boys

August 24, 1971
at Oakland
Yankees 1, Athletics 0

The stats: IP H R ER BB SO
              9 3 0 0 3 5

Author's note: The interviews in this chapter were conducted and the chapter was written in 2004, when Stottlemyre was the Yankees' pitching coach.

Mel Stottlemyre darted through the clubhouse and into the hallway filled with the inspirational signs George Steinbrenner requires at the Yankees' spring training site in Tampa, Florida.

"God willing—and given the chance—let me carve my name on something more important than a locker room bench," one giant billboard read, capped by the Yankees' logo.

Stottlemyre stood opposite it, about to enter the coaches' room. The man who had guided his family through his son's death and his own cancer battle—because he just kept going—had little time for inspirational phrases.

He was too busy working.

The Yankees pitching coach had returned for another season in 2004 after contemplating retirement the previous October. Now he had to mold a new starting rotation.

That meant plenty of work, little time to stop and even less for chit-chat.

In a suit instead of pinstriped uniform pants, Stottlemyre would be a principal. Try interrupting his routine and you're met by a pair of hawk's eyes framed by arching eyebrows peering out from behind his glasses.

If you need something, better make it quick and better make it worth-while.

His favorite game?

He paused.

Thought.

Smiled.

Suddenly, the principal was gone, the ex-ballplayer back and Stottlemyre's eyes softened, then widened. A smirk replaced the stern school-master look.

"Yeah, I know it," he said. "I know it."

There were 164 wins to consider, including a World Series victory over the great Bob Gibson in one game and a pitcher's fantasy of knocking out five hits in another.

But neither was the choice.

"I beat Vida Blue, 1-0, in a regular-season game," he said.

Stottlemyre laughed at the surprised reaction, letting out the first hint this seemingly meaningless game had carved itself into a lot more than a lock-er-room bench.

For a moment, Stottlemyre was neither a principal, pitching coach or pitcher. He wasn't a gray-haired cancer survivor or a grieving parent.

He was just a 29-year-old father about to leave his kids in an Oakland hotel room, heading for work on the day they would fly home for school.

Why did he pick that game?

Stottlemyre's smirk returned.

"My boys didn't think I could do it," he said.

*** *** ***

Stottlemyre is one of those Yankees caught between time, the fan who camps out for World Series tickets and falls just short of the window.

Oh, he had his shot at a World Series and made the most of it—outdu-eling Hall of Famer Bob Gibson in Game 2 of the 1964 Series as a rookie. But he dropped Game 7 to Gibson, then watched the Yankees drop into one of their few dark eras.

Had he pitched in almost any other decade, Stottlemyre's name would conjure images of Cooperstown. But he began his career at the end of one dynasty's run and ended it before the next. He pitched for lousy teams with great stuff, winning 20 games three times and losing the same amount once.

His highest ERA was 3.58 and the mark for his career was 2.97, but there was little help earning wins. Stottlemyre could outpitch just about any-one, but—other than that five-for-five day against the Senators—he couldn't outhit them, too.

If it wasn't enough for Stottlemyre to be trapped between time, his career was torn apart.

Literally.

When he tore his rotator cuff back in the '70s, they didn't know what to do about it. So Stottlemyre retired after just 10 seasons, in 1974, two years before the Yankees returned to the World Series. Three years before they won the first of two in a row.

Mel Stottlemyre was one of the Yankees' most accomplished pitchers ... but played in one of their least accomplished eras. His favorite accomplishment? Beating Oakland phenom Vida Blue in 1971 because his little sons didn't think he could. *AP/WWP.*

Stottlemyre could have been a part of that team, ex-teammate Gene "Stick" Michael will tell you. Could have been a World Champion.

Could have been something else, too.

"If he hadn't gotten hurt," Michael said, "he would have been a Hall of Famer."

But back then, "they couldn't fix that arm of his," Michael said. If they had, his old teammate figures, he would have pitched another five years.

So now Stottlemyre is renowned for helping develop a Yankees staff that won all the championships that eluded him as a pitcher. He's the proud father of a pair of ex-major leaguers who kept him from looking back by following in his footsteps.

His name is not the one that instantly comes to mind when mentioning Yankees pitchers, getting buried beneath Whitey Ford and Ron Guidry. It might fade more as time passes, thanks to his own assistance with pitchers like Andy Pettitte, David Cone and Roger Clemens.

Doesn't bother him so much now. Might have back then, when a rough outing would prompt his wife, Jean, to tell the kids to behave.

"Boys," Mrs. Stottlemyre would tell her sons, "you'd better be quiet. Your father's going to be mad."

"Dad was competitive," Mel Stottlemyre Jr. said. "I think he enjoyed the challenges more than the end result. He never rested on one game. Even to this day, when we play cards or get into competitive battles, the old man wins."

Yes, he still wants to win. Yes, he's still competitive. Just not as much as he used to be.

Not since he battled cancer.

Not since he lost Jason.

*** *** ***

They were angry.

At the whole damn world.

What do you expect when one boy is 17, the other is 15 and both of them just buried the 11-year-old brother who should have still been tagging along behind them?

Their Dad might not have said, "Why me?" but you weren't going to keep Todd and Mel Jr. from saying it then. And none of them could stop the question that was more like a cry.

"Why Jason?"

Brothers are supposed to trade baseball cards, barbs and maybe, in their worst moments, blows.

Not bone marrow.

Todd wasn't supposed to become a donor at age 15. And if he was, if his little brother needed help to combat the leukemia, damn it, wasn't it supposed to work?

Weren't they supposed to be playing with their dad, following him along to his job as a pitching coach the way they had 10 years earlier when he was still pitching in 1971?

When their dad was still a player, Jason was just a toddler—as apt to remember a trip to the circus as he was the ballpark.

Back then "Todd and I were at an age where we were starting to understand how big Dad was," Mel Jr. said.

By 1981, Jason had become old enough, too, to understand all the joys of raiding a major league clubhouse along with his older brothers.

"You know, it was special in that way," Mel Jr. said. "As a kid, you take for granted being grown up in baseball."

And you take for granted that your little brother isn't going to die before he reaches high school.

Weren't they all supposed to still be playing ball, showing off what they had learned?

Jason would have been the best of them, you know.

Better than Mel Jr., who'd go on to pitch in the majors before injuries forced him into coaching. Better than Todd, who along with his Dad, is part of the only father-son duo to each collect 100 wins in the big leagues.

"Jason was supposed to be the best athlete out of all of us," Mel Jr. said.

The boys moped. And burned. And cursed everything from their life to their brother's death.

"Yeah, we were big-time angry," Mel Jr. said. "We were mad at the world. We couldn't understand why our brother got taken away."

So their father, who had spent his career showing his boys what it was like to visit dad at the ballpark, made a decision.

He would come home.

No more baseball.

Not now.

His boys needed their father. Needed answers. And he knew he could provide one bigger than the rest.

The one that said he didn't have any.

"He was more there for us to lean on than he was a 'Sit down, boys, I need to talk to you' situation," Mel Jr. said. "There were a lot of things he couldn't understand either.

"He was mourning, too. I think that he was letting us know he was feeling the same thing we were. He was just letting us know and just showing us as a family he was mad at the world, too."

The boys could go to their mom and talk one way. Talk to their dad another. Instead of worrying about making him mad, the boys were now relieved their dad would allow them to be upset as well.

His job no longer mattered. Not until his boys had started to cope. So he just walked away from the sport until his boys were ready for him to return.

"I don't know how many other dads would do that," Mel Jr. said. "It's hard to say. As a son, we definitely needed him around. Those were the toughest times of our life, and we couldn't understand it."

The tough times were far from over.

Mel Jr.'s big-league career was cut short, his body cut by a surgeon's knife eight times. Like his dad, Todd faced rotator cuff problems—in between the thrill of facing his dad's Yankees team in the postseason.

Then in 1999, when the good times had come, when their father the pitching coach was winning all the titles he hadn't as a pitcher, more bad news.

He had cancer.

"For us to see our dad go through it ... we were tight as a family," Mel Jr. said. "My dad never complained. It was always about a solution, a plan of attack."

When he first heard the news, Todd echoed his anger at his brother's death. Then he remembered his father's strength.

"There comes a point where you want to call time out and say, 'Hey, I've got all the strength and character I need,'" Todd told the *Los Angeles Times* shortly after his dad was diagnosed. "My dad has been so special in my life that it rips my heart out, knowing what he's going through, but the one thing he hasn't said is, 'Why me?' or that life is unfair."

Instead, he has continued to earn the respect of his colleagues along with some more championship celebrations. It was a giddy Stottlemyre who sprinted out to the Babe's monument along with David Wells and Roger Clemens after the Yankees' epic Game 7 win over Boston in the 2003 American League Championship Series.

It is an inspiring Stottlemyre who now answers unending stacks of mail from fellow cancer paitents who write to him "because he's so positive," Mel Jr. said.

"Mel could handle anything," Stick Michael said. "He's the toughest guy in the world. You've seen what he's gone through with his son and with his health. He can handle anything. He's a tough, tough guy."

Except when it comes to his family. That's when Stottlemyre is softer than ever.

"I cherish every opportunity I get to go hunting and fishing with him," Mel Jr. said. "It has changed things. I also think he looks at life in a different manner. I think he appreciates those times he gets to spend with his grandsons or his children."

Even if some of those times are already in the past.

*** *** ***

The boys were leaving after the game. It was August, 24, 1971, which meant school beckoned back home in Washington.

Mel Jr. remembered going to the circus with Todd and taking little Jason with them. Now they were ready to see Dad off to pitch.

Hey, who's pitching for Oakland, they asked.

Vida Blue, their father said.

"Oh, Dad," the tiny voices said, "you don't have a chance."

Sure, they had seen their dad win a lot of games. Or, at least, pitch well enough to win. But they also saw the Yankees' offense turn potential wins into losses all year.

Plus, this was Vida Blue. Not to mention the Oakland A's.

The A's were a raucous bunch, who ripped apart the league. With brash superstars like Reggie Jackson and Sal Bando leading the way, the A's beat up on just about anyone in their path.

And Blue fit in perfectly.

He had burst onto the scene as a dominating superstar. At 21 and in his first full season in the big leagues, Blue blew by just about everyone who faced him.

Never mind the 24 wins. The guy barely let anyone touch the ball, striking out 301 batters.

Unbelievable.

"Vida Blue, at the time, he was the man," Mel Jr. said. "He was the one to beat. It's one of the few games as kids that Todd and I remember. Out of all the games we've been to it was one of the great games that he's pitched."

But as far as Mel Jr. can remember, *he* wasn't the one to tell his Dad he couldn't beat Blue.

"Well, that was probably my brother popping off," Mel Jr. said, laughing, of Todd. "Knowing dad, he probably said 'I'm gonna prove those suckers wrong.'"

And that's exactly what he did.

A life that included the loss of his young son, Jason, to leukemia and his own cancer battle has made Stottlemyre look at the game differently. As the Yankees pitching coach in 1996-2005 under former manager and fellow cancer survivor Joe Torre, Stottlemyre helped implement a culture of humanity along with winning. *Ezra Shaw/Getty Images.*

*** *** ***

Game of My Life
Mel Stottlemyre

"It's always been kind of special. That year, Vida Blue was just unbeatable. Had to be one of his first years. My kids, at that age, were just tremendous followers. They were about seven and nine. Very aware of what was going on in baseball circles. It was probably early September or August—they were going back to the state of Washington to enroll in school. They had flown to Oakland. The biggest thing I remember, leaving the hotel that day. When they heard Vida Blue was pitching for Oakland ...

"'Oh, Dad, you don't have a chance.'

"I was thinking, 'Thanks for the confidence for the old man.'

"Thurman Munson drove in the run with a broken-bat single over second base. That was the game's only run. The first hit they got off me was a bunt by Rick Monday fairly late in the game. Seventh or eighth inning. We ended up with two hits off Vida Blue. I didn't really think so much of a no-hitter, as much as I knew I couldn't give anything up.

"That year, he was really dealing. He had started off tremendously. He had won a lot of games in a row. He had come to New York; the radio stations had been building it up. Doing everything they could to jinx him. The priests were saying extra prayers.

"My kids were aware of all that. Oakland was dominant in those years. They were the dominant American League team.

"I kind of laughed about it afterwards. They were, 'Dad, I can't believe you did it! I can't believe you beat Vida Blue!'

"I kinda laugh about it. Both my boys remember that. I would have thought they'd at least give me an even chance. Back at the hotel, they were just shocked that I had beat Vida Blue. They didn't think I was going to."

*** *** ***

Stottlemyre, the pitching coach, grinned from the dugout of the Yankees' spring training site, a world away from work for a moment. Don't get him wrong. He loved working again, preparing for the 2004 season. And the boys wanted him back—one more year to show New York how much it's meant to him. He almost left after an aggravating season full of rants by Steinbrenner, but truth be told, the Stottlemyre family appreciates the Boss' desire to win. And they'll never forget how supportive he's been through the cancer.

But this was a memory that reminded Stottlemyre why he isn't always quite as competitive as he used to be.

"I know that it would surprise you and it would surprise a lot of people," he said of his favorite game choice. "I think the only reason I picked the game is, all the support I've gotten from my family, that was the one time I didn't."

He chuckled.

Then the smile faded.

"Maybe the reason that game is so important to me is because of some situations in my family that have happened since that time," he said. Maybe if you asked me another time, I would have picked the five-for-five game. I remember it because I've had a lot of things that have happened in my personal life. Both my kids went into playing ball. Both of them are out in Arizona.

"I lost a son who was out there (in Oakland that day). I went through an illness ... and they've always been so supportive. It's been harder for me. You look at things a little bit differently."

As he remembered the son who was lost and the boys who grew into men, Stottlemyre thought about all of them. His sons had been so grateful to have him both as a major league role model and a dad willing to reject the big-league life for them.

But he didn't release himself from worrying about his role as a parent until Todd and Mel Jr. pursued their own baseball careers. When his boys followed in his footsteps, it kept him from wondering if he had walked out of too many hotel room doors.

"The happiest thing I could see was when they tried to go into baseball," Stottlemyre said. "It put a stamp of approval on my career. That there were no feelings of, 'Dad wasn't there.'"

CHAPTER 7

Reggie Jackson:
Becoming a Yankee

1977 season

The stats:	AB	R	H	HR	RBI	BB	AVG.
	525	93	150	32	110	74	.286

WS Game 6

The stats:	AB	R	H	HR	RBI	BB	AVG.
	3	4	3	3	5	1	1.000

"Everything is magnified tonight," the announcer told his television audience. "You hit a home run, it'll be, for sure, heard 'round the country."

The broadcaster uttered his pregame prediction on a 50-degree October evening at Yankee Stadium, the Yankees about to win a championship they sought for more than a decade.

The announcer?

Reggie Jackson.

Chris Chambliss would prove Jackson the broadcaster right nine innings later, when he won the 1976 American League Championship Series with a home run off Kansas City's Mark Littell.

The blast sent the Yankees to their first World Series in 12 years, and sent fans sprinting onto the field.

"It's too bad they don't give MVP awards out in the playoffs," Jackson announced, watching from above as fans mobbed Chambliss while he raced for home like a man escaping muggers.

Let the story begin here.

Reggie Jackson's powerful swing left him with an all-or-nothing option of mammoth home runs or humbling strikeouts. In October 1977, three of those swings left the crowd chanting, "REG-GIE! REG-GIE! REG-GIE!" when they resulted in three straight home runs in a World Series game. *Rich Pilling/MLB Photos via Getty Images.*

With a jubilant Yankees team restoring pride to a franchise filled with it, but running empty for years.

With Jackson towering above it all, looking down on the action, a free agent a month from making a decision that would change all their lives.

It begins here, because the two sides were as far as they were close that night, Jackson and the Yankees sharing a shaking stadium, but not yet knowing they'd soon share the same clubhouse.

Neither side liked sharing, really.

Not from the time Jackson vowed at his welcoming press conference that, with his bat in the lineup, the Yankees would *not* get swept in a World Series—as they had by Cincinnati in '76.

"Well, excuse me," Graig Nettles remembers Yankees captain Thurman Munson muttering, a month after hitting .529 in the Series. "Who are you, Mr. October?"

This was a mismatch of epic proportions—Jackson, the three-time World Series champ, and the still-rising Yankees. It seemed destined for disaster ...

From the time when Jackson arrived in spring training camp and Munson—who had encouraged Yankees owner George Steinbrenner to sign Reggie—and most of the veterans snubbed him.

Or the time Jackson sat in a Florida hotel room that spring with reserve catcher and old friend Elrod Hendricks and outfielder Lou Piniella and complained about being treated like an outcast.

"Reggie," Piniella said, "why don't you make the effort you made with me with the rest of the guys?"

Twenty-seven years later, Jackson admitted, "I didn't exactly try to fit in."

Or when the *Sport* magazine hit the stands in May with the infamous "Straw that stirs the drink quote," Jackson reportedly saying he was the team's leader and Munson, already a beloved Yankee, was not.

Or maybe it starts way before all of that, Jackson growing up the son of a Negro Leaguer who had to work three other jobs for a few bucks a day.

Maybe it starts with Jackson growing up a "colored kid" who felt like a second-class citizen.

"There was a lot of anger in me," he said.

Maybe it starts with an American society still crawling toward equality 30 years after Jackie Robinson broke baseball's color barrier.

One in which a few of the Yankees, their respected leader and captain included, had no problem peppering conversations and jokes with the word "nigger" during a less politically correct era.

"They'd laugh and joke and say, 'We don't mean you,'" Hendricks remembered in 2004, a year before his death. "I said I don't care. I didn't think it was funny worth a shit."

Maybe it was the Jewish jokes Jackson heard around the batting cage, his head jerking up, then nodding down, wondering silently what his new teammates must have been saying about him when he wasn't around.

There were other black players on the Yankees, but none who spoke out like Jackson. There were few in sports who did. Or society.

"Ali spoke like that, but he spoke in riddles," Jackson said of heavyweight champ Muhammad Ali. "Jim Brown spoke like that. Jackie."

Or maybe the disaster really started later in the season with the manager, Billy Martin—determined to prove he was in charge—pointedly calling Jackson *boy* and threatening to kick his ass.

And maybe it was none of that. Or all of it.

Maybe, whatever drove Jackson, son of a Negro Leaguer, to open his mouth and remind the world how good he was struck right at the core of Munson, son of a trucker who reminded him he never was good enough no matter what he did.

Now it started all over again for Munson, good enough to be captain of the team and lead them to the World Series; promised to be the highest-paid Yankee, but forced to watch Jackson shoot past him in money and shoot his mouth off to reporters.

Maybe it was just one giant mess of egos butting heads, Jackson ready to prove a black man could be the Yankees' biggest star on a team that already had Munson—equally prideful in private—in charge.

A team that had won the 1976 American League pennant with Jackson up in a broadcast booth and didn't feel the need to have him looking down on them as he would when he first arrived.

Bragging about his days with the three-time World Champion A's, talking about what he could add to a team that was feeling good. And it only got worse after he was quoted as saying he was the "straw that stirs the drink" rather than Munson, the American League MVP the previous year.

"That was the way Reggie felt," Chambliss said. "That drink was already stirred. We were playing well. He added to it."

Or, as Hendricks said less politely: "These guys don't want to hear that. Those were a bunch of guys who believed in themselves and were ready to win—with or without—Reggie."

They'd win with him. Because of him, too.

And by the end of the year, full of fights and chaos, the biggest winner of all was the man who had been more prophetic than he realized the previous season.

Everything is magnified in October, especially in the last game of the season as it was in Game 6 of the 1977 World Series.

You hit a home run, it'll be heard 'round the country.

You hit three of them?

It'll be heard forever.

"Oh, what a blow!" Howard Cosell announced after the third straight homer by Jackson. "*How* this man has responded to pressure. ... Oh, what a beam on his face! How can you blame him? He's answered the whole world."

*** *** ***

He had to hit right-handed as a kid. Lady had a garden.

This was in his backyard in Wyncote, Pennsylvania, Jackson's father coming out the back door of his drycleaning shop to watch the kids play.

A bunch of seven-year-olds having some summer fun.

But if Jackson hit in his natural lefty style, the ball would go screaming over the fence and straight into the neighbor's garden.

"And she'd get *mad*," Jackson said, laughing.

He needed the laugh.

It was spring 2004 and Jackson had just returned from a conversation with Yankees general manager Brian Cashman. Cashman would later tell reporters, yes, he had enforced major league baseball's gag order on the steroid issue to Jackson, a Yankees adviser.

Jackson had spoken out bitterly in a newspaper report, not so subtly questioning the authenticity of aging, but peaking, slugger Barry Bonds.

"There is a reason why the greatest players of all time have 500 (homers)," Jackson told *The Atlanta Journal-Constitution*. "Then there is that group that is above 550. There is a reason for that. Guys played 19, 20, 25 years. They had 9,000 to 10,000 at-bats, and it was the same for everybody.

"Now all of a sudden you're hitting 50 (homers) when you're 40 (years old)."

He took pride in every one of his homers, so much that you could see him admire most before they left the park.

He took pride in the obstacles he overcame to hit them. So when he worried about the game's legends, from the Babe to Mickey Mantle to Hank Aaron and, yes, himself, Jackson wondered how they would feel if it was later discovered records were broken by fraudulent methods.

But Jackson didn't want to get into all that right after his conversation with Cashman. Reggie had stirred it up again and, at 57, he had learned to temper the tongue that couldn't be tamed at 30.

At least sometimes. (Eight years later, Jackson's comments about performance-enhancing drugs would again attract the Yankees' disapproval. He told *Sports Illustrated* in 2012 that while he considered Yankees third baseman Alex Rodriguez a friend, his admitted use of performance-enhancing drugs in 2009 should keep him out of the Hall of Fame. It was an opinion shared by many around the game, but reports indicated the Yankees did not like their special adviser offering such a candid opinion about their player, and the publicity that would accompany the comments.)

As he sat down for the interview in 2004, Jackson was thoughtful, introspective, his dark brown eyes looking down beneath shades not as tinted as the ones from his playing days.

This is the side to Jackson that surprises the far-sighted observer who sees only a big mouth to go with a big bat.

"He talks a lot, but the thing a lot of people don't know is, Reggie's very sensitive," Hendricks said.

Except when he's not.

When he's as crass and arrogant as ever, which can come the day after sensitive introspection.

Jackson is one of the most fascinating sports figures of all time, as complex and baffling a persona as you'll ever see. And to reduce him to the cartoonishly arrogant character consumed by the "magnitude of me" comments would be to miss out on a lot.

Even if you never fully understand what you're getting.

One day he could engage you in a lengthy, philosophical discussion about race, relationships and all the things that matter so much more than "Reggie hit three home runs." The next, he could be crudely talking about a female conquest, just another hound of a ballplayer seeming at home on the Howard Stern show, on which he's been known to appear.

The duality started way back, when Jackson was a young, cocky kid telling everyone around him they'd better remember his name because they'd be hearing it forever.

Except the times he thought they wouldn't hear it again.

Hendricks remembered the first time he played with Reggie, back in the Puerto Rican League in the winter following the 1970 season.

Back when Jackson had finished three full big league seasons that left people thinking he was either going to be a Hall of Famer or one of the biggest disappointments ever.

Back then, Reggie was just a 24-year-old kid wondering if he could really play the game.

Maybe he should just quit.

*** *** ***

He had gotten the football scholarship like his father had hoped. His dad wanted him to get an education.

And not the humbling one Martinez Jackson received working as everything from a shortstop to a traveling secretary and busdriver in the Negro Leagues.

So Jackson earned the scholarship to Arizona State and was determined to get his education. But Jackson was too good an athlete not to turn heads, even if he started out as a football player.

"I didn't have a special affection for baseball," Jackson said. "My father did. I was much more of a football player."

Then the baseball coach at Arizona State saw Jackson take a couple of swings and said, "Why don't you try out for the team?"

Jackson was about to become a baseball player for good.

A couple of years into his education, the A's drafted Jackson No. 2 overall. The Mets, drafting first, picked Steve Chilcott, forever known as the player drafted ahead of Reggie Jackson who failed to make the majors.

So Jackson would have to get his education later. Charley O. Finley was offering big bucks now.

And in 1969, Jackson started showing why.

By mid-summer, all of baseball was talking about the skinny, clean-shaven kid from Pennsylvania. Wondering if somehow he could chase the Babe and Roger Maris and become the single-season home run leader in his first full season.

He had 40 homers by the end of July and ...

Seven the rest of the season.

He didn't fully recover the next season, hitting .237, seemingly flaming out as quickly as he had caught fire. He took his struggling self to Puerto Rico and the winter league, as humbled as he could be haughty.

He'd work his way out of it, because he worked his butt off for everything.

Then he slumped there, too.

And wondered if it was even worth it. If he could play the damn game any more.

So when the general manager sent Jackson in to see manager Frank Robinson, he was "as low as he could get," said Hendricks, a teammate at the time.

"He broke down and cried," Hendricks said.

"'I quit,'" Hendricks remembers Jackson telling Robinson.

"I know you could go into business," Robinson told Jackson. "But you'll let down a helluva lot of people, including yourself."

Jackson listened intently. Absorbed his manager's words. Decided ...

"I'm catching the first flight out of here tomorrow," he said.

"Fine," a fed-up Robinson said. "Be my guest then. Just go."

Hendricks laughed remembering the story Robinson had relayed to him.

"Frank knew there was nothing more that he could say at that point," Hendricks said. "You want to go? Go."

Jackson didn't.

Went back to work.

Came back to lead the winter league in home runs the second half of the season.

He was on his way.

*** *** ***

As a rookie, Jackson worked with Joe DiMaggio, an instructor with Oakland at the time.

The Yankee Clipper didn't have as easy a task selling Jackson on his hitting concept as he did pushing Mr. Coffee, though.

He wanted Reggie to cut down his swing.

Jackson tried. But you might as well have asked him to keep quiet, too. Not to worry. The big swing worked out just fine in Oakland, where Jackson fit in with the raucous A's on the way to three straight World Series championships.

As it had been with the Mick, there was no in between with Reggie. He swung hard and swung big.

So the ball was either going to places you'd never seen before—as it did when his shot hit a tower atop Tiger Stadium in the '71 All-Star Game—or it was going right back into the catcher's mitt to record another strikeout.

By the time he was done, Reggie hit his way into the Hall of Fame with 563 home runs. He also struck out more than 100 times in 18 of his 20 full big-league seasons.

He was quickly becoming a leader for the three-peat A's—on the field and in controversial situations.

He'd jump on a teammate for not hustling, then get into an argument. He'd talk and talk and talk some more, and the only thing that made his teammates put up with it was the home runs that would stun them into silence.

And they won, man.

With Sal Bando and Joe Rudi? Bert Campaneris and Catfish Hunter? That was a team, man.

And Reggie became as big a part of it as any of them, winning the MVP award in '73 with 32 homers and 117 RBIs.

Then he helped the A's knock the Mets off in the Series—a year after Chilcott retired.

In October, Jackson took over.

He had two homers in his first three postseason games in '71. Hit .310 with a homer and six RBIs against the Mets in '73. And in '74 he added another homer and five RBIs as the A's took their third straight World Series title over the Dodgers.

Life was great, except Finley and the advent of free agency were chasing the A's out of Oakland.

The run-ins increased between the game's biggest slugger and one of its maverick owners and in '76 Jackson was sent to Baltimore a year before he would become a free agent.

There he could only imagine the future.

"If I ever played in New York," he reportedly told some Orioles teammates, "they'd name a candy bar after me."

*** *** ***

Billy Martin was a Yankee first, a hot head second.
Or was it a hot head first and Yankee second?

The Yankees were his greatest love. His temper the greatest threat to make his greatest love spurn him.

It had happened as a player when the Yankees sent Martin packing after an infamous brawl at the Copacabana in 1957. They were tired of Martin and Mickey Mantle tearing up the town along with American League opponents.

It broke Martin's heart to leave the Yankees.

So when he returned to New York 18 years later as manager, with new owner George Steinbrenner looking to rebuild the Yankees tradition, it was a dream come true.

And the whole '76 season was a dream for the Yankees, who finally came together.

All the acquisitions from the past few years, from Chambliss at first to Willie Randolph at second to Graig Nettles at third, were paying off.

And the catcher, Munson, the cocky kid who came up like he owned the Stadium, had developed into such a leader Steinbrenner named him the first captain the Yankees had since Lou Gehrig.

They were a close bunch of guys learning to win together, playing hard together, on and off the field.

Jackson was off in Baltimore feasting on crab cakes and pitchers, doing his thing for the year.

The Yankees were on their way to their first pennant in 12 years, capped by Chambliss's mob-inducing blast over the wall in right.

"It was wonderful," Chambliss said. "Lot of satisfaction doing it in New York. We were proud."

And along came the Cincinnati Reds to dent that pride.

The Big Red Machine featured a roster's full of Hall of Famers and, uh, would-be Hall of Famers, including Johnny Bench, Joe Morgan and Pete Rose.

The Yankees, having barely survived the Royals in five games, were overmatched and swept by the Reds in four.

"It took a lot to get away from the playoffs, No. 1," Chambliss said. "No. 2, we were facing one of the better teams in history. We had done a lot to get to where we were. I think it prepared us for the next two years."

But nothing could prepare either side for Reggie's arrival.

*** *** ***

"Go get the big man," Munson told Steinbrenner shortly after the Yankees' World Series loss, according to the *New York Times*. "He's the only guy in baseball who can carry a club for a month. And the hell with what you hear. He hustles every minute on the field."

Steinbrenner didn't want to lose again. The World Series appearance was nice, but there was another step to take and he was going to do everything he could to take it.

It was a new age with free agency and Steinbrenner was one of the first owners to jump on it, fretting not about the extra money, but eager to find a new way to win.

New York, starved for a winner after the drought caused by the cost-conscious CBS ownership of the recent past, loved him for it.

There were two spots Steinbrenner thought the Yankees could shore up—shortstop and right field.

Early in the '77 season, the Yankees would trade for Chicago White Sox shortstop Bucky Dent to add the final piece.

But right fielder Reggie Jackson was the man Steinbrenner really wanted all along.

And when his captain told him the guy played hard all the time, Steinbrenner was determined to get his man.

Even though it would end up meaning a broken promise to that captain to keep him as the highest paid Yankee on the team.

The Steinbrenner-Reggie marriage made as much sense as it created the chance of obstacles.

In many ways, they were the same guy.

They were both driven to win and perform on the biggest stage and loathe accepting anything less than the best. They both could be as hated for their bluster as they were beloved for their results.

And they both had the split personality of a man ready to kick your butt all over the room, then pick you up and pay your hospital bills.

So when Steinbrenner waited for Jackson for several hours at a hotel during the courting process, Reggie knew he'd become a Yankee.

Two teams offered more money. The Montreal Expos—yes, the Expos—and San Diego Padres threw extra cash at Jackson, but George *wanted* it, man. You had to respect that.

A superstar persona that stormed into the Yankees' American League championship clubhouse in 1977 helped leave Jackson feeling alienated from his teammates. *Rich Pilling/MLB Photos via Getty Images.*

And the $2.96 million for five years wasn't exactly chump change. It made Jackson the highest paid player ever at the time.

"It was like trying to hustle a girl in a bar," Jackson said at his introductory press conference, a lavish affair at the Americana Hotel which seemed more fit for royalty than a right fielder. "Some clubs offered several hundred thousand dollars more, but the reason I'm a Yankee is that George Steinbrenner outhustled everybody else."

Maybe if he had stopped talking then, everything would have been different. Maybe if he hadn't said things like, "I didn't come to New York to become a big star, I brought my star here," the transition would have been smoother.

Maybe Munson, who helped him lift his jersey, wouldn't have been as cold later.

Maybe not.

Martin hadn't even attended the press conference, the manager's huge ego already placed on alert.

When the manager found out the Yankees had signed Jackson without consulting him—a month after he led his beloved team back to the World Series ... well, he had one thought.

"I'm gonna show him," Martin told reporters, "who's boss."

*** *** ***

"Ellie, why don't you come over and watch the college basketball game?" Hendricks remembered Jackson telling him in spring training '77.

But Hendricks "knew it wasn't about a college basketball game," he said, smiling.

Piniella, the Yankees' veteran outfielder and one of the only players able to remain close friends with Munson and Jackson, was there, too.

Reggie was upset.

Hendricks could recognize the same type of feeling he saw back in Puerto Rico seven years earlier. This time, Reggie wasn't ready to quit.

But he needed someone to listen.

"As the day went on, he was down and you could tell he was depressed," Hendricks said. "He talked about baseball, about life, about Reggie. He felt not being a part of it; he's a very intelligent man and he felt he wasn't being accepted."

"Reggie," Hendricks told him, "talk to the guys. Talk to them and they'll find out Reggie isn't the guy they think he is."

"It's tough," Jackson said. "They won't talk to me."

"Why don't you make the same effort with the other guys you made with me?" Piniella told him. "You'll find out they're not as bad."

By the time the three men wrapped up and finished watching the game, "it helped," Hendricks said.

Things would get better. Reggie would realize he didn't have to go around bragging about the championships he won with Oakland. Reminding everyone how much he'd accomplished.

He'd make the effort.

And then Hendricks, along with the rest of the Yankees, saw the infamous *Sport* magazine article that forever marks Jackson's first season as a Yankee.

The one in which he was quoted as saying "I'm the straw that stirs the drink. It all comes back to me. Maybe I should say me and Munson, but he really doesn't enter into it. ... Munson thinks he can be the straw, but he can only stir it bad."

"I started laughing," Hendricks said. "'You $#)@#$* crazy, Reggie? You're crazy.'

"He said, 'What?'" Hendricks remembered. "Gave a sly laugh. I said, 'What the #$@)* is that?'"

*** *** ***

To this day, Jackson contends he never said it.
That he was misquoted.

To this day, he's met with skepticism whenever he contends he never said it.

This is Jackson's recollection of his conversation with *Sport* magazine writer Robert Ward:

"I was sitting in the Banana Boat bar, which was where Mickey and Whitey used to go," he said of the bar near the Yankees' spring training site at the time. "I did not want to do a story. The writer caught up to me there. I said I was one of the guys, the final ingredient. He said, 'So you're like the straw that stirs the drink.'"

All of which possibly explains how Jackson further alienated himself from the team and its captain.

Which makes you wonder if Jackson was unfairly treated from that point on after being misquoted.

Though the reaction Munson had to Jackson's friend and the club's back-up catcher, Fran Healy, has even made Jackson chuckle.

"Misquoted?!" Munson told Healy. "For three #$)*#@$ pages?"

Maybe he didn't say it.

But there's one more reason to question Jackson's contention. If his comment was misrepresented in spring training, was it again misunderstood in July by another writer?

That's when, according to an October '77 *New York Times* column by Dave Anderson—a Pulitzer prize-winning sports writer for whom Jackson has the utmost respect—Reggie made another cocktail-oriented comment.

"I'm still the straw that stirs the drink," the column quotes Jackson as saying. "Not Munson, not nobody else on this club."

*** *** ***

Jackson's season did not get easier as it went on.
Martin refused to bat his new star slugger in the coveted cleanup position.

Then on June 18, amid a five-game losing streak, Martin tried to show Jackson who was boss.

And the Yankees were never the same.

The Yankees had already lost one game to Boston, dropping 1/2 game back in the standings after a 9-4 defeat at Fenway Park. Now they were getting it handed to them again, the Red Sox in the midst of another rout.

The Yankees trailed 7-4 when the Sox put one on with one out for slugger Jim Rice.

He was one of the most feared hitters in the league and Jackson, who had been struggling defensively, played him in deep right.

Rice offered a check-swing at a pitch by Mike Torrez, blooping the ball to right.

As Rice watched the ball go off his bat, he hesitated, watching it for a second before running to first.

In right field, Jackson shared Rice's hesitation.

Ever so slowly he started for the ball, seemingly taken aback by the bloop. By the time he retrieved it, Rice was on second with a double, and Boston had runners on second and third.

In the Yankees dugout, Martin went beserk.

He screamed for outfielder Paul Blair, often a late-inning defensive replacement for Jackson, to grab his glove and sub for Jackson.

In the middle of the inning.

On national television.

When Jackson arrived at the dugout, Martin charged him, cursing. The scene has played out on video forever since, the manager restrained by coaches as he strains to get at his right fielder.

So, did Jackson loaf?

"At that time Reggie had lost his confidence playing the outfield," Healy said. "I think Reggie would tell you he probably could have made a better effort at the ball. But this guy didn't lack effort on the field. He was a *gamer*. He was as much a gamer as I've seen."

Which is why he missed a World Series with the A's after injuring himself sliding home on a double steal during the ALCS. Why he earned Dodgers manager Tommy Lasorda's ire in '78 for an instinctively smart play, letting the ball bounce off his hip to break up the double play on a relay thrown by L.A. shortstop Bill Russell.

Jackson's answer as to whether he failed to hustle can be found in his assessment of his manager's opinion.

He said the man must have been drunk.

After the scene, which received plenty of air time on NBC, Jackson waited in the clubhouse to have it out with Martin. But Healy—as he often would—calmed Jackson and told him to leave.

Later, in a hotel room, Jackson spoke with a writer for the *New York Times*, finally revealing the frustration he shoved aside after the game.

"The man took a position today to show me up on national TV," Jackson told the *Times* reporter. "Everyone could see that."

(Twenty-seven years later, when discussing the incident, Jackson remembered things differently. "I never really thought of my being embarrassed or anything like that," he said. "I just didn't think like that, you know?")

"It makes me cry the way they treat me on this team," he told the *Times* reporter then. "The Yankee pinstripes are Ruth and Gehrig and DiMaggio and Mantle. I'm just a black man to them who doesn't know how to be subservient. I'm a big black man with an IQ of 160 making $700,000 a year and they treat me like dirt. They've never had anyone like me on their team before."

On the surface, the quotes seem unrelated to an incident in which Martin called out a player for failing to hustle. But push Jackson further and he'll reveal the type of anecdotes that led to them.

Such as a few days later, when Martin and general manager Gabe Paul set up a meeting.

When he arrived, Jackson remembers Martin remaining as adversarial as ever.

"Billy said, 'I want to kick the shit out of you, *boy*,'" Jackson remembered, flinching at the racial connotation of calling a black man "boy" back then. "I said, 'Gabe, you're Jewish. How do you think that makes me feel?'"

How big a role race played in Jackson's adjustment is up for discussion and debate.

Hendricks, who was only around for a handful of games after spring training, but had spent time around the club the previous year, admits hearing racial jokes that bothered him at times.

Other black players such as Chambliss said, "Nobody said anything to me."

And Healy, Jackson's good friend, said, "I don't buy it," when asked if race had anything to do with Jackson's adjustment.

"I think at that time in our society baseball players were frowned upon if they popped off," said Healy, who is white. "I'm not saying it was a racial thing, but at that time I'm sure there was something to that, but not like it would have been 20 years prior to that. But in baseball, they didn't want you popping off, whether you were black, white or red."

Then there's the case of another quote involving Munson and Jackson, one far less famous than Reggie's "straw that stirs the drink" comment.

Again, it appears in a *New York Times* column by Anderson, one of the country's most respected sports journalists.

It's a joking, off-the-cuff comment from Munson to Jackson after Reggie's three home runs in the World Series. The pair celebrate their championship after all the tumult.

But Munson's celebratory words come with shock value decades later.

"Hey, coon," called the catcher, grinning. "Nice goin', coon."

Reggie Jackson laughed and hurried over and hugged the captain.

"I'm goin' down to that party here in the ball park," Thurman Munson said, grinning again. "Just white people, but they'll let you in. Come on down."

"I'll be there," Reggie Jackson said. "Wait for me."

Later in the column, Munson, who talked of wanting to be traded that year, comes back.

"Hey, nigger, you're too slow, that party's over, but I'll see you next year," the captain said, sticking out his hand. "I'll see you next year wherever I might be.

"But you know who stuck up for you, nigger, you know who stuck up for you when you needed it."

"I know," Reggie Jackson said.

When shown the column in 2004, Jackson became frustrated, animated.

"Why would you have to ask me that?" he said. "Or wonder to write it? To wonder what was going on around then? Stuff like that, I let it dangle."

A few moments later, as his car waited, running, in the Yankee Stadium parking lot, Jackson became reflective. There was no animosity toward Munson, of whom Jackson later said, "We made up, we had a good relationship."

There was a sadness instead.

"What a terrible thing to read," he said. "My father was a Negro Leaguer. I have a lot of young people I know, especially more so with young whites, they have no concept of what I'm saying about what it was like in the past. They just don't understand. So I guess things are changing."

Asked why he would hug Munson at such a moment if he felt the comment was hurtful rather than harmless, Jackson said, "We all deal with the social faux pas. We all tolerate it within our social circles."

What is the impact of the n-word for Jackson?

"When I was young, I was a 'colored kid,'" Jackson said. "You were a second-class citizen. There were places you weren't allowed to be. Then you get angry with it. There was a lot of anger in me."

But the anger has faded over the years. Jackson knows, as Hendricks said, racial tensions weren't relegated to the Yankees dugout.

"It wasn't just them," Hendricks said. "It was America."

And Jackson knows his own ego was as big a factor as anything in his alienation his first year as a Yankee, even if he thinks the team wasn't used to having a black star as outspoken as he was.

Jackson, who grew up loathing his second-class status, might just have caused problems with his teammates by trying too hard to act like he was a class above them.

"I didn't exactly try to fit in," Jackson said. "Because I was ... You look at the great Yankees—Whitey Ford, Yogi, Don Mattingly ... I understand with those guys, the ego is much more controllable than mine was. But it's just as big, no doubt. I've learned to control it more."

He worries more, too, about what people think. He wonders about the cheers he receives, all those "REG-GIE! REG-GIE! REG-GIE!" chants that still pepper his ears.

"Most of the minority people, their sensitivity is high," he said. "Minorities have a higher sense of what you like them for—if you like them for what they do in a game or how they perform or their character."

As for Martin and Munson ...

Well, Reggie thought he had patched things up with Martin as they celebrated the '77 World Series title. But by the next year there was another near-brawl, a five-game suspension for Jackson and an eventual resignation from Martin after he said of Steinbrenner and Reggie—"One's a born liar, the other's convicted."

But Jackson and Munson did make their peace. The pair put aside their differences to win two World Series titles together and whatever social faux pas each threw on the other were forgiven. Enough so that Jackson was as stunned as anyone when news of Munson's death in a plane crash shocked the Yankees community on August 2, 1979. On videotapes of the Yankees' first game after the crash, Jackson can be seen sobbing in right field.

"I would say we made up," Jackson said. "We had a good relationship. I would say the hard feelings were gone and we had a relationship."

*** *** ***

Munson did stick up for Jackson along with other veterans like Piniella. The veteran Yankees begged Steinbrenner to have Martin bat Jackson cleanup down the stretch of the season and end any vendetta he had.

So Martin did.

And Jackson responded.

In his last 50 games, Jackson drove in 49 runs and helped lead the Yankees to the American League East title.

But come the postseason, Jackson didn't seem ready to change his "Mr. October" nickname from sarcastic to legendary.

He was one for 14 in the ALCS against Kansas City when Martin decided to bench him in the decisive fifth game.

Martin benched one of the most prolific postseason performers in history, a risky move that could leave him wide open to second-guessing. He also left his dirty work to Healy, one of Jackson's closest friends on the team.

"Do it yourself," Healy said, ticked off. "You're the manager. You do the #)*#@ thing."

But Healy knew, as usual, he had the best shot of keeping his teammate from causing a scene.

And, Healy said, "he handled it fine."

When he was called to pinch hit in the eighth, Jackson knocked in a run with a single to center, bringing the Yankees within a run of the Royals. In the ninth, they rallied for three runs and won, 5-3, to enter their second straight Series.

No one yet knew Jackson was about to come out on top of the whole, wild season.

*** *** ***

He started off as cold as he had left off in Kansas City, with a one-for-six mark as the Yankees split the first two games against the L.A. Dodgers.

Didn't matter. That was about to change.

In Game 4, Jackson showed his first sign of October magic, hitting a homer for an insurance run in the Yankees' 4-2 win to give them a 3-1 Series lead.

And the Yankees felt ready to return to glory, set to win their first World Series title in 15 years—and against their old transplanted Subway Series rivals, too.

They would have to do it at home.

The Dodgers smacked them around the park in L.A. in Game 5, winning 10-4.

The Yankees' last run came on Jackson's last swing of the game in the eighth when he homered.

"Man," Healy thought as he watched Jackson take batting practice before Game 6. "He's putting every ball over the wall."

In the last three games, Jackson had gone five for 11 with a pair of home runs.

He didn't get a chance to do anything his first at-bat. Burt Hooton walked him on four straight pitches.

He came around to score though, and the Yankees tied the game, 2-2. So the Dodgers answered with a run off Mike Torrez, the Game 2 winner, in the third.

Munson singled to lead off the bottom of the fourth and Jackson came up.

He swung on the first pitch he saw, his first swing since his homer at the end of Game 5.

Gone.

The packed Stadium crowd jumped up and down, celebrating the Yankees' 4-3 lead. Jackson trotted around the bases and met his teammates at the plate.

That was it for Hooton, who gave way to Elias Sosa.

Except, Jackson didn't know anything about Sosa.

So he called up Yankees scout Gene Michael from the dugout phone.

"He said he wanted to call the braintrust," Michael said later, laughing.

He'd get the chance to test out his new information in the fifth, with one on and two out.

The pitch came in from Sosa.

The ball went out.

The Stadium went to chaos.

"REG-GIE! REG-GIE! REG-GIE!" the fans chanted.

The camera found Jackson in the dugout.

Once it found him there about to fight his manager.

Often it found him strutting.

Now?

It discovered a little kid just wanting to tell his parents about a great report card.

"Hi, Mom," Jackson waved, grinning. He put up two fingers, one for each home run. "Two. Two."

And the Yankees led, 7-3.

Torrez was cruising, and the game was in control.

The Yankees were going to finally bring home a title. Jackson's bat would lead the way just as he promised.

Now there was just one more question left.

Could he do what no one had done before? Hit three home runs on three swings in a World Series game?

He was on deck in the seventh with two outs when knuckleballer Charlie Hough struck out Munson to end the inning.

All Jackson could hope was that Dodgers manager Tommy Lasorda would leave Hough in one more inning.

I can hit knuckleballers, Jackson thought.

Now the whole stadium was waiting to see if he could hit this knuckleballer. Hit his way into history.

After a season full of chaos, Jackson had a shot at immortality.

He led off the eighth and the "REG-GIE" chants began again.

The knuckler came in from Hough ...

Jackson swung, his legs crouched and pointed, his hips twisting, his head turning into view behind those shades he always wore, his eyes beneath them watching the ball disappear.

He did it.

He did it.

And as Jackson circled the bases, grinning and pumping both fists, everyone in the Stadium from the fans offering their "REG-GIE" worshipping chants to Martin and Munson couldn't stop smiling.

"Nothing can top this," Jackson said after the game. "Who in hell's ever again going to hit three home runs in a deciding World Series game? I won't."

But he did.

And more importantly than that, he had survived the whole long season.

*** *** ***

Game of My Life
Reggie Jackson

"There's a lot of games, man. And what's the name of your story?" "Game of My Life." (Long pause—38 seconds. Stares. Thinks.)

"There's a couple things that stick out, stand out. ... I remember when I started hitting clean up for the Yankees in '77. Billy would not hit me fourth. And Piniella and Munson went to talk to Billy Martin in Milwaukee and said, 'You need to let this guy hit fourth. He's hurting the ballclub.' And I drove in 51 runs in the last 40-some games, you know? With 13 homers. I remember the game that Billy, in Boston, that he believed I loafed. Accused me of loafing.

"And ... he ... Jim Rice was the hitter. Took a big swing. And I played right field and the first thing I did with the big swing was back up on the ball. And the ball was in. And I ran in. And rather than have the ball get by me or anything ... it took a little bounce, a nothing bounce ... so I fielded the ball. And the ball fell in for a single or a double, I don't know which one. And so he trots Paul Blair on the field. And I kinda see Paul Blair coming; I kinda look around, I wonder what's going on. And Blair just went like this (gestures), 'I'm in for you.'

"And I went in the dugout. I went like, 'What's going on?' And he was so mad. He said, 'if you're gonna embarrass this team, I'm gonna embarrass you.' And I said, 'What are you talking about?' He said, 'You loafed on that ball.' Huh? I said, 'You must be)#$@*# crazy.' I said, 'All that alcohol you're drinking must be going to your head.' He went nuts. He said, 'I'll kick the shit out of you.' I said, 'You must be dreaming. You weigh 160.'

"And I turned around and went in the clubhouse. I went inside and I sat there and I figured, you know, this guy thinks he's such a tough guy, I'm gonna wait for him after the game. Bucky Dent was inside. He'd just got pinch-hit for early in the game and he was gonna have it out with Billy. And he looked at me and he saw I was so mad and he said, 'Hell, what's going on here?'

"Fran Healy came running in from the bullpen. And he says, 'Reggie, you've gotta get out of here. You can't wait here. If you wait here, you're gonna do something you'll regret. Something may happen whether you think you're gonna do anything or not, or whether anything ... it's just too volatile. You need to get out of here so nothing happens.

"'You need to get out, you need to get out, you need to get out, you need to leave.' And he pounded on me for at least an inning or two. And, uh, I finally got showered, got dressed and walked home. Walked out the back, walked back down to the Sheraton. Wasn't more than a 15 or 20-minute walk.

"That was *big* because if something happens, I'm branded, you know, for a long time. No matter what happens, you can't hit a manager. I mean, it has to be just such an obvious instigation from the other side. It wasn't something I wanted to do, as a black player being in New York. Something else happened...

"In '77, at the end of the season, I'd had a pretty good year. Hit .280, drove in 100 runs. Hit 30 homers. And the last game of the playoffs ... I was not swinging the bat well, against Kansas City. I don't know who was pitching. Either Paul Splitorff or Larry Gura. I wanna say it was Splitorff. And Billy sat me down (on the bench). And he told Fran Healy to go tell me. And Fran said, 'Here's what I'm telling you—whatever you do, don't make a big stink out of this. You're gonna look selfish. You're gonna look bad. The camera's gonna be on you all night, watching for some kind of reaction.' And he told me to go tell the writers. Fran said, he told me, to go tell the writers.

"I just thought, I said to myself, 'Boy what a horseshit thing to do to a guy who's played hard for you all year.' My thought was that simple. 'I've played hard for you. I've had a good year. Why would you do something like this in this situation—that's so non-sports like?' And I came in late, got a base-hit to tie the game up. We went on to win. Top of the ninth or something like that and, I just thought that was a huge moment—maybe not a big game for me—but it was a big game for me in the game of life.

"A week later, I became the record-holder of most home runs in a series, all that, three home runs in one game. I really thought Billy and I genuinely were going to become friends. That things were mended. I knew what was going on the whole time. I'd hit two in L.A. When I hit the third home run (first of Game 6) it put us close. And then when I hit the next home run, I really felt like it would help us win; we were gonna win.

"And when I hit homer No. 4 (second of Game 6), being a baseball fan, historian, just a lover of the game, I knew I had tied the greats of the game for four home runs in one World Series.

"I mean, I snuck my transistor radio to grade school to listen to the World Series, Dodgers and the Yankees. I knew what Hank Bauer and Duke Snider had done; Mickey and Yogi. I knew all that; followed it. You know, I knew what the Babe had done. I knew the Babe hit 15. Mickey hit 18. I mean, I knew all that stuff.

"And so it was really a neat thing to be part of that when I hit the fourth home run. And then when I hit the fifth home run, I probably guess I would

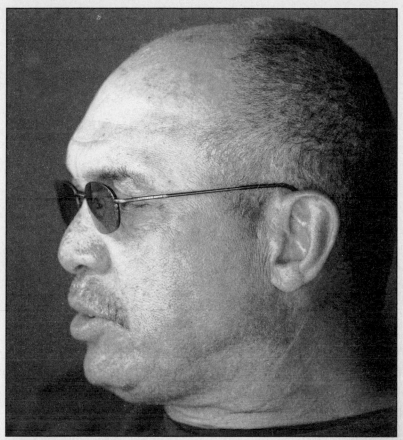

Somewhere between his sensitivity and arrogance, humility and intelligence, Jackson has become one of the most
fascinating sports figures of all time, and one who cannot
be as easily defined as his brash nature would suggest. *Eliot
J. Schechter/Getty Images.*

say I was trying to hit one. I really couldn't believe they were bringing in a
knuckle-ball guy, because I hit knuckle balls pretty good.

"I learned to hit knuckle balls from Sal Bando. Timing. 'Just time the
ball. Get a full swing.'

"So at that time I knew I had broke the record, you know? I was excited for myself as a fan. Not so much as a player. I was more excited as a fan
because I was living a dream, you know, by listening to all the World Series,
all the great players, all the success they'd had, and I was the guy that had done
it, you know? So it was pretty cool. It was a neat thing to experience. My dad
was there. My family. Some of them were there. It was kind of like being a
fan—and doing it, too. It was cool.

"You know, I just really felt good for my family, myself and the owner—George. Because, you know, he had made it happen for me to come here. And there was a lot of stuff in the newspapers, 'This is George's guy, George's guy,' this and that. And, you know, it was nice to have performed and done something to make it all right, if you will.

"I know the first part of the season, man, I was so confused. You know, caught up in just trying to find myself and fit in. And luckily, I had a lot of ability and I played pretty good the first half, but boy it was a struggle. Emotionally and socially and fitting in—and then the *Sport* article came out and it was tough, man. It was really tough. Maybe that was my big game, just being successful that year, because it was a make-or-break year for my career and for me as a person."

*** *** ***

They all admired Jackson now, even his opponents.

L.A. first baseman Steve Garvey couldn't help but applaud in his glove when he thought no one was looking.

He would keep hitting home runs and earning "REG-GIE" chants for the Yankees the next four years.

He became one of the most popular players the club has had, setting the crowd against Steinbrenner upon his return as a California Angel in '82.

Disappointed by the '81 World Series loss and thinking Jackson's skills had deteriorated, the Boss let him go.

And Jackson, as always, struck back, homering in his first game as an Angel, sending the fans into another delerious chant.

Still, he felt enough of a bond in his five years to enter the Hall of Fame as a Yankee in '93.

The applause and "REG-GIE" calls never seem to stop for Jackson. He had his jersey retired in Oakland in 2004, a couple of years after the Yankees gave him a plaque to go with his retired No. 44 in Monument Park.

His home runs were heard 'round the country, but he wants more to be heard. He wants people to look past the big swing and the big mouth and see as many aspects of Reggie Jackson as they can.

All these years later, Mr. October wants to be seen as more than just a guy who got his own candy bar.

More than just a name at the end of a chant, even if he can never hear enough cheers.

CHAPTER 8

Ron Guidry:
Hunting for History

June 17, 1978

vs. California
Yankees 1, Angels 0

The stats:	IP	H	R	ER	BB	SO
	9	4	0	0	2	18

Ron Guidry heard the fans clapping their hands sore, the stir starting with two strikes on a batter.

He saw the mystified faces of the hitters returning to the bench, sapped of their pride, engulfed by a Yankee Stadium crowd building strength with each strike.

Up in the broadcast booth, Phil Rizzuto was "going beserk" as Guidry would say later, screaming with the spirit of a child for each strikeout.

Hooooly Cow, Louisiana Lightning did it again!

Yankee Stadium was under Guidry's command, along with the California Angels.

Of all the people to own New York, the guy they called "Gator" didn't figure to be one. This was as far from Lafayette, Louisiana, as you could get, but Guidry, a pinstriped straight pin, felt as close as ever.

This was as simple as shooting ducks and quail back in Louisiana, his great-grandfather putting an arm around Guidry's tiny shoulder and pointing him toward the game.

Now Guidry was punching out the Angels and it was all guided by the same logic he used back home.

Why did he hunt?

To make his shots, get some kills and put some food in the freezer.

Why did he pitch?

To make his pitches, get some wins and put some food in the freezer.

It was that simple. Even if, years later, ex-Angels approached Guidry, sheepish grins revealing their awe.

We gave up on trying to get hits halfway through the game, they'd say. *We were just trying not to strike out.*

Then they'd mutter ...

And you got us anyway.

By the seventh inning, Guidry's catcher, Thurman Munson, jokingly threatened bodily harm if Guidry didn't go for the strikeout record. By the end of the game, Guidry didn't get Nolan Ryan's then-major league mark of 19, but passsed his idol Whitey Ford's Yankees record with 18.

That was a thrill.

Ford had been Guidry's de facto babysitter growing up in Lafayette. Guidry's mother confined Ronnie to the couch on weekends so she could catch the Yankees on TV rather than chase her son.

But Guidry tried not to think of any of that as he closed in on a piece of history.

Amid all that clapping and chanting and holy cowing and with the stadium shaking, Guidry did what he always did on the mound.

He remembered why he was there.

I'm just here, he told himself, *to pitch and win the game.*

He was used to blocking it all out by now.

His father and grandfather instructed him to do just that when he left Lafayette.

"Don't forget," they told him, "when you get to New York, you're there to play ball."

There was a job to do, so you do it. And that's all you do.

Guidry's father, grandfather and great-grandfather had all taught him that from the time he was six years old. That's when Guidry—barely big enough to carry the gun—learned to hunt in Lake Arthur, Louisiana, an hour from his home.

They were Cajuns, and Cajuns cook, see. Shoot, anything tastes good if you cook it right; quail, duck, you name it. Ron cooked because he wanted to drive, his father forbidding him to go for his license until he made a meal worth driving for.

But there wasn't always enough food to cook in the Guidry home. Ron's father, Roland, did a man's work but didn't always get a good enough day's pay. Sometimes he'd come home from that long day at the railroad station to discover this was his dinner:

A piece of bread. A glass of milk. Maybe a peanut butter sandwich.

So in the winter, Ron's grandfather Gus would call great-grandad, John.

"We're coming over Saturday," Gus would say. "We're gonna bring Ronnie to go hunting."

For supper, not sport.

With a slider he learned from Sparky Lyle, Ron Guidry became known as "Louisiana Lightning" after blowing by 18 California Angels in 1978. *Rich Pilling/MLB Photos via Getty Images.*

"When I learned to hunt in the 1950s, my father was never a guy who had a lot of money," Guidry said. "So hunting for us was a source of different food you could eat, and that's how I learned to hunt."

That was in the winter.

In the summer, Guidry was locked on the couch, the Yankees becoming his favorite team.

Now Guidry was pitching his best game for his favorite team, the one it had taken him so long to make.

It had been two years since that frustrated trip to the minors led him to an intriguing intersection at I-81 in Pennsylvania.

Go north, head back to the minors in Syracuse.

Go south, say the heck with it and go home to Louisiana.

His wife, Bonnie, nudged him north. Soon his career headed in the same direction.

Soon it would skyrocket past all expectations. The kid who was supposedly too short, too weak to start a season's worth of games, won 16 and helped the Yankees to the World Series title in '77.

By '78, the slider Sparky Lyle taught him became so nasty hitters cursed the reliever for teaching it to him.

Guidry would have one of the best seasons a pitcher's had, going 25-3 with a 1.74 ERA and 248 strikeouts.

He had already won 10 games without a loss when he took the mound on June 17, though he hardly felt ready for win No. 11.

He thought he had nothing.

He was wrong. He had everything, so the Stadium was as loud as the skinny Cajun kid was quiet.

He just zeroed in on batters as he did rabbits and ducks.

So when Munson told Guidry to go for Ryan's strikeout record entering the ninth, the pitcher worried only about protecting a 4-0 lead.

"I'm just worried about the game," he said.

But by that point Guidry had earned too much respect from the captain of a team whose players battled for each other as much as they did against.

This time, Munson insisted, Guidry—the Gator who always kept his mouth shut—would go for a piece of glory.

Or else.

"If you don't go for it," Munson growled, "I'm gonna break your ankles before you get back to the dugout."

*** *** ***

"OK, see those trees along the fence line?" John Guidry would tell his great-grandson. "See the big oak tree? See the big pecan tree? Go underneath the oak tree because they're all going in the pecan trees."

John had been the family's advance scout, spending a week scanning the trees, searching for game.

They'd hunt everything. Because a Cajun can cook anything.

"Everything that you can shoot is good to eat if you can fix it right," Guidry said, his Louisiana accent—like his slider—softly inviting with some bite at the end. "Doves. Quails. Rabbits. Ducks. Geese. All of that is great to eat when you know how to fix it. You can pot roast 'em, bake 'em, barbecue 'em, put 'em in a gumbo, saute 'em. ..."

He was a good hunter. He made his great-grandad proud.

But his grandfather, Gus, taught Guidry to hunt, too. Gus was a tough, old trucker and he'd as soon as put his fist through you as he would a wall if you crossed him.

But he loved Ronnie because the boy knew what it was like to be a team player long before he got to the Yankees.

"I always gave him half of what I got," Guidry said. "If I shot two birds, you get one, I get one. If I shot 12 rabbits, you get six, I get six. He always made suppers and dinners for us when we came back.

"But my grandfather used to say he always loved having me over because I always halved everything with him."

And they ate every last piece of meat. Had to. It was only proper.

"It was instilled in me that that's the way that it should be," Guidry said. "If you're gonna rob the land of something, then you have to use it."

*** *** ***

When he wasn't hunting, Guidry started pitching. Turned out he was pretty good at that, too.

He'd practice by himself and when he did, he was always Ford. When he was younger, he'd try to hit like Mantle, but as he got older, Guidry knew he'd be a pitcher and Whitey was the man.

And the coach would use him just like Casey Stengel used Whitey. Forget rotation. Guidry, just like Ford, only pitched against the other teams' best guy.

He'd cruise on through, striking out 22 in a game and leaving the other team wondering why they came. Eventually, folks in the "little league cult" caught on that he was good, Guidry said.

It would take much longer for him to get the Yankees to be aware of who he was.

He had gotten tired of the Yankees yo-yoing him back and forth from the minors in 1976.

Guidry knew he could pitch in the majors, but he didn't think it would ever happen in New York.

His father told him to stick with it, that he was making good money. But Guidry's pride tore at him, wondering when and if the Yankees would ever give him the chance to prove his short, skinny frame wouldn't keep him from being a starter.

The last time they sent him down in '76, he had it.

Lyle had taught him a nasty slider, but Guidry's excitement was curtailed by his frustration.

"I can't wait to show it, but I might not be able to show it to anyone," he thought.

So when they told him to go back to Syracuse, Guidry was ready to just go home.

His wife, Bonnie, remained silent in the hotel room, offering just a whisper.

"OK, I'll pack," she said.

She was pregnant at the time and knew there was no way she was driving 28 hours to Louisiana. But she wasn't ready to tell her husband that.

So, two miles before the junction at I-81, she turned to Ron.

"You really want to do this?" she said.

He surprised himself when the answer was no.

He wanted to keep pitching. He wanted his shot.

He'd end up back with the Yankees and everyone was pitching for him to pitch.

Lyle and some other veteran Yankees pitchers went to manager Billy Martin. Martin went to general manager Gabe Paul.

Forget about how small he is, Martin said. The guy can pitch. I'm putting him in the rotation.

And so he pitched. Won 16 games and helped the Yankees to their first World Series title in 14 years.

That was nothing.

*** *** ***

He had won 10 games in a row when he warmed up in the bullpen on June 17, 1978. Countless times, the Yankees had been on a losing streak that ended when Guidry took the mound.

He was that good that year. The slider became so filthy opposing hitters wanted to take their bats to Lyle's skull for teaching the kid the pitch.

How could you hit something that dipped quicker than John Travolta on the dance floor?

Guidry had been in the midst of a chaotic clubhouse full of controversy. And through it all, Guidry kept his mouth shut.

He'd remember the words of his father and grandfather upon his departure from Lafayette. And he'd remember all those hunting trips.

He was here to play ball for the Yankees, where the players would become the game, the hunters all those New York reporters shooting for headlines about the Bronx Zoo.

But Guidry never gave them one.

"It made me realize that when I became an established player in New York City, 'I'm here to play ball,'" Guidry said of his family's influence. "I'm not here to berate a manager or a player or an owner. I'm here because I'm a pitcher and that's all I'm supposed to do, and that's all I did."

Even if there were plenty of thoughts filling his head.

"Yeah, but I don't have to say anything," he said. "To me, I don't need to get involved in that."

Oh, New York could have lured Guidry out of sleep and into a lot of things besides controversy. Even a good country kid from Louisiana could have seen that in a decade full of excess.

This was the era of Studio 54 when being young, famous and in the middle of New York brought with it the appeal of endless parties.

"It's tempting if you let it," Guidry said. "Then again, I'm here to play ball."

Besides, Guidry wasn't a big-city guy. His first trip into the city taught Gator to miss home.

"When I got there in '75, I didn't even have a watch," he said. "I walked in the city one of the first few days I was there. I was looking for some kind of store because I wanted to go buy some new shoes and I knew I didn't want to be late. So I stopped a guy on the street to ask him for the time and he jumped all over my ass.

"'If you want to know the time, buy a watch!' And I said, 'Hmm. I won't be coming down here very often.'"

But they'd come out to see him at the stadium. And never would they be more excited than the night Guidry struck out 18 Angels.

It started off like nothing special, the leadoff hitter confirming Guidry's thoughts about not having his best stuff.

Double.

But then he came back to strike out the side in the first. Got a couple of more in the second and already the fans started.

"Well, the stuff he had, it was obvious to the fans he had great stuff that day," Don Baylor, then playing for the Angels, said.

With each new strikeout, the crowd grew more ravenous on the next two-strike count. In the dugout, the Angels started talking to themselves and abandoned thoughts of doing anything other than making contact.

"Oh, yeah," Baylor said. "And I was not a strikeout guy."

In the broadcast booth, announcer Bill White—often the professional sounding caretaker of the more folksy Rizzuto—appeared fatherly to Guidry, a second-year starter.

"And the fans are clapping for a strikeout—that puts a lot of pressure on this young left-hander," White said.

Later, as the crowd grew louder still, White sounded almost annoyed when he announced "Gonna get him some earplugs."

Didn't need 'em.

Didn't need much of anything except that slider.

"His slider that day was so ... you had to hit it almost way out front," Baylor said. "It would just disappear. You didn't have a chance, really."

Guidry would become the new leader in single-game strikeouts for the Yankees.

And he would become known as Louisiana Lightning.

*** *** ***

Game of My Life
Ron Guidry

"I honestly thought I had nothing. That night I got in the bullpen and I was throwing hard, but everything was up. I couldn't get the ball down. All the good stuff was up. And when I tried to put it over the middle of the plate, it didn't seem like it had the same zip.

"But at the same time, if I threw it right, chest-high, it had good velocity. My slider was breaking great, but it was 66 feet. It always was bouncing in front of the plate, it was never around the plate.

Amid a clubhouse dubbed the "Bronx Zoo" for its seemingly endless calamity, Guidry was a source of calm. "You're there to play ball," Guidry's father and grandfather told him before he left Louisiana. After helping them hunt as a boy to put food on the table, Guidry listened to his elders. *MLB Photos via Getty Images.*

"When I threw my last pitch and (pitching coach) Art Fowler said, 'OK, let's go,' I turned around and Sparky Lyle was always handing me my jacket when I was leaving. And when he handed me my jacket, I looked up at him and I said—his nickname was Count—'Count, when's the earliest you've ever been in a game? Because I feel like I've got nothing.' And he said, 'You're throwing the ball good.' But he said, 'Just everything is high. Try to get everything down.'

"I went out and the game started, and I remember the game pretty vividly. Yeah, first guy 3 and 2, leadoff double. The next guy tried to bunt, and I wound up striking him out. The next guy almost tore my head off with a line drive that I knocked down to throw him out, OK? And then I struck out the fourth guy, Joe Rudi. And I eventually got him four times.

"You know, I went out the next inning, same thing. Everything was high. Ball one, strike, 3 and 2 again, make a good pitch, get a guy out. Give up a hit, struck out one guy, it was no big deal.

"The first two (innings) was like, 'Oh, Jesus Christ,' you know? But then when I went out for the third inning, it's like everything just started to fall into place. Everything I was throwing, they were swinging, missing, in the strike zone. And it just worked out like if I threw a fastball, they were looking for a breaking ball; when I threw a breaking ball, they were looking for fastballs.

"And then they just started swinging. I mean, they just started swinging.

"Because Nolan was on the bench that night, and Nolan had 19 and he said that they actually tried not to strike out to protect Nolan's record at 19. Well, I thought it was a great compliment but then Donnie told me, he said, 'And the compliment that I have to give you about that game was the fact that you still continued to strike guys out when we were actually trying not to do it.'

"When they flashed on the screen in center field in the seventh inning that I had just tied Whitey's record at 15—I was sitting in the dugout when people started clapping. And I didn't know why they were clapping. Until Munson and I looked at the scoreboard and they had flashed 'with his 15th strikeout, Ron Guidry has just tied Whitey Ford's record.'

"And Munson and I looked at each other. He looked at me and he said 'I didn't realize you had that many.' I said, 'Well I'm not counting strikeouts. I'm just worried about the game.'

"He said, 'Well you've got 15. We've got two more innings.' He said, 'You can go after the record.' I said, 'I don't want to go after the record.' I said, 'I wanna just make sure we win this game. So he said, 'Well, I tell you what, I'm not gonna worry about the next inning. If you can get one or two in the next inning, when you get in the ninth inning, whatever you need we're going after it.'

"So we went back out for the eighth inning and I got one guy. I got 16. But when I came back in for the dugout he looked at me and he said, 'You've got 16. The record is 19.'

"He said, 'You're going for it.' He said, 'If you don't go for it, I'm gonna break your ankles before you get back to the dugout.'

"And that's the only guys I tried to strike out. I got the first two, which gave me 18, and then I gave up a basehit and I got the next guy to ground out and the game was over.

"That's when the two-strike clap originated. Somewhere in the middle of the game. ... The third inning, I got three. The fourth inning, I got two. The fifth inning, I got three. In that time is when it started. After a while I caught on because it was just with two strikes. I mean, I got strike one, nobody said anything; all of a sudden, strike two, people were clapping when I went into my delivery. And if I got a guy, it was a tremendous roar. They must have had somwhere in the neighborhood of 35,000 people, 40,000, give or take.

"I mean, it was a great crowd for in the middle of the week. but I remember every time I got two strikes, the place erupted.

"Louisiana Lightning—yeah, that's the time I got it from Rizzuto. What came about it was, at the time of that game there, I was still in the neighborhood of 10-0.

"There was a couple that used to always sit in the first section above the main ground floor area of the mezzanine or whatever. There was a family that sat there, and every time that I pitched, they broke out this big poster that had the state of Lousisiana, and there was a lightning bolt through it and they had on it 'Louisiana Lightning.'

"It had been there the whole time. But that night, since it was so electrifying and Rizzuto was going beserk on the announcing 'Hoooly cow!' ... and somewhere in that monologue of his, he said something about, 'Hoooly cow, Louisiana Lightening got another one!' You know, he said something to that effect; I don't know.

"I recall somebody mentioning it, and when I saw the replay from the stadium department, I heard him say that and it stuck. I mean, that's when it stuck for the rest of the time."

*** *** ***

It's the best game of his life, but ask him what it means, and Guidry will shrug.

"Just another game," he said. "Just another big game we had to win."

Sure, it was a thrill to break Whitey's record, but it would have been just as great to end in a tie.

A few weeks after the game, Ford came by to congratulate Guidry.

"What's it like to strike out 18?" Ford wanted to know.

"You know, just three more than 15," Guidry joked back.

"You have a camaraderie because he knows the job that you did," Guidry said. "He came over to shake my hand and tell me that he had seen it on television."

Lots of folks were ready to shake Guidry's hand after the '78 season. After the Yankees rallied all the way back to overtake the Red Sox in their classic playoff game—another Guidry win—and went on to repeat as World Series champs, the Gator was in heavy demand.

Among the requests, a popular one was to see Guidry in his natural environment. Everyone from *Sports Illustrated* writers to beat reporters wanted to go hunting with Guidry.

And that was all fine.

On one condition.

"Well, the only way I agreed to do all of that," Guidry said, "was if my grandfather came with me and my dad came with me."

CHAPTER 9

Bucky Dent:
A Bleep in the Screen

October 2, 1978, Divisional Playoff

at Boston
Yankees 5, Red Sox 4

The stats: AB R H RBI HR
             4 1 1 3   1

Hour after hour, inning after inning, Bucky Dent didn't budge, riveted by the scene on his television.

He knew all about this kind of intensity, each pitch offering the chance to make history.

On the television, Yankee Stadium buzzed with chants of "*Nine*-teen, *eight*-teen" and ringing taunts of "Pedroooo, Pedrooooo."

The Yankees and Red Sox celebrated their 25th anniversary of one classic duel with another in October 2003.

This time, Dent watched from his sofa in Florida, just another suspense-filled fan.

His wife sat beside him, the scenes from Game 7 of the American League Championship Series providing the only light in an otherwise dark house.

The Yankees and Red Sox were going inning for inning, late into the night, the kind of struggle that seemed like it would never end. The Yankees protecting their tradition, Boston trying to overcome it.

Someone has to do something, Dent thought. Someone has to keep it going.

"Deep to left ..." The freeze frame of history remains alive in the minds of Yankee and Red Sox fans, the latter forever dubbing the batter Bucky "Bleeping" Dent for his famous 1978 home run at Fenway Park. *AP/WWP.*

Just a few weeks earlier, he had thrown his mind back into this kind of chaos, replaying for the 10,000,000th time the home run that forever gave him a bleepin' new middle name in Boston.

Again, he and Mike Torrez—the pitcher who served up the 1978 shot he said Boston fans are still "crying about every night in their beer"—combined to charm the press on a conference call.

After signing countless shots of "the shot" and even uniting to recreate it when Dent unveiled a mini-Green Monster replica at his baseball school, the pair had become like an old vaudevillian team.

Torrez, the goat, fired a verbal equivalent of the fastball he had jokingly aimed over Dent's head on old-timer's day a couple of months before.

"I tell him the bat was probably corked," Torrez said. "Whether it was corked or not, the bat boy came out pretty quick so we couldn't check it."

Dent played an easier part, the Roadrunner to Wile E. Coyote, the Harlem Globetrotters to the Washington Generals, the ...

Well, the Yankees to the Red Sox.

It's been that way since the Red Sox sold Babe Ruth to the Yankees. And created the so-called Curse of the Bambino.

Even worse, the curse carried subway fare.

Over in Queens in 1986, the Mets stunned the Red Sox in typical Yankees fashion, tying the World Series on the infamous Bill Buckner error.

Dent had been as big an obstacle as all of them, sandwiched between the Babe and Buckner—and he clearly enjoyed his status as one more Boston tormentor.

The day after his home run at Fenway, a good friend asked if he had any idea how much his life would change.

The 27-year-old shortstop, in the midst of preparing for the next round of the playoffs against Kansas City, muttered, "No, I don't."

But the 52-year-old gray-haired version of Dent sitting on his couch as night turned to early morning in October 2003 did.

He had become a pin-up boy in New York, his sparkling white smile no less admired than that of '70s TV star Erik Estrada.

He could not walk in Boston without some kind of bitter greeting, a fan cursing or staring, pleadingly, wondering how a demon had inhabited such a harmless looking—and light-hitting—young man.

And when he sat atop the new Green Monster seats at Fenway in April 2003, Dent was sandwiched between a pair of 37-year-old men who politely informed him he had ruined their childhood.

As Dent's friend had predicted, the shot changed his world forever, an actor typecast in a role because he delivered the performance of his life.

But that was OK. He savored this role.

And, as he watched the Yankees battle the Red Sox in 2003, Dent knew something else.

He wasn't ready to give it up.

Babe. Bucky. Buckner. ...

"I was sitting there and I was going, 'OK, who's got a B in their name that's gonna do something to keep these Bs going?'" Dent said. "I said, 'OK, it's gonna be Boone or Bernie Williams.'"

So Dent watched. And waited.

Then he did something else.

"I dozed off," he said.

His wife had walked into the other room as her husband slept.

A few minutes later, she sprinted back into the room to see what they were screaming about on TV.

"What happened?" she said.

"I don't know," Bucky said. "Somebody must have hit a home run."

The TV flashed a shot of Aaron Boone taking his trot into history just as Dent had.

"Oh!" Dent said, springing from his sofa. "Boone hit one."

As the replay flashed the sight of Boone driving Tim Wakefield's knuckler over the wall in left, Dent nodded knowingly.

"Ahhh, right," he said. "It was a guy with a B. It keeps it going."

*** *** ***

It's a beautiful spring day in April 2004. Sun's shining, beers are in hand and the Red Sox have taken two straight from the Yankees in their opening series of the season.

Life in Boston is good.

The Red Sox fans mill around Fenway Park before the third game of the series, returning for another year full of their fate—never-ending faith and disbelief rolled into one.

"Cursed to first!" one hawker screams, handing out bumper stickers.

"Break the curse cookie!" another yells.

It's Year 86 of the Curse, but for all the grief, the Sox have started to slip out of the last season's shadow. Across from an outdoor bar where a group of Red Sox fans laugh and drink, and jutting out from the sunny sky, a billboard greets Red Sox fans. It welcomes them to a new season, trying desperately to ease the pain of the past 85.

"Keep the faith," it reads.

Red Sox fans' faith would eventually be rewarded in the most improbable fashion imaginable that October, when Boston would, of course, rally from an 0-3 deficit to beat the Yankees, then win its first World Series since 1918. But Sox fans didn't yet know that.

So, despite the dawn of a new year and the peace of winning two in a row, they were as bitter as ever when asked about Bucky ...

"Bucky $)#@@#$* Dent," the guy with the dark shades and black goatee spits out like warm beer.

He pauses. Tries to settle down. Grins sheepishly.

"I'm sorry," he says good-naturedly. "I just couldn't hold it in."

"Where was I?" another fan repeats. "Sticking a gun in my mouth."

On Yawkey Way, Barry Phillips wears a matching "Yankees Hater 5" T-shirt with his girlfriend. Unlike his younger mate, he wears the scar of watching the Dent game live.

He can still remember it. The Sox were going to win.

They had come all the way back after the freakin' Yankees came back on them. They had won eight straight games the last week of the season to tie the bahstads.

And it was all unfolding perfectly.

Mike Torrez on the mound, pitching a shutout. The Sox getting to Ron Guidry for two runs. Guidry. They were beating Guidry. And he was freakin' unbeatable that year.

This was it.

Then Dent came up with two on and two out in the seventh.

Then ...

"My jaw just dropped to the floor," Phillips said. "What was Bucky Dent? He never did anything."

He almost didn't even play baseball.

*** *** ***

When the White Sox told Dent about the trade to the Yankees in April 1977, the shortstop started "jumping up and down."

The Yankees were always his favorite team.

Of course. Join the club.

Except, it hadn't always been his dream to play baseball.

Sure, Dent grew up in Hialeah, Florida, watching Mickey Mantle and Whitey Ford just as his teammate, Guidry, had in Louisiana.

But when you grow up in Florida, you do so with a football all but placed in your crib. And the older you get, the more attention you get.

So as Dent went through his years at Hialeah High School, he started focusing on football.

That's what everyone wanted. Go get a scholarship. Go to college.

Everyone told him to do that.

Except his brother Jim.

"They were pressuring me not to play baseball because I had a football scholarship," Dent said of his friends. "(Jim) was like, 'No, go get your glove and play.'"

Thoughts about his small frame taking a pounding in football worried him, too.

"What happened was, I liked baseball (and) I didn't think I was going to go very far in football because of my size, so I started taking baseball a little more seriously," Dent said. "(Jim) wanted me to play baseball and see what happened my senior year. You know, we had a real good team and we had a chance to win the state championship—which we did. He wanted me to not limit my opportunities at the time."

But baseball still didn't provide the rush football did. Baseball didn't bring those wild, crazed fans filled with years of traditional rivalries.

Baseball—even the state championship game—didn't send Dent and his high school mates to play in the Orange Bowl.

Football did.

They were ranked second in the state in 1969, taking on the No. 1 team. Fifteen thousand people showed up.

Dent had never seen anything like it. He couldn't imagine a game this big, demanding this much attention.

As he would realize eight years later, that was nothing.

*** *** ***

"I don't think we liked each other," Guidry said.

He was talking about the Yankees and the Red Sox in the '70s, but he might as well have been talking about the Yankees and themselves.

This was the heyday of the Bronx Zoo, one of the most tumultuous seasons the Bombers have ever seen.

Just about everyone on the team was miserable at one point.

Reggie Jackson and Billy Martin nearly brawled over a missed bunt.

Captain Thurman Munson moped near season's end, determined to force a trade away from the mess and closer to the family he cherished.

The Yankees' top starters, their big bonus babies, all faced injuries at one point or another. Catfish Hunter. Andy Messersmith.

Then Martin got himself fired after a barroom boast to a reporter that claimed of Reggie and George Steinbrenner—"one's a born liar, the other's convicted."

Steinbrenner, who had been convicted of making illegal campaign contributions to Richard Nixon, reacted in standard, swift form.

He fired Martin.

In came the mellow Bob Lemon, who promised to get out of the players' way and just let them play ball. The move, along with the New York City newspaper strike that summer, is often cited by players as a key reason for their comeback.

Before that point, the Yankees weren't too happy with each other, blasting teammates in the press and bumbling through a would-be World Series title defense.

On July 17, the Yankees were 14 games behind the Red Sox.

They were living up to the words of outfielder Lou Piniella, who told reporters following the '77 World Series victory, "We'll be a good fourth-place club," if tensions continued.

But if there was anyone the Yankees hated more than each other, it was the folks north on I-95 in New England.

The brawls had started in 1975 with run-ins at home plate between catchers Carlton Fisk and Munson. The two best catchers in the league had as much contempt for each other as pitchers had for facing either of them, and it often spilled into bench-clearing brawls.

Fisk would take out Munson on a play at the plate. Piniella would barrel over Fisk.

And the fisticuffs would start.

And, as it always has between the Yankees and Red Sox, it was raised another notch or 20 with each Yankees win.

"I knew it got pretty heated because we beat 'em for the next three years," Guidry said.

They weren't doing a good job of that in '78, when the Sox had battered them all season.

But suddenly the Yankees' pitchers started getting healthy. There were no problems with the manager because Lemon looked like a grandfather and offered little more than a pat on the back.

And all that bickering and backstabbing in the papers? Gone.

So one of the greatest comebacks in baseball history began. The Yankees entered a four-game series at Fenway down just four games on September 7.

By the time the Yankees left town, Boston's lead, much like its pride, had disappeared.

With each game, the Yankees bludgeoned off the last of the Sox' lead, winning all four games by a combined score of 42-9.

That was it. After the "Boston Massacre," they were set. Ready to run away with it.

Not so fast.

The Sox came back. Won their final eight games and tied for first when the Yankees lost on the last day of the season to Cleveland.

There would be a one-game playoff.

This was it.

Finally.

"All the things that we had gone through that year," Dent said, "and it all boiled down to one game."

*** *** ***

Guidry arrived at the park early and sneaked into the trainer's room for a nap. Didn't want Steinbrenner or the reporters to bother him with silly questions.

He was pitching on three days' rest, so he was hoping he could just hold the Sox to two runs and keep the Yankees in the game.

And that's exactly what he did.

But Torrez, who had won two games for the Yankees in the previous year's World Series, did even better. He pitched six innings of shutout ball and Fenway was starting to sense victory.

The demons had not yet driven the Boston fans into hiding.

That would come in the top of the seventh.

Torrez walked to the mound feeling great. He had thrived under pressure the previous year.

If not for Reggie Jackson's historic home run trifecta in the 1977 World Series, Torrez would have been the Yankees' MVP. He had won two games for them, leaping in the air to punctuate the final out after fielding a popup. But the Yankees chased free agent Goose Gossage to stack the bullpen in the off-season and decided to let Torrez go.

Now it was his chance to stick it to them, and he was doing just that, outdueling Guidry, 2-0.

As he reached the mound for the top of the seventh, Torrez glanced at the flags atop the fence. They had been still all game. Now they blew out to left. Huh, Torrez thought.

Chris Chambliss and Roy White singled, and the Yankees had their first chance in a while.

There were two on and two outs when Dent stepped into the sunny shadows and walked to the plate.

Dent would have been gone for a pinch hitter. But there weren't enough infielders. Lemon had checked and double-checked. No choice. Got to let the kid hit.

The Yankees were not exactly confident.

"You think he can handle him?" first base coach Gene Michael whispered to White at first, worried Dent was overmatched by Torrez.

"Only if he hangs a slider," Michael remembers White responding.

*** *** ***

There are only a handful of times when immortality has been prefaced by impotence.

With the glaring sun shielded only by his cover-boy eye black, Dent fouled a pitch off his shin and collapsed to the ground in a shot.

He looked as imposing as a week-kneed teen meeting a pin-up idol.

The image of what came next plays on forever now, whether it be in the minds of Red Sox fans ready to curse, Yankees fans ready to cheer, or a VCR as it did before a Yankees-Red Sox game in spring 2004.

Dent hobbles back toward the dugout. Trainer Gene Monahan looks at his shin.

Teammate Mickey Rivers looks at his bat.

"Homey, you got the wrong bat; that one's cracked," Rivers tells him.

Before the game, White had suggested Dent use one of his bats. He had recently gotten a shipment and passed them on to Rivers. It felt good in batting practice, so Dent stuck with it during the game. But this one had a chip on the handle.

"I didn't want to use your game bat," Dent tells Rivers.

Rivers has the bat boy exchange bats with Dent.

All this time, Torrez is getting antsy. Later, he would lament his decision not to call time and talk to the ump.

"I should have thrown some warmup pitches," he said of the extended delay.

He wouldn't get any warmups once Dent stepped back in the box.

The flags are blowing to left, but Torrez has no time to think of that now. He needs one out to escape the jam. Seven outs to finally put away the Yankees.

He releases the pitch—a fastball, not slider.

As he does, Torrez has no idea he's forever letting the rest of his career go, too, as far as Boston fans are concerned.

Deep to left! Yastrzemski ... will not get it! It's a home run! A three-run home run for Bucky Dent!

For all of Yankees announcer Bill White's bellowing in the broadcast booth, the rest of the park is stunned.

Dent jogs around the bases, little sound in the whole place other than his pants swishing together and a few cheers from his teammates.

"And *look* at those Yankees come out of the dugout!" White says.

In the stands, down the third-base line, Yankees owner George Steinbrenner, his hair not yet fully gray, his frown not perfectly formed, bolts up and claps repeatedly.

Passing by the latest incarnation of the endless tape, this time on an April 2004 day in the Yankee Stadium press box, broadcaster Jerry Remy—the Sox second baseman in '78—turns to a pair of Boston writers.

"One of these days we're gonna watch that and we're gonna win," he says.

But they won't.

Because Reggie Jackson will add another homer for a 5-2 lead. Because the Yankees will hold on, 5-4, even with Gossage struggling. Because, in the ninth, Remy will be robbed of an extra-base-hit by Piniella in right field. Piniella makes a blind stab into the sun to snare the ball and save the game, keeping Rick Burleson from going to third, where he could have scored on the next fly ball.

Then with two outs, Yastrzemski sends a pop-up to Nettles at third. He clutches it, and the Yankees clutch each other, their wild ride against the Red Sox over, their trek toward another World Series title just starting.

It had been another season of chaos and comebacks for the Yankees, who came all the way back from a 14-game deficit to force a one-game playoff against the Red Sox. Here they celebrate one more after Dent's homer gave them a one-run lead on the way to a 5-4 win. *AP/WWP.*

Dent would continue to mystify the baseball world by bombarding the Dodgers with hits in the Series, taking home the MVP award.

"We've got some big hearts on this team," an ecstatic Dent said after the World Series. "People say we're the best team money can buy, but you don't buy their hearts. You don't buy what's inside of them. I think this is the best thing that ever happened to baseball. What we've done will give a lot of teams years from now incentive. They'll say, 'Hey, look at the '78 Yankees. They didn't quit.'"

*** *** ***

Game of My Life
Bucky Dent

"I just remember how big a game it was. You know, the two teams, the two cities, you know, coming down to the last day of the season. And one game meaning either you're gonna go home or you're gonna go on. Just the total impact of what the game was.

"I mean, one-game playoff? Two teams, Red Sox-Yankees? In a one-game playoff? And I mean, especially after we had come from so far back.

"Absolutely, I was nervous. Absolutely. When the game started, you know, once you get into the game, all that other stuff's out the window. The only other time that it really hit me as far as a pressure moment where you kind of got like caught for a second was the ninth inning. In the ninth inning, there was first and third, it was Gossage against Yastrzemski, and I remember standing at shortstop going, 'OK, this is it.'

"And Goose threw a fastball right down the middle and he popped it up to third. Just for a second in your mind you go, 'Here it is—Goose against Yastrzemski. This is it.'

"When I was up, I thought, 'Just get a basehit.'

"(Was his bat corked?) Nah, you know, Mickey and I actually started joking around about that. I think it was one of my first old-timer games I was at and we were in the clubhouse and there was something going on about a corked bat that year. And I said, 'Hey homey, wouldn't it be interesting if we told everyone that bat you gave me was corked?'

"I hit it on a line—and there's kind of a shadow over there—and I hit it on a line, and I never did see it 'til I rounded first and I saw the umpire signal that it was a home run.

"You know, people ask, 'What were you thinking?' All I was thinking rounding the bases was, 'Hey, we're ahead.' That's it. I've been in enough games at Fenway to know, 'Hey, 3-2 lead, anything can happen.'

"The one thing I remember is, rounding third, how quiet and stunned the crowd was. You could hear the Yankee fans, kind of, you know, you could hear them cheering. But it was kind of a weird, dead silence. Like a stunned silence. But nobody said anything in the dugout. I mean, we were ahead for the first time but, 'We've still got plenty of work to do.'

"It kinda grew at the end of the World Series. Because we went right to Kansas City and started playing the next day. So you didn't really have time to kind of, like, sit back and go 'wooo.'

"My brother called that night. We kind of just talked about the game. 'Hey, you know, we beat those guys kind of thing.' It's just part of sports. To be a part of history and tradition, hitting a big home run. I think every guy that puts on the uniform as a kid, right on through, dreams of doing something like that.

"I got to do a lot of things. I got to play for the team that I wanted to play for. I got to play in a World Series, win a World Series on the team I wanted to, I got to play in one of the biggest games ever played. I mean, there's a lot of things in my career that all came true."

*** *** ***

Dent would have been pleased to see the T-shirts that had surfaced by Game 1 of the 2003 World Series.

"Babe. Bucky. Buckner. Boone."

But the World Series did not go as well for Aaron Boone as it did Bucky Dent.

Unlike Dent, whose momentum carried him to a World Series MVP award in '78, Boone would strike out in a critical spot. Then he would make a more critical mistake.

He tore a ligament playing basketball back home in the off season, an activity banned by his contract. When the Yankees suddenly discovered they could replace Boone with, arguably, the game's best player in Alex Rodriguez, they made a decision both difficult and amazingly easy.

They would void Boone's contract.

Later that year, he signed with Cleveland.

"Oh, man," Dent said, his voice turning somber, when asked about Boone in spring 2004. "Yeah, that's a tough thing, boy."

Dent enjoyed all the cheers he earned in '78 for the next few seasons.

But after the Yankees faltered in the '81 World Series, Steinbrenner decided to shake up the team in '82, importing more offense and shipping Dent off to Texas. He would eventually become one of the Boss' favorites, though.

One of those employees Steinbrenner yo-yos back and forth. He managed the Yankees for parts of 1989 and '90 then coached in Texas. Then he came back to manage Triple-A Columbus.

But he knows what it was like to be one of those famed "B"s in a big moment of Red Sox-Yankees.

"Going to spring training the next year, it was different. It was different."

Different enough to change his life forever.

CHAPTER 10

Graig Nettles:
A Glove Story

October 13, 1978, World Series Game 3

vs. Los Angeles
Yankees 5, Dodgers 1

The stats:	AB	R	H	PO	A	E
	4	1	1	2	5	0

The guy had to be kidding, right?

A couple of hours before Game 3 of the World Series and he hits Graig Nettles with this?

There was no time to argue with the representative from the Rawlings glove company. He could do what he had to do; whatever.

Sure, Nettles had an endorsement contract, but he could give a crap about that right now.

This was the World Series.

And the Yankees were down 2-0 to the Dodgers.

Not that Nettles was worried. He knew the Yankees could come back. They had all year.

Especially with Gator on the mound. Ron Guidry had ended every losing streak.

What was one more comeback?

It hadn't even been two weeks since Bucky Dent rescued them from the Red Sox at Fenway. It had been about three months since the team finally started playing some good ball.

Kids in New York were practicing the "Graig Nettles dive" for years after the Yankees' third baseman made several spectacular plays like this gem in Game 3 of the '78 World Series. *AP/WWP.*

Shoved it right up Boston's butt and came all the way back from 14 games down. They could survive anything.

In between all that, they had watched their manager get fired—then announced as the new manager ... for 1980.

"Some kids want to join the circus and some want to become a ballplayer," Nettles had said when fired manager Billy Martin was re-hired for 1980. "With the Yankees, I've gotten to do both."

So Nettles had dealt with playing for Ringling Bros.

But he wasn't about to deal with Mr. Rawlings Bros. over at his locker a couple of hours before Game 3. So he just shook his head and accepted what he was being told.

"I had to prepare for the game," he said.

He'd have to be more prepared than he could have imagined.

Guidry had great stuff in the bullpen. But, as he would tell reporters after the Yankees' 5-1 win, "... I left it out there."

The Dodgers were on him. All game long.

But it wouldn't matter.

The Dodgers kept sending screaming shots down the line, certain hits set to break open the game. Nettles kept silencing them, diving to make the ball—and the Dodgers' chance for a win—disappear into his glove. All in a blink.

"I lost track of what I did to who," Nettles would say after the game.

So did Tommy Lasorda, who couldn't offer any bluster about his great Dodgers team. All he could do was shake his head.

"I thought we had a chance to really score some runs off Mr. Guidry tonight," Lasorda said through gritted teeth after the game. "I thought we had a chance to go ahead three games to none in this thing. I thought we had the ball past the third baseman at least three times.

"I thought all those things. Evidently, Nettles thought otherwise."

Finally, an exasperated Lasorda added this:

"I have no idea how many runs he denied us. I stopped counting."

One person in the ballpark must have been more stunned than Lasorda.

The Rawlings rep who visited Nettles before the game couldn't have felt too good. The lump must have hit his throat as he watched Nettles snare anything hit within the same zip code.

Because, just an hour before Nettles had one of the greatest defensive games in World Series history, this is what the man representing the Rawlings glove company had said to him:

"We're not renewing your contract for next year."

*** *** ***

Nettles remembers a minor-league coach approaching him back in Minnesota. At that point, Nettles was known as a power-hitting second baseman, figuring his pop at a normally puny position was his ticket to the big leagues.

"We want you to play third base," the coach said.

Third base?

Hold on a minute, Nettles thought. I signed as a second baseman. I've got more power than any other second baseman. My career's set as a second baseman.

"Why?" Nettles said. "I'm doing a good job here at second."

"We've got Rod Carew," the coach said of the future Hall of Famer. "He's a step ahead of you in the organization."

"Well, who's playing third for the Twins?" Nettles asked.

"Harmon Killebrew."

Harmon Killebrew?! He was hitting 50 homers a season.

But there was no choice.

Besides, if Nettles was going to the big leagues eventually, it wouldn't be by his glove.

That's what everyone had always told him, at least.

"I get a big kick out of people referring to my defense now," Nettles said. "I was told when I signed with the Minnesota Twins I would go as far as my bat would take me. They told me I was awkward; that I didn't have a position."

So Nettles worked at his new position, taking all the grounders he could at third.

Not that he had the assistance he would later offer.

After Alex Rodriguez joined the Yankees in one of baseball's biggest blockbusters in 2004, Nettles was assigned the task of tutoring him.

Rodriguez would move from shortstop to third base to accommodate team captain Derek Jeter and every move the multimillion-dollar investment made would be scrutinized.

So Nettles was followed almost as much as A-Rod, reporters trailing the old third baseman for clues on Rodriguez's progress.

"He'll be fine," Nettles said.

When he thought back to his own position switch, Nettles laughed.

"They didn't have any instructors," he said. "I had to kind of learn it all on my own. I didn't have a spring training to go through."

*** *** ***

Nettles was one of the final pieces of the puzzle that locked the Yankees back into another dynasty.

Gabe Paul had seen him play for Cleveland—which had acquired him from Minnesota—and decided he wanted him. So he pulled off a steal—sending John Ellis, Jerry Kenney, Charlie Spikes and Rusty Torres to Cleveland for Nettles and Jerry Moses.

Nettles arrived in New York, a laid-back, but smart-aleck Californian ready to stir it up in the big city.

He had already shown off his dry humor in Cleveland, once answering the phones when a fan called.

"What time's the game start?" the fan asked.

"Well, Nettles said, "What time can you get here?"

By the time he left New York, he would become one of the most popular Yankees of his era. He would also write a behind-the-scenes look at the Yankees called *BALLS* that made baseball history.

At least according to a blurb on the back cover.

"Never before has a book resulted in the sudden trade of its author."

Yankees owner George Steinbrenner, the rumors went, was upset with Nettles's bashing of him and some teammates in the book and shipped Nettles off to San Diego in 1984.

"I didn't even really rip my teammates," Nettles said.

Well, yes and no.

Nettles did what he did throughout his Yankees career—cut up and carve away at the egos on his team with wisecracks.

He had been both a welcome comedic break and an antagonist amid the Bronx Zoo through the years. One day, he'd offer the perfect quip. Another he'd be getting into a fight with teammate Reggie Jackson at a postgame play-off celebration.

But no barb was ever as dangerous as his glove.

Slowly, Nettles built a reputation to rival the Orioles' great third base-man Brooks Robinson. Team after team would go away muttering time after time as Nettles stole hits.

This was the formula for his Gold Glove success:

For one thing, he'd play so far off the line opponents would marvel.

"I don't know how he gets away with it," then-Boston manager Don Zimmer had told reporters during the '78 season. "It makes him the only player who can close two holes simultaneously."

Not that his body provided any obvious clue to its elastic nature. While Hall of Fame Cardinals shortstop Ozzie Smith would make hitters apprehensive with his acrobatics in the '80s—he'd do flips on his way to his position—Nettles hardly seemed fit for such stretching techniques.

His body was more soft than sculpted.

By playing off the line and saving displays of his nimbleness for when he needed it, Nettles invited opponents to accept his sucker bet.

Go ahead, go for it. I can't possibly get to the ball down the line in time.

Next thing they'd know, Nettles's body would be spread out in a shot, dirt covering his pinstripes, his glove denting the chalk of the third-base line.

In an instant, he'd be up, spinning, throwing.

And when Guidry was pitching? Well, Nettles had a little more room for error.

Guidry liked it that way.

"You know, Nettles and I worked very well together," Guidry said. "Because I was a good fielding pitcher and I always told him, 'You play third base and don't worry about anything in the infield. I'll get those. I would rather have you playing routine than worrying about coming up for possible bunts or choppers or something.'"

There were times Nettles would approach Guidry before a game and, half-jokingly say, "Look, I'm not feeling too good today. I wouldn't let them hit too many ground balls to third base."

"So," Guidry said, "I'd pitch away all day."

But not on this day.

This day, Guidry would give up eight hits, seven walks and constantly get into trouble.

And Nettles would constantly get him out.

*** *** ***

Nettles started routinely enough, beginning a double-play in the second to end the inning.

Then he singled in the bottom of the inning and scored to give the Yankees a 2-0 lead.

Then he made sure it held up.

The Dodgers had a man on third with one out in the top of the third when Davey Lopes sent a liner toward left field.

Until Nettles intercepted it.

Two down, no runs in.

The Dodgers scored on an infield single and were ready for more.

Smith shot the ball over third for a sure double and ...

Nettles dived and snared the ball over the bag. Smith was out by a step.

"If we hadn't been losing, I would have stood up myself and applauded him," Smith told reporters afterward.

Inning over. Still 2-1, Yanks.

Yankee Stadium buzzed. But underneath it was a tension that had filled the place all year.

Nothing had come cheaply that season. The fans wearing their 'fros and polyester pants had found out "It Don't Come Easy" as the Yankees' season review video—punctuated by the Ringo Starr song—would announce later.

Don Sutton was shutting the Yankees down, leaving Guidry with little room to work. And between his eight hits and seven walks, Gator wasn't exactly calming the crowd.

One loss and the season full of comebacks was all but done.

So when the Dodgers loaded the bases with two outs in the fifth, the Stadium crowd grew quiet.

Up came Steve Garvey, the clutch first baseman who seemingly always came through with a hit.

Nettles had already robbed Smith of another extra-base hit in the inning, this time unable to do more than contain him to a single.

Garvey sent another shot over the bag and toward left fielder Roy White.

White would stay lonely.

"They couldn't get the ball out to me," he said after the game.

Nettles snagged the shot—later saying an extra split-second's difference between Smith and Garvey's balls allowed him to hold the second. He was only half done.

With little time and a run heading home, Nettles spun 180 degrees to get the force at second.

Inning over. Still, 2-1.

By now Lasorda was muttering to himself.

The Dodgers were taking turns cursing and praising Nettles.

And he wasn't finished.

Back came L.A. in the sixth.

Bases loaded, two outs.

Up came second baseman Davey Lopes.

Maybe if Nettles hadn't caught the ball before anyone had a chance to realize he would again, Lopes would have cursed his fate.

But there was no time.

"It wasn't until you were in the dugout that you thought, 'Oh, my gosh, what a play," then-Yankees second baseman Brian Doyle said.

Nettles snared the ball almost before it could be seen and ended the inning with another force.

By now, Yankee Stadium—which had seen every possible symbol of dominance the last few years—erupted with a disbelieving roar.

This was something entirely new.

Winning a game singlehandedly with a glove?

It was ridiculous.

Dodgers third-base coach Jim Lefebvre jogged back to the dugout, shaking his head.

"The best one-man show ever," Lefebvre said after the game.

Not necessarily.

"I've been making plays like that for eight or nine years," Nettles said nonchalantly after the game.

Oh, these were good enough for the Dodgers. More than good enough.

By now, they had all but given up.

The Yankees scored three runs in the bottom of the seventh, finally giving Guidry—and Nettles—some breathing room.

Not that L.A. thought it had a chance to score any more with Nettles guarding the third-base line more fiercely than a teenaged girl does her diary.

By the time Lopes came up in the ninth, he all but waved a white flag.

Lacking one, he instead waved Nettles over toward short, pleadingly.

The third baseman smiled.

Then picked up another out when Lopes grounded out to him.

The Yankees won, 5-1, and were on their way back into the Series. They would soon win it, capping a chaotic year with their second straight championship.

But at this point, the Dodgers still felt in control—on one condition.

"We're still ahead ..." Lasorda said. "I'll instruct all my players to hit the ball to the right side."

*** *** ***

Game of My Life
Graig Nettles

"The pressure of that one game (against Boston). There had never been pressure like that. By the time we got to the World Series, it was a relief.

"I don't know why we got behind 2-0. I knew it was an important game; we couldn't get down 3-0.

"After playing 170 games or so, it was just another game. Don't want to do anything different. I stayed loose. Oh, sure we (knew we could come back). We knew what it took to win the World Series. Even though we were down 2-0, we were still sure we could win. I had all the confidence in Guidry. He had been our ace.

"I'll tell ya what—I couldn't even remember the plays the next day. Did an interview with Curt Gowdy; I said, 'You have to put it on the monitor.' I couldn't even remember them.

"I'm sure it picks up guys on our bench. Gid didn't have his best stuff. 'Who's gonna bail him out?' It was me that day. He's bailed me out, too.

"You don't have time to dwell on it. It's all kind of a blur. I have a tape of it at home and my sons watched it. I never watch it all the way through.

"I do remember one thing. Before the game I was signed with Rawlings on a glove contract. The rep came in and said, 'We're not renewing you for next year.' So I signed up with Louisville Slugger the next year.

"It means a lot to me. That's the first thing people bring up when they meet me. 'God, I'll never forget that game you had in the '78 Series.' I've had better games in the regular season, made better plays, but when you can shine on the big stage, people remember."

*** *** ***

They remember all right.

Never mind the people coming up to Nettles saying they'd never forget.

He spurned a whole generation of little leaguers who loved trying to get dirty like Nettles.

Sometimes, you'd practice in your backyard, finding just the right spot on the stoop that would send you sprawling to the ground, trying to make the perfect Graig Nettles dive.

Even if Nettles doesn't endorse that practice any more than he does Rawlings.

"Don't practice diving," Nettles said. "I always tell guys not to practice it, because you'll get hurt. You can't do it halfway."

Lasorda remains as bitter as ever about the time the third baseman helped cost him a World Series, even if he's joking.

"That ... third baseman killed us defensively," Lasorda said in spring 2004. "We hit him five double-plays—bases loaded, makes spectacular plays, he turned them into double plays. He made plays out of his ass. I never saw anything like it.

"I went to dinner with him and I got up to speak; I said, 'Look at him, he dropped his fork three times. How come he never dropped one of them balls?'"

If Lasorda and the rest of the world wasn't used to seeing Nettles make those plays, his teammates were.

"I knew Graig was a great third baseman," Guidry said, "but the world saw it that night."

Including one rather rueful Rawlings representative.

Twenty-six years later, one of the game's greatest third basemen grinned when asked if he thought the Rawlings rep might regret his decision.

"He might," Nettles said.

CHAPTER 11

Brian Doyle:
So That's Brian Doyle

October 15/17, 1978,
World Series Game 5/6

vs. Los Angeles
Yankees 12, Dodgers 2

Game 5:	AB	R	H	RBI
	5	2	3	0

at Los Angeles
Yankees 7, Dodgers 2

Game 6:	AB	R	H	RBI
	4	2	3	2

Tommy Lasorda ran to the mound, Santa Claus belly bouncing, Goodfellas glare menacing anyone who locked eyes.

The damn Yankees had chased off another pitcher and the Dodgers manager, along with the rest of a silent Dodger Stadium, knew New York was on its way to another World Series win.

The season before, Reggie Jackson had hit every pitch over the freakin' wall. Then, a couple of games ago, that damn third baseman had pulled all those plays out of his behind.

Now, as Lasorda took the ball from Don Sutton in Game 6, he felt the Series slipping from the Dodgers' grasp. As he stood there, steaming, he was still trying to figure out how.

They had shut down Jackson. And Graig Nettles. And Thurman Munson.

Everyone wanted to know who Brian Doyle was after the
career .161 hitter batted over .400 while subbing for Yankees
second baseman Willie Randolph in the 1978 World Series.
*National Baseball Hall of Fame Library/MLB Photos via Getty
Images*

And the whole damn Yankees team that wrecked havoc on pitchers
throughout the second half of the season.

But that skinny little second baseman out of Cave City, Nowhere—or
wherever the heck it was—had just singled in another run with his sixth
straight hit in two games.

So as he waited for his next pitcher, Lasorda had some questions for
Sutton—and the "great Dodger in the sky" he often worshipped.

"Who is that—Pie Traynor? Honus Wagner?" Lasorda screamed. "Who
the #$)*#@$*(@$# is Brian Doyle?"

Good question.
Gonna take a while to answer it.

*** *** ***

Start here, on the little league field in Cave City, Kentucky, population 1,500. Simple town. Hard-working, church-going folk.

It's a good life.

Now look at the little kid younger than the rest. His dad, the coach, wants him to play with the big kids; so at six he's playing on the nine-year-old team. One son is already in the big leagues, and Jake Doyle is determined the rest of his boys are going to learn to play baseball right.

See the way little Brian Doyle struggles to pick up the bat? Can't even swing the thing, right? Poor kid. Gonna get hurt.

Also gonna get something else.

Three hits.

Doesn't need to swing the bat.

The kid lays down three straight drag bunts.

Drag bunts.

At six.

His dad taught him to pay attention to all the details the big kids wouldn't. He set up towels and sticks in the backyard. Drew a line.

"Placement first," Jake would tell his sons. "Then run. Don't run before you bunt. Deaden the ball. If you put down a good bunt, you're safe."

So after it worked in a game and the kid who could barely lift the bat reached base three times, he realized something.

"Hey," he thought, "I don't need to be the strongest guy on the team to play this game."

The thought stuck. Good thing, too, because he didn't end up growing much.

By the time he debuted in the big leagues on April 30, 1978, Brian Doyle was five-foot-nine and, he figures, 140 pounds.

But that didn't matter when starting second baseman Willie Randolph battled injuries all year.

"They needed someone who could catch the ball," Doyle said. "And I could do that very well. Anything else was a bonus."

He had been up and down from the minors five times throughout the season. So, when Randolph went down with a hamstring injury before the playoffs, the Yankees worried only about getting the clearance to put Doyle on the roster.

An exception would have to be made for both the American League Championship Series and the World Series, and the Yankees were forced to wait until the final hours before game time. Once Doyle was cleared, so were any concerns for the Yankees about second base.

Pitcher Ron Guidry said, "If Brian is in the line up, as a pitcher, I know I've got a good defensive back-up to Willie. Hey, if he hits anything, that's just extra.

"He was just a good, solid, fundamental player."

So that's Brian Doyle.

No, not yet.
There's more.

*** *** ***

Nancy Bass answered the phone at the baseball camp in Winter Haven, Florida in 2004, as she had since she moved from Cave City so many years ago.

Her words tell you you've reached the "Doyle Baseball Academy." Her voice makes you think you've called one of your favorite aunts.

"These guys, they've been great to me," Bass said, cheerfully, of the Doyle brothers.

And, she said, they're great with the kids. Not just with baseball. The woman of faith takes pride in working where she does, because she likes what she sees.

"When you have two guys telling you you need to go to church and you need to read your Bible and they have World Series rings on, it means more than if you have your pop or your grandfather," she said of Brian and Denny Doyle. "They've had a pulpit right here at Doyle Baseball."

But it still wasn't quite the pulpit Brian Doyle wanted.

He still loves teaching kids about drag bunts and other little elements of the game. He still loves baseball enough to work as an agent.

But, Doyle will tell you, he loves his Lord more.

So, brothers Denny and Blake will have to take care of things at the baseball camp.

Now you can find *Pastor* Doyle at the First Baptist Church in Fort Lauderdale.

"He battled it all the way through November and October and December," Bass said of Brian's decision in the winter of 2003. "Right before Christmas was when he told me he was definitely going to do it.

"I said, 'Go for it, kid. I hate to lose you but ...'"

Lose him? She had almost never left the Doyle family; not since she was a teacher working in the school where the boys' father was a custodian. They were always good boys and she kept in touch with the family even as they grew.

So when they opened the baseball school in 1978, fresh off Brian's star-studded World Series trip, Nancy made her own decision.

She offered her resignation to the school and became the administrative director of the camp. Nancy's daughter, Lois, not only attended camp but would call Brian for help when she went off to play softball for Stetson College.

So, sure, it would be tough not seeing Brian around as Nancy always had. But she understood.

And Brian decided he didn't have a choice.

Wasn't that what this had been all about anyway? Hadn't this been his calling all along?

I mean, how else do you explain it? Sure, he was a smart player. Yes, he had prepared for that '78 World Series as much as he could.

But he was realistic, too. Brutally honest.

He was never a very good major league player.

If he wanted to lie to himself, his .161 career batting average wouldn't let him.

No, he had known all along his .438 batting average in the '78 World Series, and his six straight hits had happened for a reason.

He would still serve his love of baseball as an agent trying to help develop young players.

But he would serve his other love first.

"No, I wasn't a good player, but I can say I got to play up there," Doyle said. "Here I am, nobody in the world of sports, and because of just a little bit of something that I had ... a good name is worth more than silver and gold. It gave me a platform. Right now, ever since that Series, I've been teaching baseball and, then, more importantly, being able to share what I believe in and my faith.

"And it's been a great platform speaking on the truth of life, on God as our creator. Jesus has just been No. 1 in my life and that's why."

It's an important platform to Doyle. One he treasures.

He knows he can affect people.

But maybe even he doesn't know just how much of an effect he can have.

*** *** ***

"CLIMB, CLIMB, CLIMB!" the voice on the headset screamed in Lois Bass's ear. "EVADE! EVADE! EVADE!"

Just a week into her assignment in Iraq, Bass's helicopter had flown in on a blackout mission, cruising through the darkness.

Suddenly, spotlights from below—in a country mostly devoid of electricity since the United States' Shock and Awe mission—flashed on Bass's aircraft.

"CLIMB! CLIMB! CLIMB!" screamed Bass's IP—Instructor Pilot. "EVADE ... Bank left! Bank right!"

She had barely arrived in Iraq. She hadn't flown in a year.

And now, on one of her first missions, Bass's heart raced as fast as the thoughts in her head.

The spotlights are on us. They have us locked. I'm gonna die.

So she climbed and sped up and ... and she evaded.

She'd made it. She was still alive.

Bass hadn't counted on any of this when she enlisted in the army in '96. She wrote poetry. Was sensitive.

"A tree-hugger," she joked.

But she didn't want to mooch off Mom any more, and this would help pay for graduate school, so she'd do it. The other thing that helped pay for school was softball. She had a scholarship, which kept her from ever thinking of quitting as she had throughout high school.

Back then, one of the people who kept her from walking away from the sport was Brian Doyle.

"I can't tell you how many times I wanted to quit softball," Bass said in April 2004. She had returned home safely from her tour of duty the previous week and was back to changing diapers for her one-year-old. "Just because I thought I wasn't good. My mom would say, 'No, you can't quit, you can't quit.'"

And, when she got frustrated with an at-bat or a play, Doyle would tell her, "You can do it."

She had grown up around his baseball camp, tagging along with her mom. Sometimes, she'd be the only female athlete, an experience that gave her a preview of her military life.

Eventually, the camp expanded to softball and Doyle would work with her.

When she thought of quitting, Doyle would chase the thought the same way he had chased his nerves during the World Series. Back then he didn't have time to be nervous, he said, because he was so busy studying for every little advantage.

So he occupied Lois's time the same way.

"He'd tell me, 'Practice, practice, practice,'" Lois said. "I was lazy in a sense. He would preach to never do anything haphazardly. 'You have to take full advantage of every moment.'

"Brian is such a sweet man," Lois said. "Even though he was busy, he always took time out."

So Lois stuck with softball. And sports. And began to excel. She earned her scholarship to Stetson, sometimes calling home for more tips that would be relayed by Mom.

"'Where's her head? What's her shoulder doing?'" Nancy Bass remembered Brian asking her. "He could diagnose (Lois) just from me telling him," she said.

The air over Iraq, with attacks always possible quicker than a rapid heartbeat, is a world away from Bass's softball concerns. Here, a mistake in fundamentals meant your whole crew, all 11 people aboard the craft, were dead.

No room for errors.

So it's a different world.

But one Bass said she's survived in only because she didn't quit playing sports when she was younger.

"Sports has shaped my whole life, period," Lois Bass said. "You're not gonna find a woman in the military who doesn't have a sports connection. You've got to have kind of a (tough) attitude about you to take all the crap you have to endure, that's for sure."

She can't imagine doing everything she's done in the military without sports. And she can't imagine continuing in sports if it hadn't been for Doyle.

He spoke. She listened.

Why?

"Just out of respect for how good he was," she said. "If somebody tells you something and it works, you're gonna listen."

Well, it didn't always work for Brian Doyle.

But it did that one October.

*** *** ***

Doyle wasn't worried about how he'd play in the '78 postseason. He was worried about if he would.

Randolph's injury had come after the playoff roster was set and Doyle wasn't on it.

The Yankees needed permission from the commissioner's office and the Kansas City Royals—their ALCS opponent.

At the stadium, Doyle found out.

OK, kid, you can play.

So he hit .286 and made his defensive plays, and the Yankees advanced to the World Series.

Again, Doyle was left waiting until the last minute.

He had gotten into a cab with Catfish Hunter to ride to the park as he usually did. Yogi Berra, then a coach, hopped in as well.

"You're eligible," Berra said.

That's how Doyle found out he'd be the starting second baseman in the World Series.

"Well, I was thankful that I found out in the cab because in Kansas City, I didn't know until we were in the clubhouse," Doyle said, laughing.

Besides, he was ready.

The boy who learned to drag bunt at six had turned into a man who would study every quirk for any advantage.

So he knew "I would have a blast," Doyle said.

Didn't seem so fun after the Yankees dropped the first two games. But they won the next two, setting up a pivotal Game 5 at Yankee Stadium. Lose and the Yankees would need to fly to L.A. and win the final two.

The Yankees rallied with four runs in the third to take a 4-2 lead. They scored three in the fourth—a rally started by Doyle's single to center.

They'd break open the game in the seventh with four more runs—again with Doyle contributing a single to the rally.

Two hits in a World Series game. Not bad for the small kid from Cave City.

But it would get better.

Don Sutton was on the mound for L.A. in Game 6 and Doyle had picked up on something. The result was three hits, giving him six straight and causing Lasorda to swear up a storm.

The Yankees were on their way to a 7-2 win and their second straight World Series championship.

Doyle was nearly named MVP, earning non-official votes from his teammates, but the award was instead given to Bucky Dent, who followed up his famous homer at Fenway with a torrid World Series.

No matter. For Doyle, this was easily the ...

*** *** ***

Game of My Life
Brian Doyle

"A lot of times I'd sit in the dugout by myself or I'd just walk around the field. And I was just getting mentally prepared to play the game. Then

I would go back and get completely dressed. And I went every day. I sat on the bench and watched the opposing team take batting practice.

"I watched my opponents every minute. Me being a little guy, I was trying to see little flaws that I could take advantage of. And where could I attack weaknesses.

"I'd watch, especially, during the World Series.

"(Dodgers second baseman) Davey Lopes, his footwork was the same every ... single ... time. So I knew if I was on first base, where I was gonna break up the double play.

"I noticed where Don Sutton's leg kick was about an inch and a half to two inches higher on his fastball than on his breaking ball.

"I watched where Dusty Baker would nonchalant singles and you saw how I took advantage of that in Yankee Stadium. Bucky hit a regular single to left field, and I was on first base and I went into third. And he was, what, 120 feet away?

"The guys that I thought were fastball pitchers—my (favorite) pitch was up and in, and people didn't know that. So I made sure I was trying to go to the oppostite field so my next time up, I'd get a fastball up and in.

"And everybody said, 'Why aren't you nervous?' There was too much time that I had to be thinking, to be nervous. Everything was in analysis. I have a very strong faith. I knew that I was there for a reason because of all the circumstances before. I wasn't even supposed to be there, (but) I'm there. And my faith really subdued me, calmed me and allowed me to really focus. So I was focused those playoffs and World Series.

"I had five straight hits in a row. Did not know that I was close to tying a record or whatever. I remember (Yankees manager) Bob Lemon at the end of my last at-bat in Game 6, he grabbed me by the shoulder and pulled me back into the dugout when I was going up to the on-deck circle—and it startled me, because I thought he was taking me out of the game.

"And he said, 'Would you do something kid?' and then pushed me up the steps.

"After we won it ... my locker was the first locker as you walked into the clubhouse, on the left. I was the very first locker.

"And I remember when the guys came in, I heard Thurman say, 'Did Doyle get the MVP?' And then I heard Reggie walk in and say, 'Who got the MVP? Did Doyle get the MVP?' And it just dawned on me, 'Oh, yeah, they give one of those things away.' I didn't even think about it, because I was still focused. So having the great games and all of that, I wasn't even thinking about that. I was just thinking about winning.

"And then it dawned on me, 'Man, I'm part of a world championship.'

"Well, they brought Bucky and I in (to announce the MVP). And walking in, I'm going, 'What in the world—they don't give co-MVPs.' And they allowed me to be there when they announced Bucky as MVP. Of course, Bucky had a wonderful (series). I wasn't even expecting it.

"He had a great World Series. I mean, just a great World Series. I think the most embarrassing part is when I go and speak—and I do a lot of speaking across the country—I've been on marquis at the hotels or signs that say, 'Come and meet Brian Doyle, '78 World Series MVP.'

"I did not officially get it, but there's not a week that hasn't gone by, literally, that people say, 'Oh you were the MVP of the '78 World Series.' And it's embarrassing because I say, 'No I'm not. It's an honor that you think so, but Bucky Dent was the MVP and he had a great World Series.'"

*** *** ***

So that's Brian Doyle, the pee-wee baseball player-turned-pastor. The preacher who demands practice and perfection at your craft.

All these years later, Lasorda figured out who he was, too.

"I see Tommy and talk to him," Doyle said. "He sent me a signed picture. 'You would have only been better in Dodger blue.'"

CHAPTER 12

Dave Righetti:
There's No Crying in Baseball

October 15, 1981,
Game 3, American League Championship Series

At Oakland
Yankees 4, A's 0

The stats: IP H R ER BB SO
         6 4 0 0   2   4

I t's not a misprint.
    It's not the game you'd think.
    And, stopping short of apologizing to fans the way George Steinbrenner did after the Yankees lost the '81 World Series, Dave Righetti was afraid to disappoint you.
    He always was.
    Go ahead, dig out the tape of his July 4, 1983 no-hitter against the Red Sox.
    Fast forward to the end.
    Study his face.
    Watch what happens after he strikes out the league's hottest hitter, Wade Boggs, to complete the Yankees' first no-hitter since Don Larsen's perfect game.
    Watch him shyly throw his hands up then quickly jerk them down along with his head.
    No real elation.
    No real celebration.
    Know what he felt?

Dave Righetti will never forget his no-hitter on July 4, 1983 against the Red Sox, but he still can't call it his favorite game. While he fretted about upsetting the fans, he couldn't help choosing his 1981 win over the A's in Oakland for two reasons. It put the Yankees in the World Series. And his family came over from San Jose to watch. *AP/WWP.*

Relief.

He felt he *owed* you that kind of once-in-a-lifetime moment at the Stadium. Felt you deserved it, craved it.

"When I pitched on the mound at Yankee Stadium, I really did try to do extra special things; I did," he said. "I felt like that was part of my burden I had to carry as a player."

There were plenty of burdens for Righetti, right from the time he arrived in a 1978 trade and was touted as "the next Ron Guidry."

Then he became the "flame-throwing lefty," a term he cringed at because he had prided himself on his four-pitch repertoire.

So there weren't a lot of pressure-free moments for Righetti. Not after he started his Yankees career as the next Guidry and finished as the next Goose Gossage, taking over the closer's role.

And there wasn't a lot of enjoyment, even for the moments he'd earned a right to celebrate. At least not as much as there should have been.

He arrived in New York at 20, became Rookie of the Year at 22 and found himself caught in the cross-hairs of a changing of the guard. The Yankees were in the midst of ending an era, about to fall into their longest championship drought since the late '60s.

They would go down with a fight—among themselves.

In 1981, the Yankees reached their last World Series until 1996 and capped the Bronx Zoo years with some more chaos, but not another title.

Catcher Rick Cerone cursed Steinbrenner in a team meeting. Graig Nettles and Reggie Jackson got into a fight—at a dinner celebrating the team's advancement to the World Series. Then they lost and Steinbrenner apologized to the city—a lament the rookie Righetti felt responsible for after failing to outpitch his N.L. Rookie of the Year counterpart, Fernando Valenzuela, in Game 3.

Wasn't easy. Often wasn't fun.

And it didn't improve when Steinbrenner argued with coaches and shipped his '81 Rookie of the Year to the minors in '82. Coaches were fired. Righetti stayed mired in a slump.

By the time he was back up for good in '83, he was still determined to fulfill all that "Prince of Potential crap" he had heard from the time he was a teen.

That's why he couldn't enjoy the no-hitter as much as he would have liked. Also, it wasn't a team thing.

Unlike Game 3 of the 1981 American League Championship Series in Oakland.

That's the day Righetti—who grew up 35 miles away in San Jose— pitched his team into the World Series.

In front of his family, including the father who once thought his boy wouldn't be able to catch a ball.

You ask him for the game of his life and Righetti wants to go right back to pleasing everyone the way he did on the Yankee Stadium mound.

"See, if I don't pick the no-hitter, fans will be upset ..." he said.

But it's still not the one.

"Without a doubt, I know the no-hitter is the one everybody remembers, but for me, the no-hitter is kind of separate," he said. "It's like this separate thing because it's against the Red Sox, it's on July 4, anyone who follows any kind of Yankee baseball knows about it.

"But it was a game and the other part of it (against Oakland) was a chance for your team to go to the World Series. I get to jump around. ... I had friends coming out of the stands jumping around with me. It was a pretty neat thing for a young guy to do that.

"If you remember the no-hitter, it wasn't like I jumped around. You know what? Because there were so many labels put on me, I felt like I had to do something like that. At the end of the game, that's pretty much how I felt. I felt relieved, not excited."

*** *** ***

He's 11 years old and he can't believe he's blowing the game.

First, he gave up the stinkin' lead. Then he struck out with the bases loaded.

Yeah, his farm league team had already wrapped up the league championship. But that wasn't enough. They were 21-0 and wanted to finish the season undefeated.

"I was so upset," Righetti said.

About four years before, he didn't have such demanding expectations. Heck, he didn't have any.

His Dad sure didn't at least.

Leo Righetti taught his sons to play ball in the backyard because he had been a ballplayer. Except Leo's teaching wasn't going well and Dave wasn't having a lot of fun.

"When I was around five, he'd given up on me; didn't think I'd ever catch the ball," Righetti said of his father. "And then I went out with some neighborhood kids ... throwing the ball with me, helped me learn how to catch the ball and I was hooked."

But he was a long way from that when he sat in that dugout with his team's undefeated record on the line. Now he wanted perfection.

What kind of a ballplayer was he, anyway? Giving up the lead on the mound. Making an out with the bases loaded.

The A's never did that when the family went to the Oakland Coliseum in the early '70s watching Reggie and Campy and the rest of Oakland's dynasty.

Righetti's not sure exactly what he did in the little league dugout.

Maybe screamed. Shoved some stuff. Might have, to be completely honest, cried.

But he does remember, out of nowhere, the voice in his ear, the hand reaching into the dugout and pulling at his shoulder.

It was his Uncle Butch coming down from the stands.

"What are you upset about?" his uncle said, forcefully. "Keep your head up. Let's go."

The boy was stunned.

This wasn't his dad on his case as usual. Or his mom telling him, as always, how he should act.

This was his uncle. Charging down from his seat in the middle of the game, ordering him to stop whining.

This was serious.

"I mean, you're 11 years old," Righetti said. "You're worried about which shoe to put on first or whatever. That was the first time I. ... You always hear it from your parents, 'Act good' and, 'Don't do this, don't do that.'

"I realized how I acted. It must have been important for him to come down and tell me that. So I started caring about how I portrayed myself on the field or out in public or anywhere else."

It was a valuable lesson. One that would serve him well his rookie year in New York.

*** *** ***

He's 22 years old and he can't believe what he's hearing.
It's after midnight.

Righetti's supposed to be preparing his packed bags and leaving for New York. Supposed to start his big-league career.

There were four young pitchers in camp, and Righetti knew he was one of the two best, along with Gene Nelson.

But the Yankees weren't ready to admit that at the start of spring training.

"They said, 'Two of you guys are gonna make the ballclub,'" Righetti said. "They wanted us, obviously, to compete against each other, which we did."

So, fine. Good. No problem.

He would compete.

He would win.

He knew that much.

Especially when they told him to "pack your bags for New York" at the end of camp. Then they had him start the last spring training game in Miami. He goes seven innings, then prepares for New York.

But the Yankees realized they needed to make another move. Fill up the spot on the roster.

So, shortly after midnight, Righetti was told to take those packed bags with him to Triple-A Columbus.

"It was heartbreaking, because you think you're gonna be on a ballclub," he said.

But eleven years after his Uncle Butch had yanked him back to reality, Righetti found it on his own, in 1981.

"When it didn't happen, instead of pouting about it, I ended up going to Columbus and doing something about it," Righetti said. "I ended up 5-0 at the beginning of the season with a low ERA; I think, around 1.00. I showed them I belonged."

It worked.

The Yankees made a trade, made some room for him. He got sent up to New York.

His fastball started taking off and so did his career.

By season's end, he'd go 8-4 with a 2.05 ERA, earning the A.L. Rookie of the Year.

Trouble is, the season almost ended too early.

The players went on strike on June 12, the first step in setting up one of the most bizarre seasons and playoff scenarios in history.

Worried the strike would consume too much of the season to make it fair as a whole, Major League Baseball decided to call it a split season.

Teams in first place on the strike date would be awarded first-half division titles and play the second-half winner in a divisional series round before advancing to the league championship series.

This meant the Yankees—up two games over Baltimore—had clinched a share of the "title" before resuming play. That was comforting. Less soothing was the talk of sending Righetti down during the strike.

"They were debating whether to send me down again, 'So he doesn't get stuck in the strike,'" Righetti said. "I was hoping they wouldn't because, to be quite honest, I had enough of minor-league pitching by then. I had a feeling I'd be ready when I came back and I did—I got off to a nice start.

"(But) the second half we just played lousy."

The Yankees struggled the entire second half and limped into the play-offs. Not a good sign against second-half winner Milwaukee, which featured a potent lineup that would win a World Series of its own the next season.

But the Yankees heated up and, with Righetti winning Game 2, took a 2-0 lead in the best of five.

They were just about set. Soon, they would be off to Oakland and ...

They lost the next two games.

So Steinbrenner lost it.

He ripped the team, going at the players as only he has been known to do.

But then catcher Rick Cerone ripped back.

He told the owner, the Boss ... well, he told him off.

The team had played hard. They were one game from advancing.

In the middle of all this, Righetti was told to get ready. You're pitching.

"They came up and told me ... it wasn't like 'You might pitch,'" Righetti said. "It was, 'Guidry's going four, you're going three, Goose is going two and that's it.' It was like, 'Wow. All these guys, and you want me to do that?' I'd never been in the bullpen before.

"It worked out. We won."

Guidry had a shaky four innings, giving up two runs. Righetti held the Brewers to one run over three and Gossage shut them down the rest of the way.

And Cerone backed up his words, smacking a late home run to help the Yankees win, 7-3.

Righetti picked up his second victory of the series and was set up to pitch Game 3 of the ALCS.

In Oakland.

In front of the family that had never traveled east to see him pitch. In the stadium he went to as a kid.

With a chance to send his team to the World Series after the Yankees took a 2-0 series lead.

This was ... this was ...

"My greatest thrill," Righetti said.

*** *** ***

Righetti knew he'd have to keep leadoff hitter Rickey Henderson off the bases. The future Hall of Famer and stolen base king was in his pesky prime, distracting pitchers with his speed.

If Henderson got on, Righetti would have to deal with Dwayne Murphy, Cliff Johnson and Tony Armas, all of whom could drive in a pair with one swing.

What Righetti didn't know he'd have to deal with until game time was the antics of his past and future manager Billy Martin, then with Oakland.

Oakland starter Matt Keough started the game with a pitch high and tight to Yankees outfielder Jerry Mumphrey—as per Martin's orders— and the Yankees grumbled from the dugout.

After the game, Mumphrey told reporters, "If he did it again, I would have gone after him."

And Righetti was ready to go after A's leadoff hitter Henderson in retaliation, but manager Bob Lemon told him to just pitch.

So he did.

Righetti locked in against Keough. They threw five scoreless innings apiece before Willie Randolph gave the Yankees a 1-0 lead in the sixth with a homer.

Righetti took that and handed the ball to Ron Davis after the sixth.

Overall, Righetti said he didn't have his best stuff, but the results looked pretty good.

Six shutout innings. Four hits. Enough to help the Yankees to the World Series.

*** *** ***

Game of My Life

Dave Righetti

"My parents had come to have lunch with me. And this was early. This was back when nobody went to the park early. It was like 3 o'clock or something. Was gonna go have lunch with my parents and go to the ballpark. I had my bags out there, because the season was basically over and I kept what I needed for whatever length of time we had. All the extra luggage I carried during the season I was able to give to my parents to take it home.

"Then George Steinbrenner comes by. 'Get those bags and get over to the park,' and next thing you know I've gotta get to the ballpark early. It didn't fluster me. It flustered my parents. My dad. You don't know my father. He didn't say much.

"That was my first time my dad and mom had seen me in a professional game so that was a big deal (for them to see me pitch). They were on the West Coast; I was playing (minor-league ball in) West Haven, Connecticut, places like that. They weren't about to get on a plane and go back there. In fact, my parents never did even come to New York.

"I was one of the first guys (at the ballpark), which was dumb. But I was comfortable there. I felt like it was almost like going home anyway, so I don't remember being nervous.

"It was the first time I ever saw the wave in person. Crazy George Henderson, this guy; he started it out on the West Coast. I didn't know what was going on. It might sound funny to people now, because it's done in every ballpark, but nobody had ever seen anything like that before. They had it so organized, in unison. You know, at one time I turned around and said, 'What the hell is going on?'

"I think in the first inning, Dwayne Murphy might have pulled his rib cage. I had a fastball that really took off and a lot of times guys had trouble holding up. In this case, it happened to Dwayne. He hurt his ribs. He pulled a rib muscle and he was out of the game, trying to hold back on a high fast-ball. And Rickey did the same thing and busted up his hand. In fact, he tried to bunt with two strikes and he had to come out of the game.

"In the eighth inning, Graig Nettles hit a bases-loaded double to center that ... it was a tough play. Rick Bosetti was out there, so they made a big deal out of it, (Murphy) not being out there. But Murphy played shallow actually, so who knows? It may have gone over his head easy.

"I got a double play early. I didn't pitch that great, but obviously, they didn't score. Rickey got on in the first inning. I thought I was doing a good job of holding him on; he stole second. So just getting out of the first inning without any damage and stuff was good.

"(The A's) were excited, all the stuff going on. They were gonna come back and beat our butts. In fact, I had a dilemma the first batter of the game.

"Matt Keough was pitching; he threw at Jerry Mumphrey's head, basi-cally, and knocked him on his rear end. And that was a message Billy wanted Matt to send. I pitched for Billy, so I understand him. Matty never came close to anybody the rest of the game. Anyway, I had a dilemma whether to drop Rickey or not or just pitch the game and not let it bother us. And Lem told me to go ahead and pitch. He said, 'You'll probably hit somebody anyway; you don't have the greatest control.' And I might have. I'd knocked down a few people.

"But I felt like I wanted to do it. I'd do it in a minute. Especially then, I was a wild kid. 'Yeah, sure, thing, what do you want me to do?' .

"I ended up getting (Henderson) anyway. Ended up knocking himself out of the game later on on a pitch I threw; he had to leave.

"I got through it for six innings; I didn't give up any runs. Ron Davis came in and pitched the seventh and eighth. So it was my first playoffs to be a part of it. I actually felt really part of the team then. Before ... that team seemed a lot older. Cerone was probably the next youngest guy. I bet he was.

"I remember running (to celebrate) from the dugout. The big, long run. And I probably shouldn't have done it, but I asked Lou Piniella ... 'You think it'd be all right if my dad ..?' My family had to come back through the inter-view room. I was one of the last guys to get dressed and the bus was gonna be late. And I brought my dad back to the clubhouse area so he could meet some of the guys and say hello and stuff. (Lou) says, 'Yeah, bring him on the bus— it's only from here to across the street basically, to get to the hotel, it's no big deal.'

"It had to be cool (for my dad). I mean, I knew it was for me. That I was able to do it for him. So that's why the whole thing is special for me.

"Because it was so much more family-oriented and team-oriented. When you throw a no-hitter, there's so much attention brought on you, you feel—at least I did—I wasn't uncomfortable with it; I really enjoyed being able to do that, because I know how much it meant to the fans and still does. But, you know, you're always leery about enjoying too much success about your-self.

"I don't know. Just being able to have my brother there and my dad there; to me that's special. When I threw the no-hitter, me and Nettles got to go do something together (after the game), but it wasn't like I could turn around and hug my mother or wife or see my kid or anything like that."

*** *** ***

It looked like Righetti would have just as much fun in the World Series.

It was set up perfectly all over again.

The Yankees had taken a 2-0 lead on the Dodgers in New York and Righetti was up against his rookie phenom counterpart, Valenzuela, in L.A.

Actually, if you ask Righetti, he wonders if it was set up a little too perfectly.

"I sat eight, nine days ... I always felt they put me up against Valenzuela for the (public relations) and not for the pitching," Righetti said.

But that was fine, too. Again Righetti's family had come to the stadium. But this time there was a problem.

Not enough tickets.

Trying to please their guests, Righetti's parents allowed everyone else to enter the stadium and remained outside, unable to see their son pitch in his first World Series game.

That's when Nettles's cousin, Jim, was stunned to see Righetti's parents on the concourse.

"What are you doing out here?" Jim Nettles asked.

"I can't get in, couldn't get the tickets," Leo Righetti answered.

So Nettles tracked down his cousin, and Graig soon relayed the news to his teammate.

"Hey," Graig told Righetti, "your parents can't get in the game."

"Now I'm thinking about that as I'm walking out to warm up," Righetti said. "I never told anybody that. Nettles went in and took care of it somehow. I think, in fact, he went to the Dodgers and they got the tickets. So that was probably not a good omen.

"I got caught in the first inning. Didn't get my feet under me. Almost did. First two guys got on. Then I struck out (Steve) Garvey and popped up (Dusty) Baker. And then I made a real bad pitch to Ron Cey and he took me deep. I made a mistake to the wrong guy and he nailed me good.

"By the time I came out, we were behind 4-3. I was always disappointed by that."

The Yankees would lose, 5-4. Then the Dodgers would get hot and come back on them as the Yankees had to L.A. in '78. The Dodgers won the next three to win the Series, 4-2.

An irate Steinbrenner held a news conference apologizing to the fans of New York for a World Series loss.

When he did, his club's rookie of the year felt the apology was aimed at him.

"I always felt blamed for that World Series," Righetti said. "The apology; I felt bad. Here I am, I'm just getting in the big leagues, have a great year, I'm rookie of the year—couldn't enjoy that.

"In fact, I didn't even go back to New York to get the award. Basically, I felt lousy."

He'd feel worse the next spring.

Steinbrenner vowed revenge for the loss. Instead, he ended up with one of the worst renovations in history, setting the Yankees on a course that would lead to a 14-year playoff drought. Right in the middle of it was Righetti, who was sent to the minors.

"I got into spring next year and coaches were getting threatened to get fired over me because, if I didn't pitch well they're gone and this and that," Righetti said. "(Steinbrenner) was mad at me. Matter of fact, the next year we had three or four pitching coaches."

That's Righetti's job now, out in San Francisco. He enjoys it. He appreciates all his time in pinstripes now too, even if it wasn't always smooth.

He adjusted to the role of a reliever in 1984 after Gossage left and the Yankees named Righetti his successor. He set a then-single-season saves record of 46 in '86.

But he said he didn't throw his hands up too high over that one, either.

Nope. None of them felt like that first trip to the World Series.

CHAPTER 13

Jim Abbott:

The Pitcher Who Threw a No-hitter

September 4, 1993

vs. Cleveland
Yankees 4, Indians 0

The stats: IP H R ER BB SO
9   0 0   0   5   3

He wasn't different.
Not out on the field, where Jim Abbott's dad helped him learn how to play catch with his one good hand.

Sure, he looked different.

Played different.

None of the other kids had to do that rapid-fire drill of switching the glove onto one hand, fielding the ball, switching the glove back, retrieving the ball, then throwing.

They just fielded and threw the way their two functioning hands allowed them to.

So when Jim Abbott started learning to play ball because his dad, mom, teachers and friends took the time to figure out how he could, he still looked different.

But he wasn't.

"It was a way for me to get out and not be different but be good at something," Abbott said.

Jim Abbott pitched the Yankees' first no-hitter in 10 years on September 4, 1993 against Cleveland. When he was on a major league mound, Abbott proved he could perform as well as any other pitcher, despite being born without a right hand. *AP/WWP.*

Out here, no one would feel sorry for Abbott or tease him. And if they did, they would quickly learn to shut up and play the way he did—unless they wanted to lose.

This was the one spot Abbott always felt like he fit in, and it's all he wanted.

A kid's life is easier when you fit in.

Wear the wrong shirt, bring the wrong lunch, and it's fodder for feverish little minds to rake you over.

Have one hand?

Well, the kids could be as creatively vicious as they were cruel.

So, when Abbott talks about first playing ball, he says he didn't dream of playing in the big leagues.

He just dreamed of playing.

Years later, as he got older, grew taller, played better, he began to realize how much more he could do. Then it was no longer just about playing, but playing better than the people around him.

Just playing was no longer enough for the same reason it once had been.

He wanted to fit in. He wanted to be like everyone else. And to fit in in the big leagues, you had to be the best. Or, at least, good enough to stand out long enough to stick around.

So when all the comparisons to Pete Gray began, Abbott tried to be polite.

Yes, he had heard of the one-armed outfielder for the old St. Louis Browns. Yes, he knew Gray made it to the big leagues when no one thought he could.

But Abbott knew something else.

Gray played only one season.

That wasn't enough.

Not after Abbott endured every last kid who thought he couldn't play. Every well-meaning neighbor who thought it was sweet he wanted to, but he should find something more realistic.

Not after he earned his first college win, nailing a guy who thought he could steal home when the catcher threw the ball pack to Abbott. Or becoming an All-American at Michigan. Or pitching the U.S. to its first gold medal with an Olympic win over Japan.

Or jumping straight to the majors, proving wrong all the folks whispering about a publicity stunt, by posting 12 wins and a 3.92 ERA his rookie season.

See, the thing is, part of him *liked* all those people asking all those questions.

Because he could answer those.

If a guy took off for home thinking Abbott couldn't handle the ball in time, he could prove him wrong. If a team wanted to bunt on him six straight times, he could pick up the ball each and every one and get them out.

See? No different. I can get you out like anyone else.

It was a lot easier here than it was back in school or just walking down the street. Nothing he could do to silence those snickers or combat the sideways glances.

Baseball gave Abbott a place to provide answers, find some equal footing. But to find that equal ground, you first had to stand out.

So when they'd ask about Pete Gray, Abbott would correct them.

"I want to be like Nolan Ryan," Abbott said of the Hall of Famer, "not Pete Gray."

Baseball was happiness. His refuge.

He wanted to stick around. Didn't want to walk off the field too quickly.

He knew what it could be like when he did.

"You may have some success in the sporting field," Abbott said, thinking of his childhood, "but inside the classroom, somebody may say your hand looks like a foot."

He's lived with the fact so many people are always going to see him as the pitcher with one hand. Now that his career is over, he no longer has to compete. Or prove anything.

So he can put aside the natural athlete's ego and acknowledge his success is about more than wins and losses.

He'll make motivational speeches sounding as much like Tony Robbins as a former big leaguer, his A.D.A.P.T acronym preaching Adjustability, Determination, Accountability, Perseverance and Trust.

But aside from his 10 big-league seasons, that great rookie year and the 18 wins he picked up in 1991, he always has that one day at Yankee Stadium.

That's the day when, in the stretch run of a pennant race and in front of an unforgiving Yankee Stadium crowd, Jim Abbott gave himself a label to replace the "one-handed" tag he couldn't shake.

That's the day Abbott became the pitcher who threw a no-hitter against the Cleveland Indians.

"I think there's some credibility that came along with it," he said. "It's the dream of a lot of people to throw a no-hitter."

It separated him from the rest of baseball. For one day, Abbott proved he belonged by fitting into an exclusive club.

With members like Sandy Koufax. And Bob Gibson. And Tom Seaver.

Like Nolan Ryan.

*** *** ***

The Abbotts wouldn't let their son use excuses. There was still plenty he could do and he would do it.

When their child was born without a right hand, the Abbotts adjusted. God wouldn't give their boy more than he could handle, so they'd all just have to learn how to deal with this.

"My parents were incredibly supportive and encouraging," Abbott said. "Their words were always that of bearing the challenge and rising to it instead of shirking away from it.

"You just learn to do things.

"I guess it wasn't me learning things differently; it was people who took the time to figure things out, and they were very generous. Even though they knew to tie shoes with two hands, they took the time to tie it with one hand. Just adapting and finding a solution."

Look, Abbott was lucky, he'll tell you. He had mostly positive reinforcement from his parents to the coaches to the other kids. Today, he'll stay late after a speech to talk to kids.

My coach won't let me play, one will say. They don't think I can do it, another will add.

And it breaks Abbott's heart.

Because he knows how much it hurts.

He didn't play baseball to become tough. He played to get away from what made him weak.

"I was a fairly sensitive kid, so I tended to take it in and probably be hurt by it," he said of childhood taunts. "Keep trying—working at it. There was a certain element of skepticism. Particularly, when you play sports, it can be very challenging out there.

"I think kids can be cruel. I think there's a certain amount of teasing. You can be set apart, unfortunately."

*** *** ***

He had outlasted all of it.
The cruel kids.

The doubting coaches.

The opponents determined to exploit weaknesses Abbott proved were not there.

Still wasn't enough.

Because after becoming an All-American at Michigan and pitching in the Olympics, Abbott became the player to watch for the California Angels.

The Angels liked what they saw. So Abbott became one of the few players to jump straight from the draft to the majors, with no time in the minors.

Amazing. After a lifetime of people thinking he couldn't play because he had only one hand, now everyone thought that's precisely why he was playing.

"I think there was a little bit of speculation that maybe it was something that was done as a publicity stunt," Abbott said. "But if you knew the people involved—manager Doug Rader, pitching coach Rene Lachemann—they were old school.

"You had to earn your way."

There are few places more brutally honest than a major league clubhouse.

It is one of the least politically correct places left in society, a place where being different can leave you wide open for barbs.

Unless, of course, you can play.

If you help a team win, they'll forgive you for anything from multiple drug offenses to domestic violence. So, whether you had one hand, one foot or anything else, they'd accept you on the field based on performance.

"You got here, kid," veteran pitcher Jack Morris said when Abbott first came up. "Now the trick is to stay."

Abbott knew he'd have to deal with the hype and questions about his arm as well as his pitching.

Countless times he'd recount how he learned to catch and throw, down to his glove-switching technique. Eventually, the questions would become more balanced as Abbott went several seasons without an error.

That's how he wanted it then, working with the Angels public relations department to allot only a certain amount of time for talking about the obstacles he'd overcome.

"I weighted heavily my priorities on performing," Abbott said. "I didn't seek out the role model platform."

By the end of his rookie year, Abbott had shown he was worth more than a publicity stunt. His 12 wins sent people the same message fielding six straight bunts once did.

See? No different. I can get people out just like anyone else.

He started to adapt to California, enjoying it with his wife. He won 18 games in 1991 and everything settled down.

But he lost 15 the next year, and the next thing he knew ... he had been traded to New York before the 1993 season.

The good news was, the Yankees were developing into a solid ballclub and that excited Abbott. The bad news was, he didn't exactly embrace the idea of putting on pinstripes. He had been an Angel his whole career. He liked California. He and his wife would have to pick up and move across the country.

And the Yankees? Well ...

"I wasn't a big Yankee fan," he said. "I was indifferent to them, to be honest with you."

*** *** ***

By the time Abbott arrived in New York, all thought of novelty was gone. He was a successful pitcher and the Yankees were desperately trying to return pride to a franchise with 22 world championships in 90 years ... and zero playoff appearances in the past 12.

After a 76-win season the year before, the Yankees won 88 games and finished second to eventual world champion Toronto in '93.

He would not have a consistent season. But in New York Abbott knew he would have no concerns about being looked at as just a pitcher with one hand.

The city is an unforgiving equalizer, the demanding fans passionate, loyal and ready to boo your head off no matter who you are if you don't come through.

In the '93 season, with the Yankees giving the fans their first shot at a decent team in a while, it would be all about the performance.

Just as Abbott had always wanted it to be.

He would go on streaks, finishing the year at 11-14 with a 4.37 ERA.

In May, he'd provide a perfect example of his inconsistency—as well as a peek at his potential—by taking a no-hitter into the eighth inning against the White Sox. But he gave up a basehit, then a homer, losing the no-no and the shutout in a shot.

Later, as the 27,225 cheered him and the adrenaline rushed against Cleveland, he would remember how quickly it could all get away.

But as he headed into the Indians game on September 4, 1993, the least of his concerns would have been keeping a no-hitter intact. He had faced them in his last start, an intimidating lineup featuring a young Kenny Lofton, Carlos Baerga and Albert Belle at the top.

It did not go well.

He gave up seven runs on 10 hits in 3 2/3 innings.

So when he took the mound at the Stadium, he was hoping to give his team a better chance to win. Especially since, for the first time in a long time, every win counted. With a month to go, the Yankees were still in the pennant race.

But they had a loose bunch, so Abbott enjoyed joking with them and was relaxed when he arrived at the Stadium.

Especially when he realized it was a cloudy kind of day.

Cool.

He liked pitching on days like this.

*** *** ***

Game of My Life
Jim Abbott

"I remember, the thing about my no-hitter was that I had just pitched against the Indians my last time out and really had a rough outing. I was focused. I knew the challenge was to bounce back from that—against a team that just clobbered me. I also remember it being a lighthearted day. Joking with teammates.

"I just remember the first few innings doing an imitation of (fellow pitcher) Scott Kamieniecki. I'd bounce off the field like him, just to get him to laugh and Jimmy Key. Usually I don't do things like that, but for some reason, I was just a little more at ease and confident.

"It was very early in the game, and I remember looking up, and the dugout was sort of your refuge between innings and you try not to get too caught up in it, but they hadn't scored.

"In the sixth inning, the Yankee fans started cheering. At that point the lightheartedness started to melt away.

"I don't remember there being a real seriousness until later in the game. And there is a real tension there. Like I said, earlier in the game, I felt relaxed so I tried to keep that same frame of mind. The battle becomes bringing it back to now and not hoping (about what could happen.)

"You know what's on the line, but you can't focus on results. Just letting the ball go out of your hand. It's very tough, a real mental challenge, and that's one of the most rewarding things of the game that it was such a battle to keep fighting off those thoughts.

"I have an acronym I use (in motivational speaking)—A.D.A.P.T. The last one is "Trust," believing in yourself.

"The chaos of Yankee Stadium, sort of that swirling noise, the fans and teammates and bringing it back to a real small, narrow, precise focus.

"I remember the ninth inning, of course. I remember the building, the excitement growing, sort of a countdown kind of thing. The three more outs.

"Breaking things down into manageable parts. In that game, you really start breaking things down. I remember those feelings.

"I remember Kenny Lofton making an out, the first batter in the ninth inning. I think it was Felix Fermin was next, then Carlos Baerga. Then that unbelievable feeling of seeing that ball roll through the thick grass to Randy Velarde ... and the throw to Donnie Mattingly.

"There was sort of a big huddle, cramming together, high-fives. It was a very nice scene. I had been in the clubhouse, and the fans were cheering. I think I formed a permanent bond with (catcher) Matt Nokes that I'll always appreciate. Besides that, I was really excited. We were still in the hunt at that time. I was just excited to do it with the Yankees in New York City.

"I went out to dinner with Donnie and the early editions of the paper were out. People had me sign it. Those things wouldn't have happened if I pitched for any other team. It's taken on a defining characteristic of my career that I didn't imagine it would have, to tell you the truth.

"That's really what a lot of people remember about me is pitching the no-hitter. It all has to do with that day."

*** *** ***

By the time he retired in '99, there were enough moments for Abbott to look back on that he no longer avoided the role model platform. Now it's one he embraces, because he understands people are looking to him for inspiration.

"I'm a really, really fortunate person," he said. "I've met so many kids in life who've faced much greater obstacles than I've faced. I've seen kids out there who have the exact same obstacle as me, whose coaches don't give them the opportunity to participate, and I see the hurt in their eyes.

"All of that adds up to a feeling of gratefulness and a feeling of being able to give back in some small way."

Though, as a guy who once shied from comparisons to a one-armed player, Abbott appreciates it when young players overcoming obstacles look elsewhere.

"It's funny," Abbott said in 2004. "Not too long ago, I remember reading in the *L.A. Times* about some young player. He said he didn't want to be the next Jim Abbott. He wanted to be the next Randy Johnson. Echoed the same things I had said."

Abbott paused.

"I'd like to think I was good, too, though," he said, laughing. "I don't think we want to be labeled at the end. I think we want to be remembered."

CHAPTER 14

Don Mattingly:
Donnie Playoffs

October 3/4, 1995, ALDS Games 1/2

vs. Seattle

Yankees 9, Mariners 6

Game 1:	AB	R	H	RBI	HR
	4	1	2	1	0

vs. Seattle

Yankees 7, Mariners 5

Game 2:	AB	R	H	RBI	HR
	6	1	3	1	1

Delirium.

Cars honking. Stogies burning. Screams. Cheers.

Music blares from a speaker outside a Times Square restaurant and hundreds of giddy Yankees fans respond, moving their feet as far as the guy whose body is jammed against them will allow.

They dance. Sing. They're drunk on more than the beers they knocked off.

The Yankees just won the World Series.

Finally.

It had been 18 years—an eternity in Yankee time—and the folks spilling into Times Square in October 1996 would have their party, Yankees or no Yankees.

The team was still savoring its championship, running laps inside a shaking Yankee Stadium. Wade Boggs hopped on a horse. Joe Torre fought tears.

He always wanted to know how he'd perform under playoff pressure, and Don Mattingly finally found out in 1995. Thanks to a leg kick he discovered near the end of the season, he hit .417 against Seattle and reminded Yankee fans of the swing that earned him his "Hit Man" nickname. *Stephen Dunn/Getty Images.*

The fans in Times Square cheered for all of that as they watched on TV. They celebrated the moment the last out was recorded and announcer Joe Buck bellowed "The Yankees are champions of baseball!"

Then a few of them began a chant.

Suddenly, the fans who couldn't stop smiling looked at each other.

Wait ... Is that ...

The chant spread from person to person, partier to partier.

The slow look of recognition and remembrance found their faces before one after the joined in, their chant becoming a cause.

DON-nie BASE-ball

Clap-clap, Clap-clap-clap

DON-nie BASE-ball

Clap-clap, Clap-clap-clap

Again and again, the celebrants sang their salute, their faces as pained as they were pleasured.

Like the Yankees celebrating at the Stadium, Don Mattingly had no way of knowing every last fan streaming out of the midtown bars was chanting his name.

Unlike the rest of the 1996 World Champions, Mattingly was not preoccupied with his own celebration.

He was where he had been all year—back home in Evansville, Indiana.

The moment Charlie Hayes caught the last out, perhaps about when Buck announced "The Yankees are champ-" Mattingly rose from his sofa and shut the TV.

Silence.

All Mattingly could do was make the same choice he had the previous season, when a bad back and a good family forced his hand.

He walked away.

"Yeah, pretty much as soon as it was over," he said. "Like, I was happy for those guys, but it was tough to watch. It really was. It was hard to watch."

There was only one consolation for Mattingly and the fans still screaming his name while celebrating a championship scarred by his absence.

When Donnie Baseball finally reached the October stage the previous year, he *owned* it.

*** *** ***

The "Hit Man" poster still hung on a wall in the Queens, New York, batting cage in 2004, 20 years after it first emerged.

It was a dark, grimy place, no windows, little light. Just the hum of the machines swallowing the dimpled balls and spitting them out to the people trying to hit them.

Click. Whirr. Smack.

Click. Whirr. Smack.

The ping of aluminum against the giant, yellow baseballs that looked better suited to golf continued, scattershot with the one in the next cage.

The scenes could play out daily.

In one cage, a little leaguer might hit balls into the net, his father shouting for him to "Keep your eye on it!" from behind the fence.

In another, a softball player ready for another run at the Sunday league, trying to find the pride he had in high school, could curse himself for getting under the pitch.

Then, when it was time for a break, a drink, they could stop and take the walk down the hallway, blister-filled hands toting the bat.

Atop a soda machine hung the poster, as outdated as it was perfectly fitting a place where Donnie Baseball could be considered a patron saint.

He was young on that poster, a budding superstar just taking over ownership of New York City.

The advertising agency added some flash to a "Hit Man" nickname earned sweating and swinging in the same kind of inauspicious anonymity of the folks who now unstrapped the velcro from their batting gloves and fumbled for coins to quench their thirst.

On the poster, Mattingly stood proud, decked out in a pinstriped suit and fedora, a violin case holding his weapon, a grin sheepish and sly all at once on his face.

The poster was faded now, another relic in a place badly in need of renovation.

Any little leaguer who grabbed a drink wasn't likely to give it more than a glimpse, wondering where the shots of Derek Jeter, Bernie Williams and Alex Rodriguez were.

But the softball player would be more apt to linger, staring at the old poster in the dingy hall until he could picture it in bright color.

As it would have been 20 years before in the sporting goods store in Manhattan, where his dad might have pulled him by the hand once, down the stairs, the poster staring larger than life.

The Hit Man.

Donnie Baseball.

The softball player could close his eyes and picture the batting stance Mattingly's major league peers flocked to the cage to watch when he was in his prime.

He'd start in a bouncy crouch, seemingly designed to set a trap. The pitcher would stare, then find a focused glare framed by eye black, even the hairs on Mattingly's perfectly manicured mustache seemingly snapping to attention.

The pitch would come and Mattingly would spring up, his slingshot swing just smooth enough to be violently serene, his cheeks puffed by anticipation, not yet ready for exhalation, veins straining against his neck, as eager to attack the ball as was the rest of his body.

He'd shoot the ball toward the wall and shove himself to first, all arms and legs, rounding the base like an out-of-shape storeowner chasing kids who stole from him.

He didn't know how, but he'd get where he needed to go.

That was the guy on that poster.

Donnie Baseball.

The Hit Man.

The future Hall of Famer.

Most likely, the softball player would suddenly remember where he was, how much time had passed. Maybe reflect on how quickly an endlessly open world can close on you.

Then he'd probably take his tired self into the cage for one more round, forever wishing Mattingly could do the same.

*** *** ***

There was a church lot where the Mattingly boys would play. Wiffle ball. Tennis ball.

Don would play with his brothers, his cousins, whoever wanted to play. Dad was a mailman, worked hard, wanted you to play hard.

No pressure, you know?

"I just played, I really did," Mattingly said. "I look back on it as a real ... seeing little league games and seeing how some things are and stuff that goes on with kids ... a real blessing that I just got to play. And I really think it contributes to the love that you have for what you do. Taking extra ground balls is not taking extra ground balls to me. It's just like I'm working on getting better. It's not that big a deal to do that kind of stuff."

When you grew up in Indiana, baseball wasn't usually your favorite sport anyway. From Bobby Plump's shot in the state high school basketball tournament to watching Larry Bird shoot into stardom, you weren't a real Hoosier if you weren't a hoopster.

"I enjoyed basketball more because basketball's a game, really, you can go practice by yourself," Mattingly said.

So he'd play basketball during that season, then shift to baseball.

The high school had a great baseball program going for it; been to semi-states, states, sectionals just about every year, it seemed like.

So when the coach told Mattingly he'd play on the varsity as a freshman, the kid did a double-take.

So did the league.

Mattingly hit over .300, then started playing Legion ball in the summer. Against 19-year-olds.

They couldn't stop him either, and next thing you know, he was standing in there against some kid about to play pro ball with the Reds.

No. 1 pick, even.

Mattingly knocked two doubles off of him.

A couple of weeks later, the mail came from the post office at which Mattingly's dad worked.

And in the middle of sprinting out for another summer activity, Mattingly stopped.

Stared.

Gawked.

There it was in bright red print, the logo of the Cincinnati Reds.

"I don't even know what it was," Mattingly said of the letter expressing the club's interest. "I just remember that logo on the letter. From that point on, I thought, 'You know what? I'd better start working.'"

Crouched and coiled, Mattingly lay in wait for a pitcher, ready to pounce, his swing jolting out as his body would spring up. *Lonnie Major/Allsport/Getty Images.*

*** *** ***

The Yankees made him a 19th-round pick in '79, but they were soon to discover all that time Mattingly spent in the dark of batting cages would shove him into the spotlight.

He could hit.

He knew it.

They'd know it.

The cockiness was contained in his head, where Mattingly would challenge himself on each pitch.

He tore his way through the minors, hitting .332, though he didn't develop a power stroke until he learned to take aim at Yankee Stadium's short right-field fence.

But he turned heads in an era when the Yankees viewed their minor-leaguers as kids who should be traded, not seen.

There were about a half-dozen veteran first basemen blocking Mattingly's path when he experienced his first taste of big-league life in '82.

An ill-begotten collection of all-star names no longer exhibiting all-star talent.

So Mattingly started playing the outfield, too, because, hey, man, he just wanted to *play*. Eventually, he'd show off that elastic flexibility in spurts at first, giving glimpses of the Gold Gloves to follow.

But, shoot, before he could do all that, he just wanted to figure out how to handle this place, man.

Good thing they gave him that September call-up in '82 to settle himself.

Driving in from Triple-A Columbus, Ohio, coming up on that big Yankee Stadium sign, a blue-lit shroud standing out as you started to approach.

"Yankee Stadium, the whole deal—pretty intimidating," Mattingly said.

So were the people inside it.

"The scariest thing for me coming up was, 'Where do I meet the bus?'" Mattingly said. "'What's it gonna be like getting on the bus with everybody?' You know, I mean, you're getting on the bus with Gossage and Nettles and Piniella and Murcer and Randolph and Guidry, and these guys are world champions.

"It's like, 'Mannnnn, what is this bus like?'"

The bus, it turned out, wasn't so bad.

The batting wasn't as easy, Mattingly going two for 12. Except, Mattingly still knew it could be.

"I knew there wasn't a guy that I faced that, when I was going good, I wouldn't have hit," Mattingly said.

*** *** ***

There was an article in *Yankees* magazine printed in '84 that painted a picture of a smirking Lou Piniella.

Then the Yankees batting coach, Sweet Lou was infamous for startling roommates in the middle of the night by standing in front of a mirror in his underwear, practicing his swing during his playing days.

He couldn't perfect his swing enough. Couldn't stop practicing.

So, when Mattingly finished up another endless run in the batting cage by flinging his batting gloves and deciding "I stink!" ... Piniella knew he had himself a hitter.

Here's where Donnie Baseball was born, starting the first season of a three-year tear that left him standing as, arguably, the best player in the game.

He slapped the ball to left.

Drove it to right.

Found some power with Piniella's help and smacked 23 home runs.

Pounded dents into the outfield wall with 44 doubles.

And the average?

Best in the league.

The Detroit Tigers ran away from the league with 35 wins seemingly before anyone had recovered from their spring training hangovers, so there became only one show in the Bronx.

Mattingly vs. Dave Winfield.

Winfield, along with Mattingly, helped the Yankees win more games than any other team in the 1980s.

With zero World Series titles to show for it.

With his leaping, home-run-swiping catches in the outfield, giant strides around the bases and big swing, "Winny" etched himself in Yankees history.

But as much affection as he felt from fans, Winfield appears to hover in some kind of a pinstriped purgatory, appreciated, but not beloved.

It's how he would feel on the last day of the '84 season, when he battled Mattingly for the batting crown.

Winfield led by 1.57 points entering the final game.

But Mattingly, showing the tenacity he would the rest of his career, refused to give anything.

He smacked four hits to Winfield's one, claiming the title by a .343 to .340 margin.

The pair of players walked off the field together to cheers, Mattingly later thanking Winfield for being a "great person" and a "gentleman through this whole thing. It's good we're going to be teammates the next few years at least."

After '85, a season in which Mattingly flirted with the triple crown and finished as the league MVP, it appeared they might later be Hall of Fame teammates.

*** *** ***

It seemed like you couldn't get Mattingly out in '85.

After a 4-12 start prompted George Steinbrenner to fire manager Yogi Berra, Billy Martin returned and the Yankees played better.

They battled Toronto to the last weekend of the season before the Blue Jays clinched the American League East.

After an 11th-hour signing of free agent speedster Rickey Henderson, the Yankees had a potent offense, versatile and intimidating.

Henderson would use his speed to distract pitchers the way a supermodel's looks control her boyfriend. While they were busy obsessing over

Henderson, Mattingly and Winfield would walk all over them and drive Rickey home with hit after hit.

By season's end, Mattingly had a .324 average, 35 homers and a whopping 145 RBIs, earning him the league's Most Valuable Player Award.

He was fast becoming not only the game's best first baseman, but earning nods as its best player.

The arguments came from the other borough.

Fifteen years before the Yankees and Mets made a Subway Series a reality in October, fans of both teams were hoping to see matchups in more than a Mayor's Trophy game.

The Mets, under new manager Davey Johnson and with a ton of young talent such as Dwight Gooden and Darryl Strawberry, were building toward their '86 championship team.

The Yankees with Mattingly, Winfield and Henderson seemed formidable.

The dream matchup was Gooden vs. Mattingly, all of New York arguing who would come out on top.

Mattingly would have loved the challenge.

He loved any confrontation then—even the ones he lost.

Billy Sample, then a Yankees outfielder, remembers Mattingly facing young Seattle pitcher Edwin Nunez.

The kid got ahead of Mattingly 1-2 before dealing a slider so nasty he wanted to applaud as soon as he released it.

And Mattingly still got a piece of it.

"Nunez was like, 'OK, he hit my best, forget it,'" Sample said. "'Just go for it.'"

Threw him a fastball.

Fouled it off.

Fastball.

Foul ball.

Fastball.

Foul ball.

With each pitch, Mattingly dug in harder and Nunez refused to yield, even to the league's eventual MVP.

Another fastball.

Another foul ball.

Finally, on the fifth pitch, Mattingly swung and missed.

The kid got him.

When he reached the dugout, Mattingly screamed—in exhilaration.

"I loved it!" he said. "He challenged me!"

After the game, Nunez discovered a ballboy bearing a gift.

Nunez accepted the baseball glove containing three beers and a note, signed by Mattingly.

Now that's baseball.

*** *** ***

He was as much a part of baseball as anything Yankee fans had ever pictured.

The diving athleticism at first base. The team-first attitude that sent him to play second and third in a pinch, left-handedness be damned.

The too-cool eye black foiling the sun, and the swing so fluid it seemed as effortless as countless hours in the batting cage could make it appear.

He looked like a ballplayer.

Talked like a ballplayer.

Grinned mischievously like a ballplayer, scarfing some popcorn off a startled, star-struck little fan once.

So the "Donnie Baseball" banners surfaced in the upper deck. The crowd roared louder for each at-bat, separating Mattingly from his peers like the final actor appearing for a curtain call.

He knocked 238 hits in '86 and nearly scared Wade Boggs back into the lineup for the season's final game.

Boggs, in control of the batting race with a .357 average, sat out since the Sox had wrapped up the AL East.

The Yankees batted Mattingly lead off to give him a shot to catch Boggs.

And he took it, smacking hits in his first two at-bats before stalling and finishing at .352.

He didn't get the batting title in '86, but earned a more impressive mark in '87, when Mattingly went on an unsurpassed power streak. Mattingly smacked 10 homers in eight straight games that July.

With each game, the level of incredulousness grew, the shock starting to come when Mattingly *didn't* hit a homer.

Finally, on July 18, he hit the last of them in Texas, tying Dale Long's major league record for consecutive games with a home run.

"Did he get all of it?" announcer Phil Rizzuto wondered as the ball soared toward the left-field fence. "Did heeee? Holy cow! He did it! Mattingly! The opposite field!"

Along with the seemingly endless string of homers, Mattingly set another uncanny record that year.

He had never hit a grand slam before. Never hit one after.

But in '87, he smashed six grand slams. While the Mets' wunderkinds started to fall off—Gooden shocking the city by entering rehab, the Mets falling apart—Mattingly's Hall of Fame career was set.

Now all he needed was a World Series ring.

The Yankees of the '80s had a lineup built for success, but a pitching staff doomed to block it.

No problem. Good things would come. Mattingly would just keep working.

And why not?

All that constant work earned him his Donnie Baseball nickname.

It's what the game was about.

So no one could have known the unyielding work ethic that made him so beloved, the aspect that made him a poster child for the game ... would be the very thing that helped drive him out of it.

*** *** ***

All that rotation of his hips, for all those extra swings at the batting cage started nagging at Mattingly's back. Maybe the back would have gone anyway.

But the extra work couldn't help and Mattingly's bad back devoured him, splitting the sure-fire Hall of Famer's career in two.

There was the Hit Man who wouldn't stop, piling up 1,219 hits and 160 home runs in his first six full seasons, the player with all the Gold Gloves, parading into his prime.

Then there was the melancholy figure, the player whose bum back humbled him like no pitcher ever could.

The pain started in '90, Mattingly suddenly unable to shake the dull ache in his back.

The doctors discovered disc tissue tears and Mattingly, who lived to play, was put on the disabled list for the first time in his career.

He'd never be the same.

Gone, except for glimpses, was the power stroke that jolted the ball out to right and the fans from their seats. Gone was the endless array of hits, peppered all over the field, a chef knowing he needed to sprinkle his seasoning everywhere.

His lowest average in a full season had been .303. Now he batted .256 in 102 games in 1990, smacking as many home runs as he had fingers to wrap around the bat.

The power numbers were never the same. Neither was the average. He fought because it's what he always did, keeping his numbers respectable for a Gold-Glove fielding first baseman, which he was for five straight seasons.

Hit .288 a couple of times. Drove in 86 runs in back-to-back years, showing uncanny consistency with numbers that, for him, were mediocre.

Whispers started in the papers, maybe even channeled through the stands, though you'd never hear them amid all the standing ovations Mattingly still earned.

Even if there were questions of how long the Yankees could go without a power-hitting first baseman, how could you ask them?

The guy was like you.

Spending his life in a batting cage, just trying to get his swing right, pushing himself to see what he could do.

And it was all OK in '94, when the Yankees finally reemerged as a play-off-caliber team.

Led by ace Jimmy Key, who was nearly unhittable, and a balanced offense featuring the surging veteran Paul O'Neill and emerging outfielder Bernie Williams, the Yankees earned the best record in baseball.

Mattingly, no longer even among discussion as the game's best, was still among the most respected players in the game.

And he was using his clubhouse leadership role—he'd been named captain in '91—to push the Yankees toward their first postseason since '81.

This was the trade-off.

His back could claim his power. His consistency.

Mattingly would find just enough of it to hit .304 and drive in 51 runs in the season's first 97 games.

He'd help the Yankees to a 70-43 record, the baseball world again taking notice of the Bronx Bombers.

This is what it was all about.

"I just wanna see how I'll perform when I get there," Mattingly told reporter Michael Kay in a private moment. "I was in the playoffs in the minor leagues and I did well. I wanna see how I do on that stage."

Then they turned it black on him.

Oh, Mattingly knew all the rumblings of the strike that year. He was a good union man and, as much as he loved playing, he would support his peers above all else.

He just never thought it would really happen.

Never thought there'd be a strike.

At least not that long.

I mean, no World Series?

C'mon, man.

"I don't know; I really always thought it would settle," he said. "I really did. In my heart, I thought it would settle, you know? I thought there's no way they're not gonna have the World Series or whatever. I *really* didn't think ..."

But word came on August 12 ... Mattingly fielded a phone call at home, where he had never stopped believing his season was about to resume.

Where he expected any day to get the call to return to the field, to the cheers.

But the call didn't tell him to go back.

It told him to stay home.

Season over.

No World Series.

"That killed me a little bit, killed me a little bit," Mattingly said, smiling wistfully. "But I was convicted with the guys, the fellas—can't personally, at that point, can't worry about yourself.

"Yeah, but it's like you had your shot at the playoffs and you're not gonna make it. Just the history of everything we'd been through to get back to that. Played with some real bad teams and starting to cross the corner, you know, then you'd be like 'Oh mannn.'"

So he hung up the phone. Told his wife, Kim.

And that was that.

"Handled it," he said. "I don't know. Just did it."

He laughed.

"Got up. Had breakfast. Played with the kids. 'It's the off season.'"

*** *** ***

Jim Abbott can still picture it.

Little bit before a game, not sure which season.

Everyone's talking and laughing, joking.

Mattingly's over in his corner locker, nodding and smiling, too.

But as he does, he takes his batting stance.

He watches make-believe balls come in from the pitcher.

Practices his swings.

All of which might have made perfect sense except, "He was on the disabled list at the time," Abbott said.

He laughed.

"I get goosebumps," Abbott said. "I love Donnie Mattingly. He was probably one of my favorite players I ever played with. Great teammate. Probably the guy I admire most."

David Cone: "I have more respect for Don Mattingly than anybody I've ever played with."

Derek Jeter: "I remember growing up a Yankee fan, watching him play. Going about his business. That rubbed off on a lot of the younger guys."

So when the Yankees broke camp in '95, after the strike was finally settled and the replacement players went back to their day jobs, the team had a goal.

Get to the playoffs before Donnie Baseball retired.

"We knew we were still young," Jim Leyritz, a catcher at the time, said. "We knew this would be Donnie's last chance. We really wanted to do it more for him."

He had spent 10 full years in the big leagues. Played more than 1,600 games. And he knew deep down though he wasn't ready to admit it, this could be his last season.

Soon, it might not even be his choice, the whispers growing louder as the year went on. The unthinkable starting to get not just thought, but spoken.

As the Yankees slumped in the second half and Mattingly continued toward another season with a lonely, single-digit home-run total, everyone from talk radio callers to columnists started wondering if the Yankees needed more power at first.

As the season progressed, it turned out they needed a lot more than that.

Boston started running away with the division in the second half. But there was still hope.

Though it was as popular with purists as the strike, commissioner Bud Selig had implemented a new, wild-card playoff system.

There would be three divisions in each league and the team with the best record after that would qualify. The decision would ruin baseball, purists argued, complaining the new entry would defuse the fuel of pennant race fever.

Instead, it increased it.

And as irked as anyone might have been by the partycrashing nature of a non-pennant-winning team, it did offer one consolation prize for those who remained true to the game's ideals.

It gave Donnie Baseball one last shot at the playoffs.

*** *** ***

"Would I consider it?" Mattingly told then-*New York Post* columnist Tom Keegan in August, when asked if he'd go to Japan. "Sure I would. Why wouldn't I? I'm interested in playing baseball as in baseball, let's play the game as a sport. I don't think what we're doing to the game any more is a sport and it's not just baseball. It's every sport over here, really."

Mattingly didn't elaborate about his dismay with the game and sports in general.

But he was frustrated after a rough summer of rumors, a year after a strike that robbed him of his shot at the playoffs. And he was just coming off a road trip that could cost him another one.

In a trip that pitted them against the teams they were chasing, the Yankees looked like they were crawling in a sprint.

They went 3-10, dropping games against AL East leader Boston and wild card contenders California, Oakland and Seattle.

Mattingly knew they weren't finished since they were only 5.5 games back of the wild card.

"We still have an opportunity," he told the *Post*.

But maybe he was tired of the reports wondering about his bad back, wondering how he could continue to go on when the Yankees needed a power-hitting first baseman.

He thought about playing in Japan. Then he'd think of his kids back home in Indiana, remember what it was like to be on the road so long and wondered if he should be playing at all.

He was sick of it. The game was still fun, but not at this cost.

A man should see his family grow up. His dad had taught him to make the game just that—a game, no more significant than any other event for his family.

Mattingly wondered if he shouldn't be doing the same.

But his pride pricked him too.

Nagged him.

He wanted to shut up all those people saying, *He's gone 8,000-some games without making the playoffs* or whatever.

And he knew there was only one way to stop any talk of his lack of power hurting the club.

Damn well make sure it didn't.

Buck Showalter, then the Yankees manager, remembers Mattingly poking his head in his office the last month of the season.

Remembers his captain making a promise.

"'I don't know what the future holds,'" Showalter remembered Mattingly saying. "'I don't know if my back holds up, but we need a first baseman with more pop. I'm going for it.'"

He found it.

Mattingly started playing with a leg kick off his front leg. Slowly, he felt it take some of the pressure off his back.

Slowly, all those free-flowing feelings that came with a pain-free, fluid swing came back.

He could generate power. He felt good.

He felt like ... like he was back.

So were the Yankees.

They won six of their next seven to draw within a game on September 2. But the margin for error was as low as ever.

Seattle stayed hot. California, too.

The Yankees finished the season winning 11 of 12. Still, they needed to go to the season's last day to clinch.

They were back in Toronto, where the 24-year-old Mattingly, the Hit Man, the MVP, had watched one season end.

Then he knew there'd be countless ones to come.

Now, he took the field remembering the ringing cheers from the week before, the Yankee Stadium fans saluting what might have been his last home at-bat.

But this time, the Yankees' fate was in their hands.

Mattingly grabbed it.

"Mattingly rips one down the line! And ... gone!" announcer Al Trautwig told his viewers. "A home run! In the game that could send him to the first postseason of his career."

The Yankees scored twice in their first at-bat. Twice more in their second.

And when the last ball was grounded from Randy Knorr to shortstop Tony Fernandez ... Mattingly had made it.

He hugged his teammates, the sun still gleaming off his eye black.

He caught eyes with Showalter, his manager for the past three seasons. One second passed, two, three, four ... "It's just the look," Showalter said. "I took a lot of criticism that year for sticking with Donnie. ... The last out in Toronto, I tell ya, right now, I bawled like a baby."

Mattingly walked off the field, stopping short, awkwardly. He kneeled, pounded the ground, then rose.

He'd made it.

*** *** ***

The first glimpse came a couple of hours before Game 1 of the American League Division Series against Seattle.

Mattingly simply wanted to jog out and do some stretching.

The fans in Yankee Stadium wanted a lot more.

They had waited for him all day, all year, all his career.

They had waited to return this kind of roar to Yankee Stadium, but nothing short of October provokes it.

By his first step out of the dugout, the fans dropped all their banners proclaiming their love for "Donnie Baseball."

Thunder greeted Mattingly, all the fans who had spent all their hours in the batting cage like the Yankees captain sharing in his glory.

"There was just a buzz about it," Kay said. "It seemed like everybody was happier about it for him than he was for himself. I think he wanted to get there, but I think the fans were more elated than anything. They felt they were a part of a struggle with him."

When they announced the starting lineups, Showalter—the manager known to look cross-eyed at players for everything short of chewing gum—pumped his fists as Bob Sheppard called his name.

But that wasn't even the name Showalter wanted to hear the legendary PA man announce most.

"Anybody dreams of hearing Bob Sheppard announce their name ... anybody should be on that stage, but Donnie should definitely have his efforts rewarded," Showalter said. "The only way he decided if he had a good day or bad day is if we won or lost."

So, when it came time for the fifth spot in the order, the fans howled before Sheppard could even announce the name.

In the PA booth, Sheppard thought of all the years Mattingly had waited, considered this incredible connection between player and fan at the end of a seemingly impossible quest and thought ...

"Nothing special," he said in 2004. "I considered them all the same. I announced a star the same as I would a rookie. I don't shout the names."

It just *sounded* special to hear Sheppard finally announce Mattingly's name the way he had once for Mantle and Reggie and Munson on a crisp, fall night.

"At first base, Number 23, Don Matt-ing-ly," Sheppard announced, the final syllables swallowed by primordial screams.

Mattingly jogged out, ready for all of it. The leg kick had been working; making him feel like his old self. The excitement started him up, but steadied him.

"I feel new to postseason, but I know it's just a game, you know?" he said, unable to hide a grin, during a pregame interview.

He seemed fine in his first at-bat against Seattle starter Chris Bosio.

"They've waited 13 years for Don Mattingly to get this ovation," Gary Thorne announced as Mattingly stepped in to the batter's box to more verbal bearhugs. "Mattingly! Base hit right field! And the Yankees take the lead!"

They'd win the first game. Play an epic in the second that finished only after Leyritz's 15-inning, game-winning homer rocked the Stadium.

Almost as much as it shook in the sixth inning of Game 2 when Mattingly faced Mariners starter Andy Benes.

"Don Mattingly ... the fans want a dinger out of him," Thorne announced right before Mattingly drilled a pitch over the wall in right-center. "This one by Mattingly ... ohhhh hang onto the *roof!*"

*** *** ***

Game of My Life
Don Mattingly

"Just a great feeling. You know, nervous. To be honest with you, not nervous. Really, a whole different level at that time. You know what I mean? Playoffs. You can get up for games and stuff and get ready to play, but it's just a different level there, and it's really cool and I liked it.

"Lot of excitement. First time for a long time, you wake up in the morning, and all you think about is the game. I mean, obviously, you talk about other stuff, but really, anything you did was all related to the game. All day long. And then the next day it starts right over again. When you wake up the next morning, it's like, 'Here we go again. Just get ready.'

"Just coming out of the dugout to stretch. And just the feeling I got on the field, just running those sprints across the outfield, those last few sprints to make sure your legs are right—just a rockin' feeling. Soon as I walked out, you could just feel it, man. It was cool. It's unbelievable. It was like floating, you know? It was like floating. They were chanting something; it's like, just floating, man.

"Oh, it was definitely more than what I pictured. New York is something special in a big series. It was a great feeling. Yeah, it was great ... I was always able to do it in New York, basically keep the game on my mind, keep the game as my focus. It was all about the game.

"More than anything, I was turning the clock back that last month. Just because I found myself a little leg kick, really, just kinda kept me up tall and was able to stay back—I really just found it mechanically more than anything. Shoot, I could have found it two years before that and been better off.

"As a person, you want to know how you're gonna react—you don't know. You may say this, that, or the other. You think you'll do fine there, but you want to know what you'll do. How you'll react to it. And I found out my concentration level goes to a whole different zone. And then you're playing ball. You get back to 'Get a good pitch to hit, hit it hard somewhere.'

"It really gets down to the basic, simple parts of playing the game at that point. So you're still playing the game, it's still a game. It's still 60 feet, six inches, everything's the same, it's just everybody's at a different level. You really see who can focus at that point.

"I swung the bat good that whole series. I was swinging the bat good coming down the stretch; I was really confident. I remember the big righty they had; he wasn't really a hard thrower any more, Bosio. I was thinking, 'Oooh, I'm gonna get him.' My concentration was so good and I wasn't chasing everything, so I knew I was gonna hit him hard.

"(Home run in Game 2) You know what I was thinking about? Benes— he's from Evansville. More of a hometown deal going on, too, you know? (Laughs) And he got me early in the year. He got me out in Seattle and I wasn't swinging good, and I knew how he thought he could get me out.

"I was just out front in Seattle. I just wasn't swinging good. Had a lot of problems with my eyes that year. Had a lot of trouble getting it going. I *knew* that he thought I'd just chase. And I was locked.

"Yeah, he didn't have a chance. (Laughs) You know what I mean? I knew that I just gotta get a good pitch to hit. I felt like I was gonna hit hard every time up."

*** *** ***

He did.
Wasn't enough.

One of the most dramatic playoff series baseball has seen proved to be the most heartbreaking for the game's old poster child.

Mostly because of its new one.

Ken Griffey Jr. was an overgrown kid playing the game with the childlike spirit Mattingly once did. But he was young, in his prime. He didn't yet

From his trademark eye black to never-ending hustle, "Donnie Baseball" became one of the most endeared Yankees of all time. Fans celebrated with him when his postseason quest was finally fulfilled in '95—and mourned his absence during the team's World Series run after his retirement. *Rich Pilling/MLB Photos via Getty Images.*

worry about how he'd do on the playoff stage, because you figure you can do everything before age humbles you.

He just about did.

Five games. Five home runs.

The Mariners won two straight in Seattle to tie the series.

Then they faced off in a classic Game 5, Mattingly looking to extend his dream with one more hit in the top of the sixth, a two-run double.

And the Yankees led, 4-2, nine outs from advancement.

Except they ran out of pitchers to get the nine outs.

Cone was exhausted but kept going. Showalter didn't feel he had many options. It was too early for closer John Wetteland, who had struggled anyway.

And that kid, Mariano Rivera, had seemed cool under pressure, but this was Game 5.

So he stuck with Cone.

And Cone almost pitched his arm off, finally surrendering the lead and the ball after walking home the tying run.

The game went into extra innings. Again the Yankees took the lead.

But Griffey had another at-bat. So did Edgar Martinez.

The Yankees never recorded an out. And, three batters into the inning, a 5-4 Yankees lead had turned into a 6-5 loss.

The last sight on a field Mattingly would see as a player was Griffey streaking past him and all the way home, taking the division series with him.

Over.

Just like that.

Over.

In the clubhouse, Cone and losing pitcher Jack McDowell cried like kids.

Then Cone felt a hand on his shoulder.

It belonged to the captain.

His last shot at a World Series gone, Mattingly had something to say to the pitcher who had given up the lead—on a walk, no less.

"Thank you," Mattingly said.

"Rather than feeling a sense of missing out on something, he took the time to thank us," Cone said. "I'll never forget it, never forget it. Mattingly was the most gracious teammate I ever had."

It went that way all through the plane ride to New York, Mattingly fussing and fidgeting in his seat, climbing out of it to talk to another player.

From his spot at the front of the plane, Showalter could recognize the grimaces. Knew Mattingly's back again bothered him. The manager, who didn't yet know he was about to leave the Yankees himself, did think this was it for his first baseman.

"I had a feeling," Showalter said. "He said earlier, 'If I can't be what a first baseman should be for the New York Yankees, I'm not gonna do it.' Plus, he had his family he wanted to be with back home."

So Mattingly made his way through the plane.

"He was never out for himself," Leyritz said. "Everything about him is 'Team, team, team.'"

He didn't retire immediately.

He thought it over. Sent the Yankees a statement releasing them of the worry over whether to chase a power-hitting first baseman. With their blessing, he sat out a year while they signed Tino Martinez.

Then the next October, Mattingly watched Martinez, Jeter, Pettitte, Williams and the rest of the Yankees celebrate the championship that had eluded him.

How hard had it been to walk away?

"Not that hard, really, to be honest with you," Mattingly said. "The only part was not getting all the way. But even with all that, I really battled all year long, being on the road. And my kids were at home.

"I knew we were gonna be good, I knew we'd have good teams, I knew we had all these guys coming and stuff. But I knew in my heart, I was cheating. Going back to the hotel, going to the ballpark, going back to the hotel, you know? Just wasn't enough for me any more.

"It wasn't fair to (the kids) to come back to New Jersey and live and me go to the ballpark and them sit around and go to the game every night. It just wasn't enough for them. They wanted to play little league and have their own deal."

He was happy for his old teammates, even if he couldn't share their joy. It was too tough to watch it all. In January 1997 he officially retired.

The Yankees brought him out on opening day that year to help raise a World Series banner of which all the veterans said he owned an unofficial piece.

He had no way of knowing the Yankees would go on to three more titles in the next four years.

"I know," he said, shaking his head. "But you know what? I always believed I'd get there. I always believed I'd get to the playoffs. Always believed I'd get to the World Series. But you know what? That's just the way life works, you know what I mean?"

He returned as a batting instructor in 2004, and there isn't a fan at the stadium who didn't want to see him finally earn a ring as a coach, if not a player.

Instead, he had to suffer along with the rest of the Yankees in their most infamous collapse, losing the last four games in the American League Championship Series to the Red Sox, just one win from the World Series.

He would also lose his shot at managing the Yankees, when Joe Girardi was hired to replace Joe Torre in 2008 and Mattingly instead followed Torre to L.A., where he eventually became the Dodgers' manager.

He can only hope for another shot at that elusive World Series there now, though Mattingly always shoves his ego aside and makes it about his players. All these years later, the Hit Man can only take solace in knowing that when he got his shot as a player, his swing was as smooth as it ever had been.

CHAPTER 15

Joe Torre

October 1996, World Series vs. Atlanta

Yankees 4 games, Braves 2

The stats:
- Game 1—Atlanta 12, Yankees 0
- Game 2—Atlanta 4, Yankees 0
- Game 3—Yankees 4, Atlanta 2
- Game 4—Yankees 8, Atlanta 6
- Game 5—Yankees 1, Atlanta 0
- Game 6—Yankees 3, Atlanta 2

"Rocco, take your brother to the park."

The baseball life began here for Joe Torre, his infant body jolted in the carriage along a bumpy sidewalk on Avenue T in Brooklyn. Rocco rolled him to the park, mixing his mother Margaret's order for babysitting with ballplaying.

It's what you did in Brooklyn in the '40s and '50s—you played ball.

Didn't matter what kind either. Baseball, stickball, slapball. You name it, they played it. And in between screaming out for a coming "car!" you followed the bouncing ball across as many sewers as you could hit it until Mom called you home for dinner.

Joe grew out of the carriage and headed out on his own. The park, the street; anywhere he could play. The kids crowded around him, asking all about his big brother, the one making his way through the minors and into the majors.

"Hey, you hear from Frankie?"

"Joe, how's your brother?"

"He hittin' good?"

Joe fielded the questions along with the grounders, then started strategizing while everyone else just tried smacking the snot out of the ball.

Joe Torre could never have imagined the World Series celebration he waited his whole career for would become a nearly annual event, each featuring Yankees owner George Steinbrenner and former New York City Mayor Rudy Giuliani. *Al Bello/Getty Images.*

He couldn't get enough of this stuff. Besides, it got him out of the house.

Especially when his dad's car was parked out front, the sight of which would send little Joe anywhere but home.

Out on the street, the worst thing Joe dealt with were cranky old neighbors who spent their summers trying to spoil slapball games.

You'd bounce it once and try to hit it down the street—two manhole covers a double, four a homer—but the neighbors didn't want to know from such nonsense.

When they weren't peeking from behind their curtains, the housedress and undershirt crew screamed from their stoops.

"Whattaya playin' in the street for?" they'd yell after a bouncing ball came, literally, too close to home. "Why don't you play in the park?"

"Tried to explain, the ball doesn't *bounce* in the park," Joe Torre said. "Dirt. I'd have to bounce it to hit it."

Already the diplomat.

Already a manager.

"I was always looked to, to sort of organize the teams and the game," Torre said.

Maybe this was the first hint of Torre's lifelong trek toward his first World Series in 1996. Maybe this was the first sign of the calming presence that would be criticized, then commended, the first World Series title turning to a second, third, fourth.

All of them adding up to a nearly inevitable entrance into Cooperstown. But back then, no one could predict the Torre family would captivate all of New York in 1996.

Certainly, no one could have believed the made-for-TV-movie plot, Joe ending a lifetime's quest to reach a World Series while mourning the death of Rocco and celebrating the miracle of Frank's last-minute heart transplant.

How could the Torres imagine the eyes of New York on them back then? They were afraid of someone looking too close.

This is where it started for Joe Torre, in the house on Avenue T, where the boy found a baby carriage could no longer protect him.

Eventually, he'd have to come home, past his father's car, not knowing how much the man would scream today. Not knowing if he'd have to cower from another threat.

Here, his life started, even before the carriage, Joe an unborn baby inside his mother's womb—as she was thrown down the stairs by his father because he didn't want any more kids.

This was his life until his brother Frank, sick of the fear, grew big enough to challenge the old man and chase him from the house when Joe was 11.

Until then, the Torres did what any other self-respecting family on the block would do:

They kept their blinds closed and their mouths shut.

What were they going to do?

Call the cops?

Torre the adult, the man who became as calming as his father could be cruel, smiled. It was the typical Torre grin, the one that shows wisdom and vulnerability, the kind that has endeared him to New York by showing he represents it.

"Well, yeah, my dad was a cop," he said. "That was a little tough to even consider letting anything out of the house. You never let anything out of the house anyway. It was something you had to deal with. You felt that nobody else ever had to deal with this. You were embarrassed."

The embarrassment didn't leave as he got older. It hid.

So Torre the teenager savored watching his brother Frank come home to play in the World Series. He embedded that day in his brain, when Frank's Milwaukee Braves beat the Yankees at the Stadium to win the '57 World Series.

All that celebrating. All that happiness.

Joe's 17-year-old eyes studied the scene of his brother's teammates, grown men giddy as boys without a care in the world. He wanted that.

He'd become a ballplayer. He'd win a World Series.

Four thousand, one hundred and nine games later ...

Torre had buried his pain, but never felt the joy for which he aimed. He became a player, a perennial all-star. One of the most respected hitters and people around the game. Then a manager.

It never worked.

He couldn't quite get to the big game, to the Series.

Didn't have enough talent with the Mets. Time ran out on him in Atlanta. And St. Louis?

Well, his third wife, Ali, looked at him after his third firing and said, "No, no, this wasn't it."

But Ali *was* it. The first wife Torre fully recognized as a partner, the one he finally confided in.

He thinks about his previous two marriages and realizes his ex-wives didn't have a fair shot at helping him when he arrived home from the ballpark.

"Early on in my career, I wouldn't let anybody in," Torre said. "It was mine, it belonged to me, and it was my life. It didn't make me a very good husband or a father, unfortunately. But as you get older, I guess you get smarter, or more mature, one or the other.

"I didn't like myself very much when I was younger," he said. "I was more irresponsible, and that's probably why I'm a stickler for responsibility now. ... I think you realize this later; anything that happens in your life is what makes you what you are anyway."

Torre was about to find out exactly what he was in 1996.

On November 2, 1995, Torre stood up at a press conference and accepted a Yankees managing job that almost everyone told him to decline.

George Steinbrenner had just split with his latest manager, Buck Showalter, and depending on whose side you believed, the manager either quit or was forced out. The track record of an owner who had gone through more managers than turtlenecks led many to believe the latter.

"Clueless Joe," the headline in the *New York Daily News* blared, by way of welcome. "Joe has no idea what he's getting himself into" was the tease to a column.

This was Joe's return to New York.

And only one thing made it worth it.

"There's one missing piece to my puzzle in my career," he said at his introductory press conference. "I have never been in a World Series."

But there was another puzzle for Torre to complete first, a piece buried so deep he had done everything he could to lose it.

One month into the center of a New York storm bigger than any he knew with the Mets, what did Torre do?

He attended a self-esteem seminar.

Ali, pregnant with their child, insisted he join her. She prodded. He went.

And then, with all of New York waiting, ready to dissect his every move ... with the most demanding Boss in baseball ready to breathe down his neck...

Torre made himself as vulnerable as he had ever been.

"In Cincinnati; I'll never forget," he said. "We were split into groups; separated from Ali. A group of strangers. This was not something I would have normally done, but I found myself pouring my heart out about my life and crying. It was a real freedom.

"I got to figure out some of the things I was feeling."

Torre discovered he had blocked out the abuse of his dad for years.

He called his sister, Marguerite, over in Queens. Asked if his dad had ever hit his mom.

And all the memories rushed back. All the explanations why, even through a near-Hall of Fame playing career, Torre couldn't find a way to like himself more when he closed the clubhouse door and exited in street clothes.

This is what he realized as he prepared for his last shot to win in a city ready to show him just how much he could be disliked if he lost.

"Baseball was always my escape, but I guess what this did is helped me understand why I acted a certain way," Torre said. "... My confidence level wasn't ideal. But it's something you have to fight. I knew one thing by playing this game—if I got swallowed up by the insecurities, I knew I couldn't play it."

The game. It had always been his out. It would be again in '96, as much as ever.

And he was ready for a fight. He'd confront his past. Take on the present.

"In essence, I was gonna find out if I can manage," he said. "If what I do, works."

His life flashed before him the whole way in '96, daring him to honor and defy his past all at once.

In June, he heard his wife on the other end of the phone as he sat in the manager's office in Cleveland.

"Are you sitting down?" she asked.

Frank, he thought, knowing his brother had been in and out of the hospital with heart problems.

It wasn't Frank.

Rocco.

He died of a heart attack.

Torre was shocked. Rocco had been like a father after his dad left the house.

So the manager mourned.

Then he moved on, because the big brother who played ball in between babysitting wouldn't want it any other way.

A 12-game lead was trimmed to two, and Torre told his jittery players they *would* win.

Frank went back to the hosptial in August, his body demanding a new heart. The Yankees reached the playoffs.

As the Yankees led the city on an ultra-charged trip deep into October, Torre was getting attacked from every emotional angle possible.

Teary eyed and exhausted, Torre watched the last out of the American League Championship Series from the dugout in Baltimore.

He hugged his bench coach, Don Zimmer, who tapped his leg repeatedly as Derek Jeter threw out Cal Ripken.

He was going to the World Series. Finally.

Frank kept rooting his heart out and hoping for a new one.

The World Series returned to Yankee Stadium for the first time in 15 years and New York prepared for the return of royalty.

Then the Atlanta Braves made the Yankees look like a bunch of court jesters.

The Braves smacked all that Yankee tradition around the park, bashing out a 12-0 win. To commemorate Atlanta's gleeful disregard for the revered ground, 19-year-old outfielder Andruw Jones homered twice, breaking a Series record as the youngest player to hit a home run.

A record once owned by Mickey Mantle.

The Braves were defending world champions and had rallied from a 3-1 deficit to beat St. Louis in the National League Championship Series. They had scored 44 runs in their last five games.

They were throwing four-time Cy Young winner Greg Maddux in Game 2.

The headlines held as much hope for the Yankees now as they had 11 months earlier for "Clueless Joe."

The whole World Series, that had taken Torre 4,272 games to reach, seemed ready to slip away in two. All while he lost one brother and was in danger of losing a second.

If ever there was a time for Torre to decide he didn't like himself or that he could doubt himself, this was it.

But he didn't. Baseball was his out. His escape.

And this time, Torre knew what he was doing and who he was. He liked all of it.

He knew his team had been rusty after a long lay off following the American League Championship Series.

He knew he'd have to turn to his shaken family one more time and have them all stick together.

The blinds were wide open now.

No more need to hide. No more need to question himself.

He could handle anything thrown at him.

Even the Yankees' demanding owner, who, not surprisingly, was as frantic as ever.

"Joe," Steinbrenner said with a growl in the manager's office after Game 1, "this is a must win."

Torre laughs thinking about his response.

"I said to him and I was serious—even though I said it in a half-joking manner—I said, 'We're a little out of whack,'" Torre remembered. "I said 'Maddux is pitching tonight, we may lose tonight.' And that's when I got goofy. I said, 'But we'll go down there and win three, come back here and win it Saturday for you.'"

Torre grinned. That soothing grin. The one that had folks thinking his laid-back manner allowed things to spin into chaos and now shows his utter control.

"Yeah, he thought I was nuts," Torre said. "No question."

*** *** ***

After four World Series championships and six American League titles, he's become a cross between the Godfather and a magician. Before that? He was too soft.

He laughs at it, the dry, polite chuckle that barely hides a barb at the media. This is how he offers his putdowns to scribbling notebooks—with a New York wisecrack realistic enough to stop just short of being sarcastic.

"When you don't win it's soft," he said. "When you do win, you motivate your players, I guess. We're here for the players, we're here for the players.... it doesn't mean that you just run a rag-tag organization or anything. You still have certain parameters and things they have to do. I try to make sense to them."

So, three months after he took the job—and two months after he started uncovering his past—Torre prepared to address his team for the first time.

He had thumbed through a book on coaching by two-time Super Bowl champ Bill Parcells when a passage caught his eye.

"If you believe in what you do," the book read, "stay with it."

"OK," Torre thought.

He entered the room full of players returning from a devastating playoff loss to Seattle. Their captain, Don Mattingly, was gone, replaced by power-hitting first baseman Tino Martinez. There were veterans craving a title all over the room, from Wade Boggs to David Cone to Paul O'Neill.

The kid Torre would learn so much about as the year progressed, Derek Jeter, was there, giving the manager the first glimpse of the look he later compared to Tiger Woods.

"I've never been to a World Series," Torre told his players. "Every single one of these guys on my coaching staff has been to a World Series; I just want to get there."

The tone was set.

But there were plenty of other areas to tidy up.

"For some reason," he said, "stuff that had nothing to do with baseball would interfere with what seems to be going on on the field. I wanted to give my club every chance to really lock in on what we're trying to do."

So he put it all on him.

He'd handle the owner. What was to handle anyway? The guy just wanted to win.

No. *Needed* to win. And after years of not getting the players he needed at other jobs, Torre would take that. They wanted the same things; Joe just needed to shield his players.

"I knew if I was ever going to get to a World Series, it would have to be working for a man like George," he said.

The media?

No problem. He knew the media here. He knew New York.

So he shrugged off the "Clueless Joe" thing, he said, because "You knew what they based that decision on. I was basically, 'We'll see.' I had enough confidence in my ability that I could relate to people and I knew baseball.

"And to me, it was the right fit, because media is a big part of it and I felt very comfortable with the media. Here in New York, I seem to have the pulse in this. Maybe the calming stuff like Bob Lemon brought here when he took over in '78 was the type of thing I wanted to do. Let them play baseball. I don't need to show anybody what I know, other than the players play the game."

It worked.

It worked so well that all these years later, Torre no longer has to win over anyone.

They flock to the Yankees, hoping to earn his respect.

Alex Rodriguez, widely regarded as the game's best shortstop, came over to play third in 2004. Jason Giambi shifted out of first to DH before his knees forced him to do so.

And if there's more than a few peeps against Torre's team-oriented managerial style—"I'm loyal to players, yes, but loyal to the team first"—the guy can expect to pack his bags.

That's what Raul Mondesi found out in 2003 when he griped about Torre's usage of him in the lineup.

"Well, they're gonna have to be made to be the right guys," Torre said. "They just have to understand, that's the way we do things. But at that time, we hadn't proven anything."

So Torre proved as he went.

If you believe in what you do, stay with it.

Team first. Players next.

Your average star has an ego the size of the Chrysler Building, but Torre has become a bigger master of handling the ego than Freud.

Could any other manager get as many big-name players as Torre has to sit so easily?

"No, no," former catcher Jim Leyrtiz said.

But they respond when they see success.

And the Yankees outlasted everyone in '96. Even when it seemed they were done.

They came back from a deficit in the ALDS against Texas. Beat Baltimore with help from that controversial kid, Jeffrey Maier, hanging his glove over in right.

Then Atlanta sucked all the enthusiasm out of New York.

There had been endless anticipation.

Memories were sparked along the way, the Bronx Bombers finally making it back to the big stage.

In the Bronx, New York doesn't feel as big, as boastful when the Yankees are down. All through the '80s, Yankee Stadium stood as regal as ever, but was left devoid of the noise it can only make in one month.

October.

Now, with the Yankees finally honoring their history, the place shook with the banshee calls of a beast returning to devour old prey.

Except the Yankees were the prey.

They had wrapped up the ALCS too soon.

Atlanta took too long to win the National League.

Then came a rainout.

The Yankees went a week without a game, and Torre knew they'd be rusty.

Just not this rusty.

Torre's vindication and New York's elation over a World Series was met by a backhand from the Braves.

They were the defending world champions.

They were the dominating force.

Yankees tradition?

Go find Bucky Dent and Reggie Jackson.

John Smoltz, Chipper Jones and Andruw Jones didn't know from it.

And, after the Braves won Game 2, 4-0, behind Maddux, no one around baseball seemed to either.

"Get someone else in here," one columnist wrote.

"End it now: What's the point?" a headline read.

The veteran Braves started cackling, wondering exactly when they'd sip their champagne.

Never.

Torre stuck with David Cone in a big spot in Game 3, the pitcher determined not to let the season end on his watch again. Cone worked out of a jam and the Yankees were back in the Series.

Then they were right back out of it. Or so it seemed.

Atlanta jumped on Kenny Rogers for a 6-0 lead in Game 4, but it didn't matter.

The Yankees had come back all year. Torre's calming influence continued as he told them to just cut the lead in half.

Then Leyritz came up in the top of the eighth, the Yankees down 6-3, two on, two out.

Braves closer Mark Wohlers threw one of the nastiest fastballs in the league. But Leyritz kept fouling it off.

In the broadcast booth, announcer Tim McCarver pointed out you want to get beat with your best pitch.

But Wohlers threw a slider.

Leyritz was on it.

"To the track, to the wall, we are TIED!" Joe Buck announced.

A few innings later, after a bases-loaded walk and an error by the Braves, the Series was tied, too.

In Game 5, Andy Pettitte would again have to duel John Smoltz. This time, he would outlast him, throwing zero after zero, making the Yankees' one run stick.

How good was Pettitte pitching?

Torre left him in to pitch the ninth even after a pinch-hit single in the top of the inning could have given the Yankees another run.

Then Pettitte made Torre's heart jump, giving up a leadoff double. But closer John Wetteland would end a seemingly endless confrontation with Luis Polonia with a deep fly to right.

Paul O'Neill, gimpy legs and all, raced back, stuck his glove up and sealed the game, punctuating the Yankees' win with some pounds of the outfield wall.

Torre's team had done just what he said it would. Won three straight in Atlanta. Gotten within one more win at the Stadium of bringing the World Series championship back to New York.

By now, Torre's Yankees had captured New York and his family owned it.

Especially after Frank received a heart transplant the day before Game 6.

"Heart of the Yanks" a front-page headline read, over a picture of Frank Torre in a hospital bed, wires all over his body.

Then came the headline the day before Game 6, the one that appeared in the *Daily News* 11 months after the "Clueless Joe" welcome.

Now it pictured a soulful Joe, hounddog eyes looking thoughtful under his navy blue Yankees cap and above a chin full of stubble.

After his brother's miracle heart transplant, Joe Torre vows to:
WIN IT FOR FRANK.

Life as a Yankee changed everything for Torre, who returned to his New York roots and carved out a reputation of winning he'd sought his whole career. *Ezra Shaw/Getty Images.*

*** *** ***

Game of My Life
Joe Torre

"Things happened so quickly for me. I lost my brother Rocco in June and my brother Frank was waiting for a heart transplant. It's funny. He was in the hospital waiting to see how long he was gonna live, and he was still wanting me to realize my dream of, you know, getting to a World Series.

"When you realize how unselfish some people can be, I think it gives you ... it makes you feel good.

"Well, you know I tell ya, we beat Baltimore on Sunday. The National League series started later than ours to begin with, they went seven games—and then we got rained out opening day, Saturday. So we got our ass kicked the first game. There's nothing you can do—even to this day, we had a week between games.

"You don't have a week between games at any time. So the best you can do is practice. So we weren't sharp. So after Game 1, knowing what I saw in Game 1, George comes in and says, 'This is a big game.' I said (to myself), 'Well, no kidding.'

"But to be honest with ya, I was so excited about being in the World Series—yeah, you wanna win it—but it still wasn't gonna rain on my parade because of the excitement and satisfaction of getting there. ... And that's when I got goofy. I said, 'But we'll go down there and win three, come back here and win it Saturday for you. ... The one thing I felt and I told my players after Game 1—it just takes one game to change the momentum in a short series. Just one game.

"Game 3 was probably the best decision I made in having David Cone start Game 3, because of all our starters, he was the only one who pitched in the National League ballpark in Atlanta. And I didn't want any of my other pitchers going down there, pitching in that launching pad, just getting real psyched out by it.

And he gave me what I hoped for. He gave me a courageous outing. There were some tedious times in the middle there when I believed him, he says, 'I'll get 'em.' And he winds up walking in a run but he gets out of the inning.

"Game 4 ... I remember Game 4 so vividly. We're losing 6-0. Fifth inning. Players came in after the fifth inning, I said, 'Just cut the lead in half.' And we did and it was 6-3, and whatever inning it was that Leyritz hit that three-run home run to tie it up. You know, you sit there and the one thing you have to remember the advantage that I had ... over, maybe managers who hadn't managed in a National League game is, you sort of have to bide your time making sure you don't run out of players. Luckily we had Wade Boggs, hit with the bases loaded, he winds up walking.

"I remember, we started getting superstitious. I have a friend of mine, Ed Mall, who lives in Atlanta and we had lunch at the Buckhead Diner Monday. Lunch at the Buckhead Diner, we won Game 3. And then Game 4, which got through at who-knows-what time? Then you get up and the only meal you're gonna have is that one and it was getaway day and we still decided we had to go to the Buckhead Diner.

"So we went to the Buckhead Diner and went to the ballpark. And that was the toughest game for me to manage. On my way to the ballpark I just made up my mind—actually I felt it before that—thought that Cecil (Fielder) was swinging the bat better than Tino (Martinez), and I thought since we had Andy Pettitte pitching that I needed more range at third base, so I played Charlie Hayes over Boggs. And I was gonna play— in fact, I told Paul O'Neill he wasn't playing, and I was gonna play (Tim) Raines. I called them all in, single. Told them what I was doing. Tino was mad. He went, "OK." Very short, snappy. Boggs was, you know; he shrugged.

"And O'Neill sorta was discouraged. He walked out. Zimmer was in there with him. And Zim said, 'You know what, this guy has been playing with one leg the second half of the year here. He's been hurting.' He says, 'Maybe we should trust him a little bit more.' Made sense. So I called him back in. And I told him, 'That's the privilege the manager has. He can change his mind.' And when I told him he was playing, he really didn't change much expression. He just shook his head and went back out. Which, you know, that's Paul O'Neill. Very business-like guy. And as it turns out, he makes the catch in right-center field to close the deal.

"The one thing early on, when I started managing, I made up my mind I wasn't going to manage so that I would have an easier time answering questions. You know, I think the easy thing for me to do, even where my players were concerned, was to play Tino at first because it was a right-handed pitcher, Smoltz. But my heart tells me that Cecil just looked like he was on the ball better.

"That's very tough. Very tough. 'Cause you had these guys leaving their hearts on the field for ya. And you're loyal to them, but your loyalty is to the team first.

"Pettitte staying in (to hit in the ninth), that's one of the funny ones. He was pitching so well. You know, if it wasn't a 1-0 game where he's gotten everybody out with ease, I could have done some other things. When you go in the ninth inning, you do one of two things. You either leave the pitcher in or you bring the closer in.

"So I said to Zim, top of the ninth, 'I want Andy to start the ninth inning.'

"And I explained why I wanted to do it. I said, 'We've got Chipper Jones leading off (for Atlanta).' At that time he wasn't near as good a right-handed hitter as he was a left-handed hitter. And you had McGriff next. And you had Javy Lopez. Whoever else was following that group.

"So in the top half of the ninth, Mariano Duncan got on base. He was batting seventh. To be perfectly honest, I had it in the back of my mind, 'Let's just make three outs.' You sorta want to get to the ninth inning, because I think you realize by the seventh, one is gonna be it. So Duncan gets a base hit, Leyritz is the hitter, he's hitting eighth.

"And I said, 'Oh, I'll send Duncan (on a steal); he'll get thrown out, end of the inning, you don't have to worry about it. You get in trouble, in the next inning, you can pinch hit.'

"So Duncan makes it, steals second. Now they walk Leyritz intentionally, and I let Andy hit for himself. No decision. To me, I had made up my mind in the sixth or seventh inning, it was gonna be a 1-0 game. Sure, if we'd have gotten another one or two, it'd be great, but I just liked what Andy was doing.

"Well, you know, he goes up there, goes up to hit, and I think Andy was surprised. Some guy starts screaming out of the stands, and Zimmer tells him to sit down. Come to find out later on my wife is sitting there with Andy's wife. And Andy's wife, Laura, is saying, 'What's he doing? He never pitches the ninth inning.' And my wife couldn't give her a legitimate answer.

"My wife who was questioning me all of a sudden decided to stand up for me. Because she knew I needed some more soldiers on my side of the field. The only way she could do that is, 'He knows what he's doing.' And that was the reason.

"So what happens? Chipper Jones hits a double. And that's torture. Total torture. 'Cause I made a very easy decision to second-guess. I mean, I was proud of myself that I didn't let the fact that I'd be second-guessed keep me from making the decision that I felt was the one I wanted to make.

"So now McGriff is the hitter, hits a ground ball to second base on the first pitch. Now I bring in Wetteland, man on third base, one out. Play the infield up. Javy Lopez hits the first pitch to Charlie Hayes one hop. Two out.

"Now Klesko's the next hitter. I go out to the mound. And I said, 'I wanna walk Klesko. I know he's the winning run, but I want to walk him.' It's two outs. And that's another thing you could be second-guessed about, walking the winning run.

"So I went out there and I thought Pendleton would pinch hit and they brought in Polonia—but either way I would have done the same thing—and that at-bat was a torturous at-bat.

"Probably fouled off five pitches, six pitches. So the more he fouled off over our dugout at third base, (coach Jose) Cardenal moves O'Neill about three steps to the gap. And I'll be damned if he doesn't hit the next pitch to the gap. I thought O'Neill slipped at first. Looked like he stepped in a hole—it was just his legs bothering him. And he reaches up and makes the catch. And I see him kissing the wall.

"And then we went home. You know, we flew home and then early morning I get a call like at five in the morning, or six in the morning, that they found a heart for my brother.

"So we had a workout that day. Went to the workout. Surgery went well. Reggie (Jackson) and I went over to see my brother.

"I remember going out to dinner and there was a message on my answering machine ... I said, 'Who do you think this is?' I said, it sounds ... it could be my brother. There was a message. I called back. And I said to the nurse I said, 'Did my brother call me?' She says, 'Yeah. hold on. I'll let you talk to him.'

"You know, that morning he had a new heart put in his chest. He's asking me for four tickets for the next day's game. It was for one of his doctors, that they're gonna unplug him if he doesn't get the tickets so ...

"And then Game 6 was quite a game. I watched it last year somewhere, and they had Game 6 on one of those classic stations, and you forget a lot of the stuff that went on in the game.

"You know, (Joe) Girardi hit the triple off Maddux. And then two out in the ninth inning, Wetteland kept going after (Mark) Lemke, fastball, fastball, fastball, fouled one off, looked like it was interference at third base. And, you know, I'm watching it, but I seriously doubted the World Series is gonna end on an interference call at third base. So the next pitch was a carbon copy except it was up. And I remember Jeter's arms going up as he was sorta standing off to the side of Charlie Hayes. Never had a feeling like that. Happy to say I've had feelings like that since, but not quite like the first one. There'll never be another first one."

*** *** ***

As absent as he had been in World Series photos throughout his career, it's now become stunning *not* to see Torre walking off a field, tears in his eyes, hugs all around.

It all started in '96, when Zimmer suggested he take the team on a lap around the field and Torre did, the Yankees reaching out to fans who had been waiting 18 years for another title.

In the stands, his sister Marguerite wiped tears between cheers. From his hospital bed, Frank smiled and shook his head at his little brother's success.

They had all come a long way from Avenue T and they would come even further in November 2003. That's when the Torre family united to go public, telling of their abusive father on *Dateline NBC*.

Then Joe announced he was starting a foundation called Safe at Home. He wanted other kids to feel just that, without having to cringe at the sight of a parked car.

"I get so many people telling me about similarities in their youth that I dealt with," Torre said. "The kids are in a very tough situation, because if they're made aware of the fact it's the wrong thing, who do they go to? ... We're encouraging them to go to an aunt, an uncle."

For all the titles, the time hasn't been that easy for Torre. That's OK, too, he'd tell you, shrugging at the way life works.

He topped cancer in 1999, then helped his team repeat as champs. Won his third straight in 2000 and inspired the city with a playoff run in 2001 a month after the terrorist attacks.

The Yankees fell behind Oakland 2-0 in the best-of-five ALDS, but Torre donned a "It ain't over til it's over" hat he got from Yogi Berra, and the Yankees kept it from being over all the way to Game 7 of the World Series.

For all his titles, Torre took more criticism in 2003, finally going barb for barb with Steinbrenner, when he had so often chose silence in the past. He was all but ready to quit after the year, his bench coach Zimmer storming out. "I didn't want to be where I'm not wanted," he said.

But he had a commitment to his players.

And, after an epic win over the Red Sox in the American League Championship Series, Steinbrenner showed his commitment to his manager. He gave him a three-year contract the next spring and the trust Torre craved.

The trust would eventually evaporate, as it always seemed to for managers in the George Steinbrenner era. An elder George would butt heads with

Torre handled everything thrown at him through the years, from an abusive father to the death of his father-figure brother, Rocco, along with heart surgery for his brother Frank and his own cancer battle. *Rich Pilling/MLB Photos via Getty Images.*

Torre one last time in 2007 after a first-round playoff exit, this time team president Randy Levine and Steinbrenner's sons also in the fold.

Torre would consider the Yankees' one-year offer, which included a pay cut, an "insult" and he resigned, eventually going on to manage the Dodgers.

Relations were icy between the ballclub and its former manager at that point, especially after a book co-authored by Torre was critical of Alex Rodriguez and general manager Brian Cashman.

Finally, Torre returned to the Yankees in 2010, at the new stadium, to pay tribute to his old Boss, when the team honored Steinbrenner's memory after his death.

Thus began a reconcilliation as Torre, like so many other Yankees who had feuded with and thrived while working under the Boss, acknowledged his appreciation for the man who gave him a chance to win that first World Series and all those that followed.

"George is responsible for the best years of my life, professionally," Torre told reporters that day. "George, in my opinion, not only belongs in Monument Park. He belongs in the Hall of Fame."

Eventually, you can also picture the manager who once couldn't make it to a World Series in the Hall of Fame, his No. 6 jersey retired in pinstripes.

He built one of the most popular Yankee dynasties of any era, one in which the club's success drew as much respect as it did hatred. It was a model for winning in the late '90s, Torre showing how far human motivation can go.

How you didn't need to yell and scream to inspire. He knows that as well as anyone.

For so long, he didn't think he'd have one World Series ring, much less four. There's nothing like the first one. The one that revealed the Torre family from Avenue T to all of New York.

"They were all there for me though, you know," Torre said. "Even my brother Rocco, I sensed his presence, really. I know I had a dream during the World Series. I opened the door up and Rocco was standing there. 'Cause he was sorta like my father figure after my dad left."

CHAPTER 16

Jorge Posada:
The Perfect Call

May 17, 1998

vs. Minnesota
Yankees 4, Twins 0

The stats:	PO	A	E
	11	1	0

The crowd wouldn't stop cheering, all the claps, whistles and roars overflowing into one giant loop.

On the mound, David Wells lay at the bottom of the pile, teammate after teammate trying to touch him.

A tap on the head. A pound on the arm. Every Yankee wanted whatever piece they could get of Wells, knowing with it came a part of history.

In the middle of the pack, before Wells emerged to take his bow, he had to do something. In a moment, his teammates would lift him on their shoulders and off the field. Wells thrust his cap over and over, stabbing the sky to the howling delight of all 49,820 who had witnessed Yankee Stadium's first perfect game in the regular season.

And there, to his left, walked catcher Jorge Posada Jr., smiling and applauding like any other spectator.

Except Posada was far from that.

"You were *awesome*, Jorge!" Wells screamed, yanking his catcher close. "You were *awesome*, Jorge!"

Posada, still proving himself as a catcher, had called the game of his life. But the celebration wouldn't have been complete without one more call.

When David Wells finally recorded the last out of his perfect game, he couldn't wait to share the accomplishment with his catcher, Jorge Posada. *David Seelig/Allsport/Getty Images.*

The sweat hadn't yet dried as Posada, still trying to calm his nerves from having to call the ninth, dialed the phone.

His dream of making it in the majors was starting to come true. So he had to call the person who made it possible by escaping a nightmare.

"I called my father right away," Posada said. "There's a lot of emotion and he has lived every moment. That was another chapter."

The first began before Posada Jr. was born.

*** *** ***

Thirty minutes passed and Jorge Posada Sr. didn't blink.
He couldn't.

He'd rather live.

Tucked inside a humidor, the cigar boat sped Posada Sr. away from Cuba, but he remained motionless.

Moving meant capture.

Capture meant death.

Or, at least, a return to Cuba, which was no kind of life.

Posada Sr. had spent years in prison before fleeing Cuba in 1967, pushed there by dictator Fidel Castrol for political reasons.

He played sports his whole life because they provided the only refuge from the poverty the communist regime inflicted on Cuba. If you could play sports or musical instruments, you could eat a little more.

"That was the only way you could live there, play sports or play music," said Posada's son, Jorge Posada Jr. "They'd actually get a lot of food because they were doing something for the country. All the other people, it didn't matter how much money you had, it was all gone."

Playing sports meant you earned more, but you also yearned more.

Posada Sr. couldn't believe it when the call came from the major leagues. The Philadelphia Phillies wanted him.

Too late.

Castro had him.

Posada Sr. had a difference of political opinion with the Cuban president. Those debates are short-lived and, as it did with Posada Sr., can end with a jail sentence.

His son's teammate, Orlando "El Duque" Hernandez, could tell you all about the lack of freedom after his escape on a raft in 1998.

Decades earlier, Posada Sr. devised a plan to escape Cuba and join his family, which had already managed to leave.

Posada Sr. was 26 and his dream of a major league career had been locked up along with him. His youth went to Castro's Cuba.

His life would not.

There was "no futuro" in Cuba.

So when his friend the cigar boat captain came up with a plan, Posada Sr. agreed.

He would go.

With each chopping wave, Havana faded farther away. For 30 minutes, he remained still, afraid the slightest movement could betray him.

He had no choice.

"He had to do that, because if he didn't do that, he would still be in Cuba," Posada Jr., said all these years later. "Probably dead."

The boat took Posada Sr. to Greece. The freedom to choose his fate eventually took him to Santurce, Puerto Rico. He met Jorge Jr.'s mother there in 1968, and she gave birth to Jorge in 1971.

Only later did Posada Jr. realize the ramifications of his father's escape.

His father had risked his life to ensure his family would eventually have a better one.

"That's one thing I'll never forget—my dad, everything he did for us, me and my sister," Posada Jr. said. "He gave up his life to put food on the table."

Now Posada Sr. puts food on the table as a scout for the Colorado Rockies, searching for the kind of talent that once drew the Phillies to him. He has passed on his love of baseball to his son, who has developed into an All-Star catcher.

Posada Jr. learned just what it took to be a big leaguer, working hard enough to eventually impress his father's friends and co-workers.

But his father's courage would serve him well when Jorge Jr. needed it for his own son, too. The boy was born with a skull condition that has demanded too many operations and tested the family's strength.

Posada Jr. knows where he gets it from. And he knows how he got to the major leagues—thanks to his father.

*** *** ***

Posada paused at his locker in the back of the Yankees' spring training clubhouse in Tampa. It was March 2004 and he was as much a Yankee as any of them now. Two lockers down, Joe Girardi, his old mentor, was finishing up an unsuccessful bid to serve as his backup. Now Posada had become a leader, mentor.

When the Yankees bowed out in their earliest playoff exit in six years in 2002—a first-round loss to Anaheim—it was a testy Posada who snapped that some of his teammates didn't seem upset enough. The next season, he would soften the message, not deny it.

He had become a passionate part of one of the Yankees' greatest eras, earning Most Valuable Player votes in 2003, but finishing behind future teammate Alex Rodriguez.

No one knew what to expect of him in 1998, the year the Yankees would go on to their greatest season. The 114-win domination of the league serves as the centerpiece of their dynasty's run, and Posada was still developing along with it.

He had only become a catcher seven years earlier when the Yankees converted him from the infield. In past training camps Girardi embraced him, eventually passing him his starting spot.

But in May 1998, there were questions about Posada's defense as he started to share time with Girardi. Questions about his ability to call a game. To keep baserunners from racing to the next base while balls rolled to the backstop.

Lots of questions. Lots of room for doubt ...

"But I never thought about things the media said about me," Posada said. "I just kept working hard. I knew what I was. I know what I am."

And he knew who his father was. He had known that since the time he opened the trunk when his dad picked him up from school.

*** *** ***

The trunk was full.

As jampacked as his dad's schedule, leaving Jorge Jr. with an idea of just how hard his father worked.

This was the new life in Puerto Rico, Jorge Sr. finally free to earn the money he needed to make for his family.

Time wasn't as available, but he found it.

"He would be with Proctor and Gamble—he would sell all their stuff; he would sell cigars; he would sell medicine; he would sell gloves," Jorge Jr. said. "His trunk ... the trunk of his car was something else. He had files for his Proctor and Gamble stuff and then he would have another box full of balls, bats, gloves. Everything. I mean, he would have everything in there."

So Jorge Sr. would pick up his son from school and take him to his *fifth* job.

The one that didn't feel like work.

Posada Sr. scouted for the majors, but that wasn't enough.

Finding the next big star was great. Helping a boy find the game was better.

"He would have a little country club—Caparra Country Club," Posada Jr. said, rolling the "R"s in Caparrrra as though he were back in Puerto Rico. "He was a baseball instructor there."

Saturday was the best day.

That's when they'd play the games.

Posada Jr. always played for his dad, the old scout teaching his son all the tools he couldn't use. But when he turned 13, the son was placed on another team. Eventually, he faced his father.

The game went down to the last inning, Jorge Jr. coming up with the bases loaded and his team down.

And for all the hard work to teach his boy how to play and love the game...

The kid beat him with a bases-clearing double.

"Jorge," the father joked during the car ride home, "I'm not going to let you eat tonight."

Hey, that would have been fine. Who needed to eat? The boy was too excited.

"It was a big turning point for me," he said.

Well, at least a positive one.

The other came a year later when he headed to his grandparents' house on his bicycle. At that point, Posada had been split.

He was good at baseball. Good at cycling.

"Which one am I gonna do?" he wondered.

The first boy struck him with a log. Then another. Then Posada was off the bike and trying to cover himself from the attacking schoolkids.

His necklace was yanked from his neck. His bike was pulled out from under him.

Posada was left alone, the group of boys having beaten him with logs to steal his bike. As they left, his ears heard the cackles, his eyes caught sight of the blood staining the street.

Forget cycling. He would play baseball.

*** *** ***

OK, Jorge Sr. said, I'll make you a deal.

You get good grades, you can come with me.

His father was a scout for Toronto, and the 14-year-old Posada Jr. wanted this trip to Florida. He wanted to watch the big leaguers. Meet his idols.

"So I would work so hard to get good grades," he said.

He earned the first trip in '85, tagging along with his dad to Dunedin, Florida.

They started off at the minor-league camp, watching the prospects his father had signed. Then he met George Bell, took a picture with him and Lloyd Moesby and then ...

Then, he disappeared.

Jorge Sr. scoured the place.

The major league field.

Not there.

The minor league camp.

Not there.

Inside the clubhouse?

No.

The father started to fret. Where had his son gone?

Finally, Jorge Jr. appeared. He toted the broken bat he found. He had mended it with tape from another bat, the scavenger learning to make do with as little as possible. Just like his father had taught him.

"Where were you?" Jorge Sr. asked.

The boy showed his father his hands.

They were bleeding.

"You were in the cage, huh?" Posada Sr. said.

"Yeah," Jorge Jr. said. "I was hitting there for a long time."

Posada Jr. laughed at the story he remembered.

"No gloves. Never wore gloves in my life," he said at his locker in spring training 2004. "I mean, those balls were coming hard, and I'm (14) years old trying to hit those baseballs. That was fun. I mean, I got blisters and blood.

"I worked my tail off to be here, and I'm still doing it."

*** *** ***

He started off as a shortstop in high school. Then second base. Outfield. After watching his father fill his trunk with five jobs' worth of material, Jorge Jr. wasn't about to limit himself.

"I pretty much played every position," he said. "Play anywhere. I just wanted to make the team."

Every day, he would take grounders. Every day, he would hit. By the end of one year, Jorge Jr. discovered he had torn a fence apart.

It had the misfortune of standing behind the batting tee he set up.

"Everything came together, all the work, my last year of American Legion," Posada Jr. said. "And all the scouts were seeing me as a prospect instead of seeing me as Jorge Posada's son."

But his father knew this business. For all of his son's effort and, yes, talent, there were certain obstacles that wouldn't fall down as easily as that battered fence.

The boy was too slow.

"I did about 7.2 one time and my dad said, 'You've gotta break the 7,'" Posada Jr. said.

So Jorge Jr. set his course up the hill by his house. And he ran.

And ran. And ran.

One day.

Two days.

Three days.

Six out of seven days, 10 sprints a day, Jorge Jr. would chug up that hill. Finally, he tried again, his father's finger fixed upon a stopwatch.

Posada Sr. glanced at the time.

6.75.

"Go again," the father said.

"How much?" Jorge Jr. said.

"No, I couldn't get it," the father said. "Go again."

Posada grinned in the Yankees locker room, as though he seemed ready to come down the hill and check his father's watch.

"So I went again, he showed me," Posada said. "He said, 'I couldn't believe the first time was 6.75, the second time was 6.78.' He was excited."

His boy really could do it. He could make the major leagues.

*** *** ***

Posada earned his first substantial playing time in '98, a season in which he'd finish with 12 homers and 57 RBIs. He'd wait another two years before becoming the full-time starter. Then, he'd earn All-Star honors. Posada was happy to find his name in the starting lineup on May 17, 1998, to catch Wells.

The bad boy biker/pitcher who loved honoring the tradition of Babe Ruth almost as much as he did partying like him.

"This is the best part," Wells would say, pointing to a pinstriped uniform in his locker.

But this was his second year in the Bronx, having been traded from Baltimore before the 1997 season. Wells had some success, but he hadn't yet run off the string of October victories that endeared him to Yankee fans along with his, "Hey, he looks like me" beer gut.

Manager Joe Torre criticized the pitcher's conditioning, always a sore spot with the portly lefty. It was a day game after a night game and, should his autobiography be believed, Wells wasn't always in the best condition to pitch in those scenarios.

Like his fellow San Diego native and fellow graduate of Point Loma High School—Don Larsen—the Yankees' "Boomer" was infamous for being as far from perfect as you can get.

It was a beautiful day, sun shining, the Stadium crowd filled with kids ready to scream. But not necessarily for the Yankees.

It was "Beanie Baby" day, the popular giveaway of the collectible stuffed animals that helped ensure packed crowds. So if something great were to happen, there would be enough people to celebrate it.

And, after watching Wells warm up, pitching coach Mel Stottlemyre thought something could.

"How's he look?" Torre asked.

"Wow," Stottlemyre said.

Inning by inning, the fans put their Beanie Babies away, freeing their hands to clap louder and louder.

The closest the Twins came to a hit was a hard shot to second baseman Chuck Knoblauch with one out in the eighth. Knoblauch knocked it down, and made the routine throw to first.

Two down.

A pop-up to Tino Martinez later and the Yankees were three outs away.

The camera showed shots of Wells, exhaling deeply in the ninth, his pinstriped jersey opened to reveal a gray T-shirt underneath. It panned the fans, frenzied and on their feet.

With one out and a 1-2 count on Javier Valentin, Posada's glove dipped down low.

Valentin swung and missed. Posada blocked the ball and tagged him out. Two down.

Up came Pat Meares.

"How nervous is Posada?" Yankees broadcaster Ken Singleton wondered from the booth. "He's making the calls."

"Nervous as hell," Posada would admit later.

Meares swung ... Yankees radio announcer John Sterling made the call.

Swung on—he's gonna get it—Popped up to right field. O'Neill near the line. Makes the catch! David Wells! David Wells has pitched a perfect game. 27 up! 27 down! Baseball immortality for David Wells.

The rambunctious pitcher had finally earned respect and a counter to his critics. A prime opportunity to rant against those who would offer wisecracks about his weight, the perfect chance to tell everyone to stick it.

And he would do all that eventually.

"This is a dream come true for me," an emotional Wells said after the game. "Nobody can take this away from me. Ever. No matter what happens."

It was his game to cherish.

Except, before Wells told the world about his place in history he had to thank his catcher.

*** *** ***

Game of My Life
Jorge Posada Jr.

"David Wells ... he didn't seem like he was throwing hard, he didn't seem like he had anything special in the bullpen, but there was something about it ... about the way he threw strikes, he located the ball ... that got a lot of first-pitch swings, a lot of outs early. We were going along, winning. Three hours go by and we're in the seventh inning with a no-hitter and a perfect game going.

"I didn't realize what was going on. Nobody's talking to David, nobody's talking to me. I'm just paying attention to the game; I don't realize what's going on until the seventh inning. Girardi's next to me, 'What pitch was that?' and stuff, but he really wasn't talking. And I have no idea what's going on. In the sixth, I know there's no hits, but I don't think it's a perfect game, because I thought he walked somebody.

"I remember a great play by Paul O'Neill in right field. That's how it developed. Everybody was playing great behind him, and he was just lights out. He was getting better and better as the game was going along.

"Towards the seventh inning, he's not even shaking me off. I'm getting more nervous—because he's not shaking me off. So I'm like, 'If I call something here and they get a hit, it's my fault.' That's how nervous you get.

"When he came out for the ninth inning, the fans were giving him a standing ovation the whole inning. They didn't sit down. Stayed up the whole inning. I said, 'There's something going on. There's a perfect game or something.' I'm like, 'OK, I'm nervous as hell.' I'm sweating bullets.

"It's really tough. He was really hitting my spots. Especially away to righties. He had a nasty sinker. He's always had a good curve ball, but that day he was throwing it in the dirt. I remember a 1-2 pitch to Javier Valentin in the ninth inning, and I tell him to bounce it.

"(If the) ball gets away from me, perfect game goes away, and I tell him to bounce it (anyway). I mean that's how intense I'm going. 'I'm getting a strikeout. Bounce it. Go ahead, bounce it.' He bounced it. I blocked the ball, tagged the guy out.

"I was so aggressive. When games like that happen, you know what's going on, but you keep doing what you're supposed to do to get guys out. You're in a zone.

"Then Pat Meares comes up, a 1-2 fly ball to right. After the game is over, when Meares hit the ball to right field, I run. I'm running, like, after the baseball. Like pointing at it, like, 'Catch it.'

"I went all the way past first base. I mean, I've got a picture in my house, I'm running and I'm behind first base.

"And he's looking for me; you can see him looking for me, and I'm way over there. And I throw my glove up. And I just come up ...

"Looie Sojo gets there first. David Wells pushes him out of the way, grabs me. He said, 'You were *awesome*, Jorge! You were *awesome* Jorge! You did this.'

"I'm like, 'No, you did it. I didn't do nothing,' and he's telling me this. This is how excited he was. 'You did this,' he told me."

*** *** ***

Posada couldn't wait to call his dad, so he reached for the phone before he changed.

"I watched it on television," his father said.

And he was proud.

He would be proud many more times, for so many reasons.

The next year, Jorge Jr.'s son was born. The doctors told him his son had craniosynostosis—a medical condition which occurs when the bones in a baby's skull fuse together before the brain has stopped growing.

The boy was barely two when he had as many operations as he did birthdays. Posada Sr. came from Puerto Rico. Posada Jr. could barely concentrate on the field going into the surgeries.

"You get stronger, you get better as a person," Posada Jr. said. "Priorities do change. I remember going to the stadium and I wasn't there. You know I would be stretching, and I would not even be looking. I didn't hear fans. I don't remember any of the days my son was in the hospital. Any."

But he did remember one day.

"I remember the day he opened his eyes and saw me," Posada Jr. said. "I remember hitting a home run, a double. I got five RBIs. It was probably one of the happiest days in my life."

Posada developed into a perennial all-star, slugging homers from both sides of the plate and creating the kind of career his father, Jorge Posada Sr., was denied as a political prisoner in Cuba. *David Seelig/Allsport/Getty Images.*

Now little Jorge is "awesome, he's doing great," Posada Jr. said in 2004. Posada brought him to All-Star games because "It's his day, too." And to help children like his son, he started the Jorge Posada Foundation.

Posada Sr. marveled at his son's courage, his ability to concentrate on his work with all he endured as a father. The son would tell him the courage is a gift from his father, the one who worked five jobs and risked his life for the chance to do so.

And the father would tell the son he's given his old man a gift in return. The one that seemed locked away so many years ago in a Cuban prison.

"He's seen what he could have done and he's very happy that I'm doing it," Jorge Jr. said, translating as his father looked on smiling, in 2004. "... He still feels like, you know, it's him. Like I'm filling his shoes, you know? He's seeing himself in me."

CHAPTER 17

David Cone:
Déjà Vu All Over Again

July 18, 1999

vs. Montreal
Yankees 6, Expos 0

The stats:	IP	H	R	ER	BB	SO
	9	0	0	0	0	10

It all disappeared into the clubhouse mirror, the day's events blending in with his career, David Cone staring into the solitude.

Outside, the surreal Yankee Stadium carnival played on in the bottom of the eighth, Yogi and Don Larsen in the house, the whole place shaking, punch-drunk murmurs squeezed between screams ...

Could this really be happening?

"He pitches a perfect game on Yogi Berra day?" announcer Tim McCarver wondered aloud to stunned listeners. "C'mon."

Cone loved the whole damn thing, from the eerie and unending tradition to the New York fans who pushed his pulse quicker than his own demanding nature.

A few innings before, he had stood on the mound as delirious as every last fan in the place, pondering the handshake he shared with Larsen, wondering whether the old pitcher had passed on perfection.

But all of that was gone for Cone now, nothing left but the reflection in the mirror of a vacated clubhouse.

The game was all but won, the Yankees up 6-0 over a free-swinging Montreal team that had succumbed to Cone's deliciously devious slider. So,

For the second year in a row, Yankee Stadium roared in salute of perfection, David Cone's teammates carrying him off the field as they had David Wells the previous season. *Vincent Laforet/Getty Images.*

this was Cone against himself, a veteran pitcher three outs from catching the history that hissed every time he drew near.

Three times, he took no-hitters late into a game in his career. Three times he yielded hits.

And just three years before, in September 1996, Cone stunned the baseball world. An aneurysm threatened to claim not just his career, but his right arm. No one knew if he could pitch again.

Four months later, out in Oakland, Cone made the A's wonder when they'd hit.

Seven innings. No hits.

The only man to stop him then was manager Joe Torre, who chose to protect his pitcher's arm rather than his no-hitter. Torre pulled him after the seventh, strictly sticking to the prescribed pitch limit.

History had shunned Cone again.

All of those memories raced inside the pitcher's mind now as the Yankees batted in the bottom of the eighth against Montreal, Cone inside changing shirts on a sweltering day.

All of it came back.

The pitching that started with wiffle balls in the backyard with his dad to the peas he pelted by National League hitters with the Mets all the way to those moments with the Yankees when his arm tired, but his heart screamed it into submission.

He knew how many chances he'd had. How few remained.

So his 36-year-old eyes burned into the reflection, ordering the man on the other side to recognize just what awaited amid the roar.

This is your last chance. Don't let it slip away. Get it done.

*** *** ***

He loved New York.
Cone discovered this from Day 1 with the Mets, a Midwest kid suddenly feeling like he'd been adopted all those years.

He was a New Yorker.

He loved the race through the streets, people bustling into and over each other, fueling the city's frenetic pace. The city exuded energy and ego, and when you're a 25-year-old pitcher who could smoke the snot out of any batter, how could you not love that?

The people were his on that mound, the ones he first discovered at Shea in Queens and later in the Bronx. The ones working their butts off, then rushing into the stadium to blow off steam.

Other guys, they'd ignore the crowd, lock it out. Some would get swallowed whole by it, shrinking under an intensity built by thousands of fans whose daily fights for the subway, cab, cable guy, fueled the deafening bellow unleashed at night.

Cone?

He *lived* for it.

His dad, Ed, had been this kind of intensely hard worker, if not an emotional one. Handshakes were offered in lieu of hugs most of the time, but he taught his boy to work those hands raw for what he wanted. When he wasn't working graveyard at the meat-processing plant, Ed was in the backyard with David, showing him how to throw. He wanted the kid's best.

These people out at the stadium, pushing or pulling, shouting for "Coney" were like that, too—demanding, unyielding.

But it wasn't just that.

He'll admit it.

Cone loved the stage because he admired his own act.

"I think just the excitement and all the attention seemed to really agree with me," he said. "I seemed to really enjoy being part of the spotlight. Part of it was ego. A lot of it probably does have to do with background, having a blue collar, tougher background. Also, the pride factor of not wanting to let New Yorkers down. I never experienced such a passion for baseball as I did with the New York fans."

It started at Shea, a group of recent college grads from Lehigh University connecting with him immediately. Andrew Levy, Robert Michaels and Scott Saber marveled at Cone's stuff as he went 20-3 in '88.

Also, they were college grads.

They wanted attention, too.

So they hit the costume shop, picked up elongated rubber tops and became the "Coneheads," a tribute both to the Mets' new pitcher and to the old *Saturday Night Live* characters.

They created "Cone's Coner," and added another level to the New York circus.

He joined the Mets two years after their '86 World Series championship team took home the title and ticked off the rest of the league. It was an arrogant bunch of bad-asses who played and partied hard.

Cone fit right in, grateful for the presence of vets Bobby Ojeda, Keith Hernandez and Ron Darling.

"They taught me about New York," Cone said.

Then Cone learned the other side of his team, the tabloids and the city.

The Mets of his era won just one division title but plenty of back-page headlines off the field. Cone's name was in the middle of a couple of them.

He was accused of performing an indecent act in public—as public as you could get, in the Shea Stadium bullpen. He has denied doing so through the years.

Then there was the night in Philadelphia when Cone was accused of rape after a woman entered his hotel room. While he fretted the whole next day about a possible arrest, no charges were ever filed and the case was dismissed.

Philadelphia police found inconsistencies in the woman's story and said it was "unfounded," according to newspaper reports.

But while the investigation was still ongoing and the threat of an arrest hovered over him, Cone pitched in Philadelphia.

And struck out 19 batters.

So this affair with New York, steamy as it might have been, left scars. But he couldn't keep himself from craving the city.

Even after he was forced to leave.

As the Mets fell into the oblivion of an abysmal team, they traded Cone to Toronto in '92, starting his reputation as a rent-a-pitcher.

But even after helping the Blue Jays win the World Series and returning to Kansas City, Cone wasn't robotic about leaving New York.

"I never really wanted to leave," he said. "I kept an apartment in the off-season. Stayed around, did maybe 30 to 40 appearances, everything from little leagues to Bar Mitzvahs."

He returned to New York in '95 when the Yankees picked him up from Toronto, who had taken him back from Kansas City. His Mets background didn't inspire Yankee fans to claim him as their own.

But then he pitched his heart—and his arm—out in the playoffs.

He'll never forget pitch No. 143, or the 142 that came before them in the decisive Game 5 American League Division Series loss against Seattle.

He'll never forget the walk that gave the Mariners the lead and helped steal a chance for Cone and the rest of his teammates to advance.

"That was as devastating a loss as I'd been a part of," Cone said.

He would be more unnerved by the feeling that hit him on the plane ride back. He couldn't lift his arm without pain.

"That was probably the beginning of the aneurysm," he said.

The aneurysm that threatened to take his career the next year. The one Cone combated to prove just how well he fit with all those New Yorkers looking for a fight.

This is when Cone endeared himself to Yankee fans, finally earning the right to call New York home again.

He kept coming.

"It was a relative unknown as to what it was exactly," he said. "No one knew for sure after having a vein grafted if I could pitch again. All the emotion leading up to that comeback ..."

And he threw seven no-hit innings, inspiring the folks back home who watched him shut down the A's.

The next morning in Oakland, Cone's father—there to watch him pitch—pulled out a copy of the *New York Times* during breakfast.

"Not too many sports stories," Cone's father told him, "get on the front page of the *New York Times*."

A few months later, Yankee fans looked into Cone's fire-filled eyes and pleaded for him to keep them alive, down 0-2 to Atlanta in the World Series.

He escaped a jam and helped change history, spring boarding the latest Yankees' dynasty to a run of four World Series titles in five years when few thought the Yankees could win one game.

He hugged his father after, "one of the first times I can ever remember giving my dad a hug."

All of New York embraced Cone now, too.

"I kind of felt like I had found my way back home and finally found a place to hang my hat after all those years of bouncing around," Cone said. "I never quite felt so welcome, really, until that point."

The '96 champs had won the city's blue-collar crowd over with the kind of comebacks so often needed in their own lives.

The '98 team, cruising through a 114-win regular season, then dominating the postseason, appealed to the city's upper-class arrogance.

And right in the middle of it was Coney, the perfect poster child for a city with a split-personality. He had the everyman's work ethic, feeding off their fire. He had a desire greater than so many of them could understand, their cheers driving him, but his unyielding pride defining him.

For all the fans he fed off and all the tradition he took in with awestruck eyes, Cone's competitiveness controlled him as much as anything.

That's why the man in the clubhouse mirror screamed at himself louder than any of the 41,820 people outside when he was three outs from perfection on July 18, 1999.

Outside, they all rooted for the kind of unbelievably absurd story ... that had become commonplace at Yankee Stadium.

In a Yankees' era full of comebacks and heartwarming stories of honoring fallen parents and cancer-stricken clubhouse mates, the crazy thing was no longer to think the improbable would happen at the Stadium.

It was to think it would not.

So, for all the disbelief passing through the stands like a hot dog down to the middle of a row, there was expectation.

This time, New York was rooting as hard as ever for Cone.

*** *** ***

The thought started when Cone threw out that seven-pitch blip of an inning in the fourth.

Could he ...

The incredulousness wouldn't end until after the game. Then it increased.

After shaking Larsen's hand and watching Yogi hand over his catcher's mitt to Joe Girardi ... with a big, old No. 8 in honor of Yogi painted on the grass ... and play halted by a 33-minute rain delay (the uniform number of ex-Yankee perfect game pitcher David Wells) ... Cone threw an 88-pitch perfect game.

"I mean, those are just things you look at and you're like, 'Where else could it happen?'" said Mike Stanton, a lefty reliever at the time. "I mean, there have been other perfect games, but to happen on a day like that. Things just happen there that enough of them have happened over the years, you almost don't want to think it's just coincidence."

Cone wasn't thinking about the possibility as he entered the game. He wasn't thinking about much other than how good it felt to pitch on a day like this.

Plus, he had won nine games in the first half, had a solid All-Star appearance and prepared to face a Montreal team full of young hackers he could easily dissect.

To top it off, it was hot and sticky, just the kind of day Cone liked pitching on.

Michael Kay didn't find the weather as appealing.

There the Yankees broadcaster was, all set to emcee the Yogi Berra day festivities and Kay couldn't get his lip to stop sweating.

Oh, it was a great day to be at the Stadium, heat or no heat. This is the kind of stuff you don't get anywhere else.

And Yogi had been gone too long, owner George Steinbrenner finally making amends after the Hall of Fame catcher held a grudge over his 1985 firing as manager.

So, Kay loved this day.

He just hoped he'd get a quick game so he could get out of the broadcast booth in a hurry after it ended.

He had Springsteen tickets.

Luigi Castillo prepared to man his ballboy post in the right-field corner. He had grown up in the Bronx and this was the second year of his dream job. The 16-year-old loved the Yankees, and now he was getting to meet all of them, from his favorite player Bernie Williams to Cone.

Coney was great. So nice, always taking the time to talk to him. Cone helped Castillo pitch, too, making him good enough to win a league championship.

This was exciting.

Yogi's family came in from all over. His kids. Grandkids. Sister.

His sons pushed him into a reconciliation with Steinbrenner because they wanted his grandkids to understand what he had meant to the Yankees.

Cone's face could have shown them when Yogi came out and the ovation started. The pitcher couldn't stop staring, his eyes seemingly taking a snapshot for his mind.

Larsen threw out the first pitch, and Cone muttered something to him as he stood next to him.

Larsen smiled, said something back, then threw out the ball to Yogi.

The crowd roared.

A perfect strike.

The Yankees piled on five runs quickly off Expos starter Javier Vazquez. Derek Jeter homered. Ricky Ledee, too.

Cone looked sharp, getting through the first three innings without a hit.

Good, Kay thought. Let's get this thing done with quick. Gotta get to the Meadowlands for the concert tonight.

So much for quick.

It started pouring.

The grounds crew stretched the tarp out, and the players went in.

About 13 minutes later, word came they would resume play in about 20.

"Squeegie," Cone called to Castillo, calling him by his nickname, "grab a glove."

"OK," Castillo said.

Then he followed the pitcher out the clubhouse door and into the long, narrow tunnel under the stadium.

Luigi's heartbeat quickened. Coney wanted him to warm him up.

He'd never done this for a pitcher before, just played catch with the outfielders.

Plus, the ceiling was low and there were pipes. What if he hit one? What if he threw Coney off?

Five throws later, Cone said, "C'mon, let's go on the field."

So they walked out the dugout, down the line, the fans screaming "Yeah, let's go, Coney!"

Yeah, Luigi thought. Let's go home.

"I was scared, making sure I throw right to him, making sure I don't hurt him," Castillo said. "I threw one messed up. He caught it."

The game resumed after a 33-minute delay, and Cone took about two to dispose of the Expos in the fourth.

The whispers started here.

In the stands, one fan started cheering a little louder.

The Coneheads had long since graduated college, moving on to adult lives. Sort of.

Levy, one of the founders, stayed in touch with his youth by starting a career in sports.

The teenager who paid tribute to Cone in goofy, fan fashion had become his business associate. Levy knew Cone's wife, Lynn, from seventh grade. They stayed in touch. He became Cone's sports marketing agent.

So now a grown man was watching his old favorite pitch, but he couldn't contain a boy's excitement. Levy had met enough of his heroes to know he shouldn't have met some of them, but this was different.

This was Coney.

You had to root for this guy.

So when the calls started rushing in for major memorabilia deals, strangers finding out Levy's cell phone ... he hung up.

Forget business.

"I'm definitely sitting there first as a fan, and then as a guy ready to handle million-dollar memorabilia deals," Levy said. "We had gone from being the Coneheads at Shea, to sitting in the family section of the Stadium—a little more reserved, wishing there were those people around me."

By the sixth, announcer McCarver, who had called Cone's games years before with the Mets, noticed something.

"I can see it in Cone's body language," McCarver told his listeners. "He's going to be very disappointed if the Expos get a baserunner in this game."

Up in the booth, Kay no longer worried about his concert. Now he was focused on Cone, the pitcher he had to stifle cheers for.

"There was an added tension in the booth, because John (Sterling) and I really, really liked Dave personally," Kay said. "Being objective, you don't want to come across like you're rooting for him, but inside you're rooting for him. You really want him to do it."

Cone retired the first two batters in the seventh, then jumped ahead 1-2 on Rondell White. The roars he loved wouldn't stop.

Neither would Cone.

"Could this be another great memory in a ballpark full of great memories?" Kay announced over the screams. "The 1-2 to White. Swung on and missed! Heee struuuck him out ... on a breaking ball out of the strike zone ... 21 up, 21 down ... six more outs to baseball immortality!"

In the Yankees dugout, outfielder Chili Davis offered to do his part.

"Want me to go out there again?" Davis said since the Yankees had no back-up catcher available to warm Cone up.

Cone, who had lightened Wells's mood with some jokes the previous year, laughed as he pictured Davis squatting that big, old body down again.

"No, no, let Girardi do his job," he said.

Then it was back to the clubhouse, back to the mirror.

In the press box, official scorer Bill Shannon rose from his seat between innings to grab a hot dog, have a chat ... anything that would keep the game normal.

Good thing he didn't remember at the time just how similar it was to a game he scored at Shea Stadium a decade earlier.

Back then, Cone took a no-hitter late into the game. The Mets had never thrown one, and Cone was ready to claim the first and ... then a rocket was smacked back at him.

The pitcher knocked the ball down, but was unable to make the play.

Two rows of heads jerked back toward Shannon in the press box.

"Base hit," he announced amid groans.

The vets, the guys who had scored games before, like Jack Lang and Maury Allen, nodded in agreement. But the young beat writers in the box griped.

"The first one has to be clean!" they screamed.

"I never bought into situational scoring," Shannon said.

After the game, a dejected Cone confronted Shannon, trying to soften his anger with disappointment.

"You jobbed me, man," he said.

"Dave, it's nothing personal," Shannon said.

So, when it was over, Cone would know this much:

If it came down to a no-hitter instead of a perfect game, he'd have earned every last call made up top.

*** *** ***

Midway through the previous season, second baseman Chuck Knoblauch became a story.

Not the kind you like to write. Or read.

The man couldn't throw the ball to first base.

The tales pepper their way through baseball, pummeling otherwise fine careers. A mental tic develops and never leaves.

Now Knoblauch was the second baseman in a perfect game, a gaffe-filled landmine on a field where none would be tolerated.

He would say after the game he didn't think of that. Only worried about making a play.

But Cone did.

He worried—for Knoblauch.

Didn't want something like this on his conscience if things should go wrong.

There was one out in the eighth when Cone fell behind second baseman Jose Vidro. Vidro smacked the ball straight up the middle, to the right of you-know-who.

"Swings—hits a hot shot; grabbed by Knoblauch—he turns, throws ... got 'em!" John Sterling announced on the radio. "Ohhhhh, Chuck Knoblauch stole a hit from Vidro. And David Cone is four outs away ..."

That's it, Cone thought. That's the break. I'm getting this thing.

He retired the next batter and found himself three outs away, the nev-erending roars rushing him off the field.

Down the right-field line, "Squeegie" Castillo, the ballboy, tried to calm himself.

"Wow," he thought. "Coney's got a shot. Don't mess anything up here. Don't let some stray foul ball in right distract Paul O'Neill. Catch anything off the billboards."

In the stands, Levy was beside himself.

"It was so hot," Levy said, "I was nauseous from the whole thing."

In Steinbrenner's box, Larsen stared in wonder, thinking, "I know what he's going through."

And in the clubhouse, Cone paced his way to one more glaring meeting with the mirror.

He blew right by Chris Widger to start the ninth.

Three pitches. Three sliders. Three strikes.

Two outs to go.

Out in left, Ricky Ledee was as nervous as any other Yankees fielder. He waited for pinch-hitter Ryan McGuire to step up and begged for the ball to be hit anywhere but to him. The sun was messing with his sight.

So of course the ball went to left.

He had it. Then he didn't.

He lost it in the sun. Stuck his glove out.

The ball fell in.

"Oh boy!" McCarver screamed on the air. "Oh boy!"

The devouring cheers slowly shifted to silent prayers as public address announcer Bob Sheppard announced the next batter.

"Number 10, the shortstop, Orlando Cabrera, Number 10," Sheppard announced, 44 years after breathlessly calling Dale Mitchell to the plate.

One out to go.

Cone got ahead 1-2.

Then Cabrera sent a pop up into the sun toward third baseman Scott Brosius.

Sterling made the call.

Popped 'em up! He's gonna get it! ... Brosius makes the catch! Ballgame over! A perfect game! A perfect game for David Cone!"

Cone's hands reached for his head, his face turned red, exhaustion and disbelief replacing determination and focus. He collapsed on the ground, falling into a bear hug with Girardi.

The camera showed Larsen looking on, smiling. The Stadium kept shaking.

The Yankees lifted Cone on their shoulders as they had Wells the previous year.

He thrust his cap toward the crowd he loved.

"New York, New York" blared as Sterling screamed over it all.

"Yankee Stadium is the emotion capital of the world!" he said. "Boy, what a place! What a place! And what a day today!"

In the clubhouse, Cone hugged Larsen and fielded a phone call from his old buddy Wells, who was in Toronto. He took a phone call from his father.

And later, after things quieted down, official scorer Shannon made his way to the clubhouse.

"Well, this time," Shannon told the pitcher, "you didn't get me involved."

Cone's eyes widened.

"Were *you* the scorer?" he said.

Cone's stunned expression from the events of a day that reviewed his career remained locked on his face all through the night.

"It's like, even though he threw the game, it was almost like it was a dream to him," Stanton said. "The amount of stuff that David went through to get back to where he was then. With the aneurysm and all the arm problems that he had. ... To make it back with a game like that ...'"

*** *** ***

Game of My Life
David Cone

"I just remembered having a happy-go-lucky attitude before the game because it was Yogi Berra day and Don Larsen was in the house. It was just a giddy atmosphere to see Yogi in the clubhouse. I knew it'd be a good crowd.

"I was just lucky to pitch on those kind of days. I really loved those days. Old-timer's day. Anything that gave us a chance to talk to those guys.

"Just observing (Yogi), watching him float around the clubhouse. How excited Joe Torre was that day and Mel Stottlemyre. There was kind of a buzz in the air. Made me feel happy go lucky and excited at the same time.

"Care free, 'let it all hang out today.' I knew Montreal was a young, free-swinging team.

"I felt I was on top of my game. I knew I had good breaking stuff—that combination with a free-swinging young team was a good match for me. So I had a lot of confidence going into that game.

"Had a great warm up. The pregame ceremonies were tremendous. The tribute to Yogi Berra. Don Larsen shook my hand.

"I remember the first pitch, asking him if he was gonna reinact the scene from their perfect game. If he was gonna jump into Yogi's arms. "He said, 'Kid you got it wrong; he jumped in my arms.'

"It's a lot of those rare moments that you only get at Yankee Stadium.

"I never saw that as a distraction. Not at all, not at all; I thrived on it. It was an honor to be pitching that day.

"It was a hot day. I loved it. I was a warm weather pitcher and my arm started to get a little looser. I got loose very quickly. There actually was a rain delay in the fourth inning. Grabbed Luigi and warmed up.

"He looked a little shaky. (Laughs.)

"I think after the rain delay I had a real quick inning. Six-pitch inning. Got through the sixth real quick as well. Knew my pitch count had been extremely small.

"The thing that's going through my mind was, this might be the last chance I have to do something like this. After three or four times with the Mets, I had tasted it many times before. It hurts. It hurts. It's ironic because if you get close to pitching a no-hitter or a perfect game, usually if you lose it, you still win the game. But it feels like you lost the game.

"I knew at 36 years old it was my last chance to do this, so it was almost a desperate feeling not to let it slip. I was definitely thinking about it early on. There's not much you can do.

"You just sort of have a quiet determination, that you maintain this level of focus. You just do not give an inch, you do not let yourself relax. In some ways that was good for me at that point in my career, because we had already won a couple of World Series titles.

"Everyone was staying away from me. (Outfielder) Chili Davis was the only one who would actually talk to me.

"There was no back-up catcher; Chili actually had to warm me up between innings. Chili came running out there with a catcher's mask and he was saying, 'You could let it, go c'mon; I can catch, I can catch.' Just seeing him, all 260 pounds squatting like that, to see the look on Chili's face, that was enough of an icebreaker for me.

"The fans were getting louder with every pitch. Every pitch. That's the beauty of New York. One of the reasons I fell in love with New York at an early stage of my career, it wasn't just a two-strike clap for a strikeout ... every pitch, it would erupt. That's something I love to feed off. Some pitchers say they block it out; I felt it.

"Chuck Knobluach was playing second base and had some throwing problems. I got behind Jose Vidro and he hit a hard ground ball up the middle. Knoblauch wheeled around, threw a bullet to first base, right on the money. That was probably the loudest the stadium got, cheering for him.

"That (throwing problem) was something that was devastating for Chuck. When the ball was hit to him, I was, 'Oh no. I don't want this on his head, too.' I wasn't worried about myself.

"Not only did he field it without a hitch, it wasn't an easy play, too. It would have been scored a hit, without a doubt. Not only was it him not messing up a play, he made a great play.

"I talked to him afterward. He was a real quiet, introverted guy about the throwing problem. I didn't want to overplay it or say, 'Glad you didn't screw it up.' Just, 'You made a great play.'

"That was in the eighth inning and that was the break. When that play happened, I said, 'There it is, that's the break I needed.' I said, 'OK, this is my day; now I can go ahead and finish this thing.'

"It was incredible. It's hard to describe. I could almost feel my hair growing; almost like my head was on fire. The emotions, just knowing this is my last chance.

"I looked at myself in the mirror. I went into the clubhouse. I changed jerseys every inning. I had cut-off T-shirts that I would change every inning. Did the same thing in the ninth.

"'This is your last chance. Don't let it slip away. Get it done.'

"It was incredible. I was pacing around the clubhouse. Usually there are clubhouse kids, coaches running in and out. But it was just a dead city. Everybody had scattered. At that point, I appreciated it. Maybe in the seventh or the eighth, Chili could provide an icebreaker, but this was no time to fool around.

"This one's all individual. It wasn't a playoff game. It wasn't a World Series game. It wasn't even a big game. I think it feels different in terms of ...

With each pitch, David Cone realized this could be his last shot at perfection on July 18, 1999. The pitcher, then 36, had come so close to several other no-hitters he vowed not to lose this one. *Vincent Laforet/Getty Images.*

it's a little harder to breathe physically, your legs get a little heavier, whether it's nerves or anxiety, you start to feel some physical effects from the situation.

"It was completely an individual effort.

"This was just me and the guy in the mirror, looking back at each other.

"Ninth inning was a great start, three-pitch strikeout, three sliders. Threw a slider, strike one to the catcher that day, Chris Widger. Boom, boom, boom, three great sliders.

"Felipe Alou pinch hit; I think he sent up Ryan McGuire, who I had never faced before. Ran the count to 2-2, back-door slider; he hit a little humpback line drive into left to Ricky Ledee.

"Ricky said he never saw it. Ball just went into his glove. He still claims he never saw it. Saw it off the bat, ran in to get it, lost it in mid-flight. That's his story and, having looked at the replay, I believe him. It was a stab, certainly wasn't a running catch.

"And then Cabrera comes up with two outs. Pretty quick at-bat. Swinging strike. Ball. Then he pops it up to Brosius. Pretty high pop-up. I pointed up because I looked up and the sun kind of blinded me, my first instinct was to point up, in case he didn't see it, too.

"I really had no preconceived notions of how I would react. I was just living in the moment, last chance. Then when it happened I remember just being exhausted and just kind of dropping to my knees. Girardi came over and hugged me. (The team) kind of smothered me for a while. It was sort of, 'Enough of this, get up.'

"The best thing involved was that I was older; 36 years old. I knew what I was up against, what this meant. To finally acheive it was a tremendous feeling. Kind of a career-long taste. Finally catching the reward.

"I remember giving Don (Larsen) a big hug in the runway and Yogi as well. I don't remember any conversations that I had or anything specifically; just to look them in the eyes and say, 'What a day.'

"Came home with my wife, had a quick bite to eat, then went out with Tino and Knoblauch downtown and had some drinks. We were up pretty late. A couple of police officers and firemen came in and they already had the morning papers with the headlines.

"Not getting much sleep at all, getting up the next day to meet with the mayor. Mayor Giuliani had a big ceremony ... Did Regis and Kathie Lee. Just a great night. To see the morning papers come up before the sun comes up with the headlines ..."

*** *** ***

The headlines stopped for Cone in April 2003 when he brought a grim face into a press conference at Shea Stadium.

He had surfaced one last time, taking another shot as a Met. He had struggled the rest of 1999, going 2-5 after the perfect game. He had watched his talent evaporate with his age in 2000, suffering through a humiliating 4-14 season.

He had come back in 2002, winning nine games for Boston, proving his pride could trump his arm yet again.

And he even turned back the clock for his friend Levy and the rest of the Coneheads on a frigid April day at Shea.

The bunch of grown men sheepishly returned along with Cone and watched him strike out five in five innings ... against Montreal.

But that was it. Cone woke up one day and found a hip condition wouldn't let him out of bed.

It was the one thing that could silence the drive Cone could never stop before.

He couldn't move.

So he's retired.

Now he focuses on charitable work. Still keeps a place in New York. Does some broadcasting.

He'd like to look into a pitching coach job some day, but only if he's healthy enough to throw batting practice and participate. He never was a watcher.

He admits when he thinks of pitching, "I miss being good at it. I miss being able to do it well. I don't miss physically being hampered. I don't miss all the medications you have to take. All the anti-inflamatories. All the work you have to do to control the pain."

He controlled his pain as long as he could. He also made sure there were no scars of missed opportunities to heal after he retired.

He saw his last chance. He didn't let it slip away.

He got it done.

CHAPTER 18

Derek Jeter:
New York, New York

October 26, 2000, World Series Game 5

at New York Mets
Yankees 3, Mets 2

The stats: AB R H RBI HR
             4   1 1   1   1

The little boy stares intently at the television screen, concentrating.
Concentrating.
Concentrating.
"The next item up for bid on the *Price is Right*," the announcer calls from the screen, "a washer/dryer."
The boy is six years old. He doesn't know the prices.
He doesn't have a chance.

That one's fair down the right-field line! Giambi is on his way to third ...

But he's still trying to guess the prices along with his father, competing against him.
His dad could go shopping for the machines on the TV, but the boy only knows they clean and dry his perpetually dirty baseball uniform.
He can't ...
Wait. Not allowed to say that word.
Tried it a few times.
"Mom, I can't ..."

Derek Jeter didn't want to hear Mets fans gloating all over the city and making his life miserable if the Yankees lost the 2000 Subway World Series. With this homer to tie Game 5 along with a leadoff shot in Game 4, Jeter helped ensure he wouldn't have to, leading the Yankees to a Series win and earning MVP honors. *Jed Jacobson/Getty Images.*

What?" his mother would say sharply, jerking her head around. *"What?"*

... and they're gonna wave him around, the throw misses the cut-off man ...

So here he was, going at it item for item with his dad, his hero.

The man nobody could beat on the softball field, where the boy would tag along watching every move his father made.

Everyone respected him. He was the best player out there. The MVP.

A winner.

And now he was beating his son all morning long, but the kid kept playing.

He was losing. Getting mad.

"I was a little kid," Derek Jeter says, laughing, about the childhood memory. "I didn't know the prices."

But he couldn't stop.

He had to try.

Even if it looked like he didn't have a chance.

... shoveled to the plate! OUT AT THE PLATE! DEREK JETER WITH ONE OF THE MOST UNBELIEVABLE PLAYS YOU WILL SEE BY A SHORTSTOP!

*** *** ***

This could be the play. The game.

Because it was one of the best plays in baseball history—featuring the best aspects of the game.

Hustle.

Thinking.

Athleticism.

Because, when he made it, you didn't know what you were seeing until well after you saw it, after Fox broadcaster Thom Brennaman called it.

Because years later, as they think about Jeter's famous "flip" in Game 3 of the 2001 American League Division Series, his teammates' eyes still glaze over.

What was he doing there? Sure, they had practiced using Jeter as a rover, but ...

To pick up the ball ... on the fly ... midway down the *first-base line* ... and toss a perfect shovel pass behind him ... in a playoff game, with just a 1-0 lead in the seventh and all of Oakland screaming as Jeremy Giambi raced home?

You've got to be kidding.

It should be the game, because it propelled the Yankees into a series they would have lost and on to another October run they'll always remember.

Because it left the opposing manager, Art Howe, stammering, caught between admiration and annoyance.

"I didn't have any clue why he was involved in that," Howe said after the Yankees' 1-0 win that night, "but it worked out for them."

So it seems like it should be Jeter's favorite play, his favorite game.

But it's not. For the very reason he made the play—all the guy gives a damn about is winning.

"Can't be that one," he said in 2004. "We lost."

No, you won that game, he was told. Won that series.

"We lost the World Series that year," he said.

But it's known as one of the best plays ever made ...

Jeter grinned. The grin that puts him just short of cocky, the perfect shade of confident.

"Why don't you just call the book, *My Favorite Games—With These Players?*" he said.

He'd made his point.

And would do so eight years later once more. By then, Jeter was no longer the invincible captain, universally adored without a hint of controversy. Unlike when he was first interviewed for this book, he would face the fallout from his sometimes stormy relationship with Alex Rodriguez, then a bitter contract dispute that played out publicly in 2010.

He would seemingly be humbled by age, hitting just .270 in 2010 and struggling in 2011 before going on the disabled list.

Suddenly, the whispers began to mount that Jeter might just be done.

But he answered them again on the field, returning from the disabled list with a resurgence that reminded everyone of the Yankees captain's strong will.

He would provide the biggest individual highlight of his career, the man known for not just seizing, but strangling moments known to tighten other men's collars, stunning even his most loyal supporters.

Jeter would collect his 3,000th hit in grand style, going 5-for-5 and smacking the milestone out of the park for a home run against Tampa Bay ace David Price.

It would be one more classic moment to go with Jeter's passing of Lou Gehrig on the Yankees' all-time hits list, his headfirst dive into the stands against the Red Sox and his Mr. November home run.

But asked in 2012 if he wanted to change his favorite game, Jeter simply offered a slight smirk.

"Nope," he said.

He could have just been savvy, knowing changing his favorite game might mean an extended interview, which Jeter had cut down on in recent years. But it also would have meant focusing on an individual accomplishment, something the Yankees captain still was not a fan of doing.

"Nope," Jeter said again, another slight smile, when told his questioner didn't expect him to want to pick an individual honor.

Jeter won again.

Just like he did in his favorite game—the one that clinched the Subway World Series.

*** *** ***

Losing? "Can't stand it," Jeter said in spring training in 2004, spitting out the words. "It makes me sick."

He's supposed to say that. Think it.

He's an athlete. Ballplayer.

You play to win.

But there's this conviction when Jeter says it, the same even-keel coolness that marks the make-up everyone raves about every October.

Jeter is as protective of his image as any athlete in sports, keeping the usual pack of reporters at a safe distance, buried beneath a pile of cliches that grows larger than his World Series ring collection.

But this is when you get him as real as he can be, no filter, no mask.

You've seen how bad he wants to win, has to win—has to try—too many times for him to guard those feelings.

No time to worry about what he looks like, or what people think of him when the game's on the line.

So he'll go sprinting across a diamond when no one expected to see him as he did for the "flip."

Then he'll look at you like you're crazy for suggesting it was anything out of the ordinary.

"Well, we needed an out," he said.

Or he'll lock in at the plate, holding the bat high, haughty, his front arm pointing up, an arrow, the precursor to the thrust that comes with oh-so-many victorious fist-pumps. The ball will fly off his bat and over the wall as it did against Arizona in the 2001 World Series, "Mr. November" trotting around the bases, arrow of an arm shooting up in victory.

But he likes that stage because, well, you *have* to like it, bro.

Doesn't mean you're going to succeed every time, but you have to want to be there or else why are you playing?

So, most other questions raise Jeter's eyebrows, his cover-boy grin ready to fend off a reporter's query the way it would make faint all those teens proposing marriage through cardboard and magic marker-crafted banners.

"Can you speak up?" he was asked once, from the back of a pile before a postseason game.

"You have to listen harder," he said.

Tell him he was getting old as he approached 30, he'd respond with a boyish grin to counter, "old-*er*. Make sure you put the 'er in there."

This is when he gives you a glimpse of the stone-cold confidence that often leaves those around him humbled and inspired.

Which is why, when a reporter asked him about it possibly being Andy Pettitte's last start as a Yankee early in the 2003 playoffs, Jeter cut him off as sharply as his mother once interrupted him.

"It *won't* be his last start," Jeter said, confident Pettitte and the Yankees would advance amid rumors Pettitte would not be a Yankee the next season.

You're around Jeter long enough as a Yankee, and you figure you're not supposed to lose. Not allowed to lose.

He was right. It wasn't Pettitte's last start. The pitcher went on to win three games and lead the Yankees to the World Series before he left for the Houston Astros the next year.

He just doesn't get it.

No, really.

He doesn't.

Why be negative?

Makes no sense, bro.

"There's no need to.... see everyone's so negative all the time," he said. "I don't see why people look at things negatively if they haven't happened yet. Sure, when things are over, sometimes negative things happen, but I don't see why, going into it, you would think like that, because otherwise you're already defeated."

And there's your glimpse into one of baseball's biggest winners, the guy critics declare overrated in every month of the baseball year except the last.

That's when you look into Jeter's eyes and see what his manager saw from the first season, that unflinching glare so naturally confident it defies you to beat him.

"This kid, the tougher the situation, the more fire he gets in his eyes," Torre said after the 2000 World Series. "You don't teach that. It's something you have to be born with."

See, Jeter *wants* to be in the spot that has you quivering even from the comfort of your couch. The spot that forces you into a paralyzed state, save the incessant nervous tapping of your leg against the floor, your heart unable to take the tight score with your team's season on the line.

Jeter lives for that spot with a coolness you can't fully understand until you see it. And if you forget it every summer, he'll remind you every fall.

"He's amazing; he's calm in situations when other players are nervous," Jason Giambi said. "He's played in so many postseason games it's like a regular-season game to him."

He craves that spot, because he may hate losing, but he's not afraid to, and it's better to be up there in the tight spot, taking your shot than waiting for someone else.

"You have to enjoy playing in this type of microscope," he said. "Just because you enjoy it doesn't mean you're going to go out there and be successful.

"But even if I go out and make four or five errors in the game, I'm still going to tell you the same thing. Everyone is going to make mistakes, but I just enjoy being in these types of situations."

Losing may make him sick, but failure doesn't faze him. In the midst of an 0-for-32 slump early in the 2004 season, he offered the same relaxed grin and said matter-of-factly, "I know I'm going to get a hit again."

He adjusts as the year goes on, unafraid to fail. But for him, much like his demanding Boss, the season is a flat-out failure if the Yankees don't win the Series.

"We didn't win any trophy for beating the Red Sox," Jeter said, when someone asked if the epic 2003 ALCS was the Yankees' World Series.

Lots of players talk like that, say winning is all that matters. Then they gripe about where the manager bats them or how much they're making.

Jeter?

He can party like the *GQ* cover boy who owns New York—as George Steinbrenner reminded everyone in 2003. But he would do whatever it took to answer even his Boss, who made a commercial parodying his complaints about Jeter's partying with the shortstop later that year.

And for all his late-night antics and Page Six rumors of dates with supermodels, Jeter lives for the games on the field, not in the night clubs.

He certainly couldn't have looked too good in those night clubs with his perfectly pressed suit but mashed-up face in July 2004.

That's when he added one more play to his file, sprinting for a game-saving catch in a 13-inning classic against Boston, diving headfirst into the stands, emerging with the ball and a bloodied face reminiscent of Rocky.

"Total disregard for his safety," Torre said.

The next day, Alex Rodriguez, Jeter's old friend and new teammate, couldn't stop raving about the play. It had been four long years since A-Rod questioned Jeter's leadership in a magazine article, and after some initial scrutiny upon his arrival as a Yankee, the pair attempted to snuff out any controversy. Rodriguez said he apologized long ago, Jeter accepted, and A-Rod showed his respect by giving up his Gold Glove position of shortstop for Jeter as he moved to third.

A few years later, the rift would again cause a stir, with general manager Brian Cashman eventually feeling compelled to tell Jeter he needed to work on the relationship due to his role as a captain. Finally, when the Yankees claimed another World Series title in 2009 with Rodriguez leading the way, the pair was able to excel together.

But at that point, a few months into his tenure as Jeter's teammate and a day after the safety-risking play, Rodriguez couldn't stop complimenting his infield mate.

"I'm sure most players would say they'd do it," Rodriguez said of the play. "But to go out there and fight the fight and walk the walk ... I'd like to say I would do it, but until you're in that situation ...

"Watching him up close this year, I told him, 'Boy you're a lot greater player than I thought and I thought you were great.'"

Jeter was a great player who owned the city, still a kid, not yet a captain, in the fall of 2000.

Just about everything had gone his way on the baseball field, Jeter yet to learn the season usually ends in September. In his first four years, Jeter's team won the World Series three times and lost in the playoffs once.

He had been named Rookie of the Year in '96, played on the best team the game's seen in '98 and finished as a leader of the "Team of the Century" after the Yankees' sweep of Atlanta in '99.

The Yankees had won 12 straight World Series games and he was their poster child, the guy who owned New York.

Women wanted him. Men wanted to be him. And kids saw themselves in him when he offered another confident, care-free grin.

He had it all. And nothing could take it away.

Except, maybe, this.

A subway World Series.

That's when all of New York's eyes were on him, half burning into him, ready to pounce if he lost, the other half pleading with him to avoid doing just that.

Jeter, the upper East Side resident who savored his time around town, knew there was no choice but to win.

The Met fans in the street finally had a chance to jeer Jeter, the star they'd been jealous of for years.

The Yankee fans told him to treat those three little World Series rings he won in his first four years like they came from a Cracker Jack box if he lost to the Mets.

"I think that he probably had the most riding on it," Yankees announcer Michael Kay said. "Because the King of New York—the leader. If the Yankees lose to the Mets, his life is probably made a little more miserable walking around town. So I think he had a lot at stake."

A Series with the whole city watching, the ultimate Series you had to win or else listen to everyone tell you about how you lost?

Perfect.

"I mean, this was the Subway Series," Jeter said. "The biggest stage you could have in New York sports is Yankees and Mets in the World Series."

Of course, Jeter's favorite game comes from the biggest stage, when he stood atop it as the World Series MVP.

Because it ended the only way a successful season can for him—with a World Series championship.

*** *** ***

Charles and Dorothy Jeter drew up contracts between themselves and their kids, Derek and Sharlee, demanding certain promises in exchange for rewards. Had them sign it, all but notarized it. Their kids were going to learn early just what it took to get what you want.

The Jeters pushed their kids to expand their minds because, well, you have to if you want to be happy. Lots of limitations out there if you live by them.

Especially when one parent is white and the other is African-American and you live in a small, midwestern town like Kalamazoo, Michigan. Or anywhere, for that matter.

There were going to be looks. Stares. Questions.

"With me as a kid, that's all I know, is my mom and my dad," Derek said. "It's not weird to me. I'm not raised to look at someone's color. You look at the person."

A lot of people aren't like that ...

"*Most* people aren't like that," Jeter said. "You go places and you get stares, you get looks. I think as a youngster you don't realize it because you're always looking at it like, 'What are they looking like that for?' That's how it's supposed to be. But you always have ignorant people, though.

"Being very young, I mean, you get looks everywhere you went. You're darker than your mom, you're lighter than your dad. People don't know what nationality you are. You just surround yourself with good people. I mean, I had good friends from all different races. I played baseball where it was primarily white and then basketball was primarily black. So I had friends of all different races. You pretty much learn to deal with it."

Stares he could deal with.

Doubts?

No time for that, man.

Couldn't take it.

He knew he'd play shortstop for the Yankees when he was a kid. He'd go over to his grandmother's house in New Jersey all those summers, flip on the TV and watch the games. He'd see Willie Randolph turn double plays at second. Watch Dave Winfield use all of his six-foot-six frame to rob home runs or go loping around the bases and he fell in love.

The Yankees were the best. He wanted to play for them one day.

So they'd ask him in school what he wanted to be and he'd tell them "shortstop for the New York Yankees." The teachers would fret, telling another daydreaming kids' parents to monitor his goals.

No need.

The Jeters knew what their son wanted to do.

Go do it, they told him.

"People were like, 'Oh, no one from Kalamazoo's gonna make it," Jeter said. "'Kalamazoo, Michigan, it's a real small town, got all these great players from around the country. You'll never make it.'"

The Yankees drafted him sixth overall in 1992.

He was in pinstripes by '95. Rookie of the Year in '96.

Can't?

What?

*** *** ***

"I've gotta get you later, man," Jeter said to a reporter, darting into a side room amid the Yankees' clubhouse celebration in 1998.

The Yankees had beaten Cleveland and were on their way back to the World Series, this time with 114 regular-season wins, more than anyone had seen in the regular season. Jeter had been howling along with everyone else in a room containing enough champagne for your past 10 New Year's Eve parties.

But Straw was on the phone.

He'd been battling cancer.

Jeter had to talk to him.

He'd watched Darryl Strawberry as a boy. Rooted for him, too, because when you're that young you don't know Yankee fans are supposed to hate the Mets and vice versa.

He loved Darryl and Doc, the two young players who made the Mets big enough to steal some of the Yankees' spotlight for a while.

So when Strawberry arrived in the Yankees' clubhouse years later, ravaged by the hard-living lifestyle he led as the hot, young star in New York, the players bonded.

Jeter was the city's young star now and all through his first few seasons, Strawberry counseled him, told him not to end up like him.

Now Strawberry was battling cancer, undergoing chemo, and Jeter rushed to get to the phone, another human-interest inspiration for a Yankees' dynasty that seemed as powered by compassion as it did championships.

"I promised I'd spray his locker," first baseman Tino Martinez said a few minutes before the phone call, spritzing Strawberry's plastic-covered locker.

When Jeter reemmerged from the room, shared his joy over a return to the Series with Straw, he offered a rare open moment to a pair of reporters.

"I love him, man," he said. "That's the bottom line."

Not that he needed much help after his parents' influence, but Jeter appreciated Strawberry making the effort to help a young player learn from his mistakes.

"Straw's like a big brother," Jeter said then. "[He told me] what to expect in New York. He came up like I did. He took me under his wing."

The thing is, it didn't seem like Jeter needed a wing to nestle under.

Torre learned how little guidance Jeter required in the kid's rookie season.

Torre remembers that glaring mental error Jeter made to help cost the Yankees a game in '96. Remembers muttering to bench coach Don Zimmer how he would have to talk to him the next day.

Then he remembers looking up to see Jeter approaching, sitting down and squeezing in between Zimmer and Torre.

"He knew he messed up," Torre said. "I hit him in the back of the head and told him to get out of here."

Then came the game down the stretch when Jeter made a physical error. Torre was worried his rookie might have dented his confidence.

"Rest up," Torre remembers Jeter telling him. "Tomorrow's the most important game of the year."

"I didn't have any questions after that," Torre said.

*** *** ***

"Winning isn't easy, man," Jeter said over and over in '98 and '99. "We made it look easy, but it isn't easy."

In 2000, it looked every bit as hard as it was for them to do.

By the end of the season, they no longer seemed as invincible as they had the previous seasons. Not when they limped to a 3-15 record down the stretch and finished with a paltry 87-win record.

And certainly not when they followed that up with a loss in the first game of the ALDS to Oakland. It was a huge psychological blow that ...

"Who cares if you won 10 in a row or lost 10 in a row?" Jeter said in a pre-Game 2 press conference. "When you start the postseason, it's 0-0. Oakland could care less if we were struggling at the end of the year. If you're a hot team, you have to go out and try to perform well in a short series."

So the Yankees did. They went five games with the A's and flew back to Oakland for the final one.

Warming up on the field before the game, Jeter and some other veterans suddenly snapped their heads to attention.

On the scoreboard, Oakland third baseman Eric Chavez was talking about it being someone else's time to win after all those years of Yankees' domination.

Except Jeter and the Yankees didn't know about anyone else's time. They only knew how to extend their own.

The Yankees scored six runs in the first. Held on for a 7-5 win.

On to the League Championship Series.

*** *** ***

Never had the Yankees and Mets both been in this position.
Well, there was that taste the previous year, when the Mets reached the National League Championship Series. But then the Braves beat up on them and, despite a late comeback, the Mets were done.

New York had dreamt of a Subway Series since the last one in 1956, punctuated by Don Larsen's perfect game.

Actually, New Yorkers didn't dream of one back then because they'd wake up to a new one each year.

But the Dodgers left town. Then the Giants did, too. All of a sudden, the annual bonus was gone, and New York baseball fans were left short of what they had become accustomed to receiving.

Wasn't ever much chance for the Mets and Yankees to meet.

The Mets were the Yankees' kid brother. He could throw all the punches he wants, he's still not going to land any with a long arm holding him back by grabbing his head.

Finally, the kid brother escaped the clutches in the mid-80s, the Mets suddenly stealing the town's spotlight. It was the first gleam of a thought of a Subway World Series, with Strawberry and Dwight Gooden leading the way in Queens, and Winfield and Don Mattingly giving fans in the Bronx hope.

But as the Mets grew, the Yankees shrank, a few pitchers short of a chance at a championship. By the time the Yankees were ready to rumble again, the Mets were back behind their long arm, swatting at air.

That's how it was in '97 when interleague play first started and the Yankees began a run of season series won that didn't end until 2004.

But the Mets weren't worried about any of that in 2000.

They were on a run of their own.

With Mike Piazza cracking home runs louder than a chiropractor does a back; with Al Leiter looking like the ace Yankee fans lamented trading away at a young age; with "the boy from New York City," Johnny Franco, sprinting from the bullpen, his dad's old sanitation shirt under his uniform, as he set up another game, the Mets were starting to share the city.

Now it was all converging, the subway cars starting to rumble from way back in July when the Yankees' Roger Clemens beaned Piazza after he couldn't beat him.

Piazza had owned Clemens, and when the Rocket sent a fastball to his head, the Mets had blood in their eyes after watching their catcher go down in a shot.

"I used to have a lot of respect for him as a pitcher, but I can't say that any more," Piazza said after the incident.

But you had to respect what both teams were doing.

While the Yankees held on to win their division, the Mets claimed the wild card.

The buzz started as a whisper, the city's fans starting to wonder ... could they really both get there this year?

While the Yankees battled Oakland, the Mets were across the bay, playing San Francisco.

And while the Yankees played their decisive Game 5, the Mets were back at Shea for Game 4 watching Bobby Jones pitch the gem of his life.

A one-hitter.

The Mets would move on to the NLCS against the Cardinals. They were for real.

So were the Yankees.

Even if their hitters didn't seem like it at first.

Mariners ace Freddy Garcia shut them out in Game 1.

And the Yankees' bats looked anemic for most of Game 2, the Stadium crowd growing more silent with each inning, wondering if they had finally run out of cheers for their aging champions.

Paul O'Neill couldn't get a hit. Tino Martinez either. Or Jeter. Anyone.

John Halama had the Yankees off balance and, seemingly, out of the series for six innings of Game 2. Another inning of scoreless relief from Jose Paniagua and the Yankees' scoreless streak ran to 21 innings, counting the last five of their Game 5 win over Oakland.

They were six outs from going down 0-2 in the seven-game series and blowing their home-field advantage.

It was over. Everyone in the Stadium started to feel it.

Except, of course, the Yankees.

Arthur Rhodes came in for Seattle and the Yankees' collective slump went out.

David Justice started it with a double. Bernie Williams singled. Baby steps.

Tino Martinez singled. And Jorge Posada. And Luis Sojo.

Then, to cap it, with the eighth hit of the inning, Jeter provided the sixth and seven runs.

He homered.

Yankees 7, Mariners 1.

Yankee Stadium was back to its usual October sound of screaming with arrogance and anticipation all at once, just waiting for the scoreboard crew to cue up Sinatra.

They were back.

By the time they returned from the three games in Seattle, the Yankees were one win from another World Series.

Still not good enough.

The Mets were already in.

They had beaten the Cardinals, four games to one, the scrappy Mets featuring speedy rookie Timo Perez.

Perez sprinted around the bases and made life miserable for St. Louis, then finished the Cards off by putting the last out away in center, hopping up and down while he waited for the ball to reach his glove.

The fans at Shea, waiting 14 years for a return trip to the Series, shook the building.

Franco, the pitcher who grew up on Staten Island and went to his first World Series with his father in '69, was carried off the field. His dad was gone now, but he still wore that T-shirt and he couldn't believe he was getting to the Series as a Met.

Now it was up to the Yankees.

"The pressure was on us because the Mets already clinched," Jeter said.

*** *** ***

The blow came in the seventh, the Yankees down 4-3.

Jose Vizcaino singled. So did Jeter.

Up came David Justice, the slugger the Yankees acquired during the season.

In the general manager's box, Brian Cashman was munching on an ice cream bar, the GM looking like a kid, outthinking most men. There had been talk of getting Chicago Cubs home run king Sammy Sosa, but the Yankees were worried about chemistry. Justice, they decided, was the better deal.

And he had been.

And he would be.

The 3-1 ... Swung on and drilled deep to right field ... there it goes! See ya! Into the upper deck! David Justice with a three-run home run and the Yankees have come all the way back!

The fans were at their delirious best, the usual cacophony of cheering and clapping and laughing roaring over announcer Michael Kay's call.

But now there was one more element added, the one that prompted a primordial scream of satisfaction and sadism.

The one they were thinking of along with Kay even if they couldn't hear him from the stands.

"Get your tokens ready!" he screamed. "You might be boarding the subway!"

And, as they saluted Justice, a chant began. A raw, raucous chant, built by the bullying nature of the latest Yankees' dynasty as much as it was formed by 38 years worth of contempt for their baby brother in the other borough.

"WE WANT METS! WE WANT METS!" the Yankee fans screamed, all but foaming at the mouth.

Inside the Yankees' giddy clubhouse, the energy level finally matched that of the rest of the expectant city. Frank Torre, who gave his brother tickets to the last subway series, when 16-year-old Joe saw Don Larsen pitch a perfect game, congratulated him on yet another World Series appearance.

Comedian Billy Crystal, often a clubhouse regular during the postseason, thought back to the memories of the Dodgers' Jackie and Duke battling Mickey and Yogi, of the intra-city battles that used to be annual occurrences.

"There's a lot of folklore," he said, remembering when kids would argue over who was better.

Then he thought of fellow comedian Jerry Seinfeld, a noted Mets fan.

"I'd like to smack Seinfeld a couple times in this series," Crystal said.

*** *** ***

"Ya gotta believe!" the Mets fans screamed outside Yankee Stadium before Game 1.

"Ya gotta believe you guys suck!" Milton Ousland and Donald Simpson screamed in perfect harmony.

Then they walked away cackling, content to fill their roles as Bleacher Creatures.

They're the most arrogant, passionate, creative fans in baseball, the ones who reside in a chanting, cursing fog, in Section 39 of Yankee Stadium—right-center bleachers.

Now their very existence was threatened.

How could they respect themselves if they lost to the "Mutts"?

"I'm sick," said Tina Lewis, Queen of the Bleacher Creatures. "I had nightmares last night."

About?

"The Mets," she said. "I dreamt about the victory lap and all that."

If the Yankees were to—gasp!—lose, "We would have to move the Stadium to another city," Simpson said. "The Mets' fans don't care. I tried to reason with my brother. They're unreasonable."

So unreasonable that Simpson was awakened daily by his brother's 6:30 a.m. phone calls bragging about Mets' wins in the playoffs. Finally, Simpson offered his brother a choice.

"We're gonna have to stomp you," he said. "Either that or—I work for the phone company; I'll cut off his phone."

Not that all Yankee fans were in such a mess over the prospect of losing to the Mets.

"We don't believe," one banner read. "We know."

*** *** ***

Andy Pettitte dueled Leiter for five scoreless innings in Game 1, neither pitcher budging.

In the top of the sixth, the Mets' speedster, Perez, was on first with two outs when Todd Zeile smacked a long drive to left field.

Gone. Mets 2, Yankees 0.

Except it wasn't gone. Perez just thought it was. Trotted like it was.

The ball hit off the top of the wall and bounced back. As left fielder Justice gave chase, Perez jogged toward second, looked up, then hit another gear.

Justice's relay throw was off as Perez rounded third. No matter.

Jeter was the cut-off man. He raced to his right to snare the ball, throwing over his body, on the run, to home.

Perfect. Perez was out. The Mets were stunned.

"When Timo kind of broke down running there, I figured it was a home run," Mets manager Bobby Valentine said. "He did, too. It wasn't. It's a game of inches, huh?"

And pitches. Plenty of them. Ten in one key at-bat, to be exact.

The Mets still managed a 3-2 lead in the bottom of the ninth.

Armando Benitez had struggled closing out the Yankees with both the Mets and his former team, the Orioles. But he was ready to now. He might have, too, if Paul O'Neill didn't outlast him, working a 1-2 count into a walk with several foul balls.

A sacrifice fly by Chuck Knoblauch tied the game, and it would stay that way until the 12th. The fans from both teams, the ones who had waited 44 years for another Subway Series, would have to endure the longest game in World Series history.

But it would contain the usual ending.

With runners on second and third, up came Jose Vizcaino, who Torre had started on a hunch because he hit Leiter well.

He didn't do too bad, against Turk Wendell, either, singling to left for his fourth hit, the game-winner.

He pumped his arms wildly, hopping up and down around first. Jeter leapt over the dugout railing, his trademark fist-pump in place.

"New York, New York" played, but only half of the city sang along.

"I'll tell you one thing," Franco whispered in a quiet Mets' clubhouse. "Anyone who thinks this thing is over is kidding themselves."

In another corner, Mets longtime public relations man Jay Horowitz approached Wendell. He slapped him on the back.

"So," Horowitz said softly, "you #)@$* up."

*** *** ***

"Why would he throw it? He was angry? He was angry so he threw the bat?"

This was as angry as Torre had been in public as Yankees manager, tossing back questions at reporters as violently as his pitcher, Roger Clemens, had thrown a shattered bat toward Mike Piazza in Game 2.

Torre was so angry he left the press conference early before calming down and returning.

It had been the confrontation everyone anticipated and the moment when Piazza stepped in against Clemens added an even bigger buzz to all the Subway Series hype.

"I saw on ESPN today Piazza got hit 36 times in 36 seconds," Torre said before the game, sarcastically referring to all the replays of Clemens's July 8 beaning.

But no one could have anticipated this.

A foul ball. A broken bat.

Clemens whizzing it past Piazza on his way to first.

"What's your problem?" Piazza said, walking toward Clemens.

"I thought it was the ball," Clemens said, a response as irrational as flinging the bat.

The Yankees won 6-5. Clemens dominated the Mets, who rallied for five runs in the ninth to remind the Yankees they were ready to give them as big a test as anyone had in the postseason.

Clemens was fined $50,000 for throwing the bat. The Mets called for his head, some of Piazza's teammates foolishly claiming their catcher had been less than manly for failing to charge the mound.

"It's the bleeping World Series," Piazza wrote in a diary column in the *New York Post*, pointing out he couldn't afford to get thrown out or suspended.

Either way, two games in, the Yankees owned the stage as usual.

Then they didn't.

In Game 3, the first World Series game at Shea since '86, the Mets cut into several layers of Yankees invincibility.

Orlando Hernandez had eight wins and zero losses in the postseason.

He lost.

The Yankees had won 14 straight World Series games.

They lost.

Benny Agbayani's late double gave the Mets a 3-2 lead. They'd go on to a 4-2 win.

All over the stadium, you could hear Mets fans starting to believe again, roaring at game's end, whispering on their way out.

They were alive.

"I can clearly remember being with the other teams that play the Yankees, there was a feeling of invincibility the Yankees portrayed that other teams tended to buy into," Zeile, then the Mets first baseman, said. "When we lost, 'We gave it a good shot' but it was expected. But with the Mets ... there was something about that club that gave us the feeling 'I'm gonna find a way to win.'"

They had knocked the Yankees down.

Now they just had to keep it up.

"We've *GOT* to win all three games at Shea if we're gonna win this thing," WFAN overnight radio host and big-time Mets fan Joe Beningo told his audience, trying to temper his glee. "We've got to win all three games."

*** *** ***

"First pitch, 8:31," Yankees announcer John Sterling said, starting off the Game 4 broadcast. "... And Jeter swings ... it's a high drive to left. It is high ... it is far ... it is gone! First-ball fastball! Deep into the bleachers in left field ... and on the first pitch of the game, the Yankees take a 1-0 lead!"

*** *** ***

Just like that, Jeter answered.

Just like that, the Yankees reminded the Mets why they had won 14 straight World Series games before finally losing one.

"They had felt pretty good about themselves because they had won that Game 3," Jeter said. "And that's, what, the first World Series game we had lost ... we won like 12, 13, 14 games in a row, something like that, in the World series. So they had beat us and that was huge.

"I was leading off; always aggressive. He throws the first pitch; why not try? I'm always aggressive. I was looking for a pitch to hit. He threw me a pitch, middle in. Got it. You wanna score first. When you score first, you

obviously give your pitchers a comfort level to start, and I think that probably set the tone."

Jeter reset it in his next at-bat, leading off the third with a triple to center. With the Yankees already up 2-0, Luis Sojo's grounder drove Jeter in and
the Yankees were up by three.

Until the Mets' star answered.

In the late '90s and early 21st century, Jeter and Piazza shared the city's
spotlight. Both were young, attractive future Hall of Famers, each known to
sample a different aspect of the city's nightlife.

Both were rumored to date models and stars, Jeter linked once with
Mariah Carey, Piazza palling around with Playboy playmates.

So it made sense in their showdown they'd each take a shot at the other.

In the bottom of the inning, Piazza struck back, the ball screaming off
his bat with baseball's loudest crack for a two-run homer.

The Mets wouldn't let the Yankees go that easily.

But that's where it ended. The bullpens took over from there, and the
Yankees held on.

They were up three games to one.

"That was a huge game for us, because, obviously, you don't want them
to be in the Series," Jeter said.

But now Game 5 was the Mets' last chance to be in the Series, shrinking
opportunity that it might be. They had their ace, Leiter, on the mound, the
former Yankee, the Jersey kid who grew up dreaming of pitching for the Mets.

"You don't have to worry about pitch counts," Valentine remembered
Leiter telling him before Game 5. "I could throw 150 pitches. I'm going to
give everything I have, and I'm going to be the guy to get the victory tomorrow."

*** *** ***

Bernie Williams hurt Leiter with a homer in the second, but other than
that, Leiter was about to singlehandedly keep the Mets alive.

The Mets knew Andy Pettitte would be just as tough considering his
postseason pedigree. Knew runs would be hard to come by.

Which is why, when they had two on with two outs and the notorious-
ly poor-hitting Leiter up, he improvised.

He laid down a perfect drag bunt, chugging to first like a middle-aged
man afraid to miss his bus to work.

Safe. The Mets tied the game.

Then Agbayani sent a roller to third baseman Scott Brosius, who mis-
played it and the Mets led, 2-1. That was it. Leiter was giving everything. He
was going to get the victory. He retired the next 14 of 16 batters he faced.

There was one out and no one on in the sixth when Jeter stepped up.
Jeter looked cutter. Leiter hung a changeup. Jeter swung. The ball shot out to
left.

"Derek Jeter's gone deep again!" Fox announcer Joe Buck called. That's
when, Jeter said, he knew they'd win.

It happened in the ninth. Leiter had cruised past the first two hitters, the game tied at 2-2. But Jorge Posada, showing the paitence that marked the Yankees' era, drew a walk on a nine-pitch at-bat.

Brosius singled to left.

Leiter's pitch count was up to 141. Valentine didn't make a move. It was Leiter's game to lose. And he'd lose it on the next pitch.

Sojo—the Yankees' modern-day Brian Doyle along with Vizcaino—bounced a single up the middle. The play at the plate was going to be close. The throw from centerfielder Jay Payton was on line. But Posada got there first. The ball bounced off of him and away from the plate, Brosius racing in for a 4-2 lead. Jeter hopped the dugout rail again and pumped his fist, the sight Yankee fans love and opponents loathe.

And when Mariano Rivera limited Piazza to a long fly ball with one on and two outs in the bottom of the ninth, the Yankees had their third straight championship.

The Mets had their usual inferiority complex, and suffered the greater indignity of watching the damn Yankees celebrate on their field, lifting a teary-eyed Torre on their shoulders.

Jeter had a World Series MVP trophy to go with the one he'd earned at the All-Star Game. He also had something else, the thing that made his victory even sweeter. Respect for the team he had just helped beat.

"This, by far, was the best team we played in the five years I've been here," Jeter said after the game. "All five games could have gone either way."

But they didn't.

Jeter's status as king of the city, along with his Yankees' championship defense, was safe again.

*** *** ***

Game of My Life
Derek Jeter

"It started building up the year before, when we made it and the Mets lost to the Braves. That's when it started, and then the following year, the Mets made it; they clinched before we did. And that's all you heard about in New York, everywhere you went—the Subway Series. Yankees fans saying, 'You have to win, you have to win, you have to win.' Mets fans telling you how bad you are. That was a pretty big series in terms of, I would have had to move out of the city if we lost to the Mets.

"(Getting to the Subway Series) was huge. There was a lot of pressure on us. We played Seattle and Seattle was tough. Going into Game 5 against Seattle, we had to win otherwise we had to travel back to Seattle for Games 6 and 7. And the Mets had already won, so it put pressure on us to go ahead and get it over with. Then you get so excited you beat Seattle, the next thing you know, you've got to get your mind right because that means absolutely nothing unless you beat the Mets.

"It was nuts. Everyone was talking about it. Everywhere you went. Every person you ran into, everywhere you went. Walking down the street, driving down the street.

"[In Game 5] we had a chance to finish it. You know, we didn't want to have the next day off, go back home, play Game 6, possibly Game 7. We've always been good, when we have the other team down, step on them. We didn't want to give them any hope.

"It was close. Leiter was pretty much cruising. I mean, Bernie got him for the home run early on, but other than that we didn't have him in too much trouble. They scored first; they were up 2-1. That's when I hit the home run to tie it.

"Leiter was always throwing cutter, cutter, cutter, cutter. And in that particular situation he threw back-to-back changeups. And I don't look off-speed. I hit the ball the other way, pretty much most of the time, so I was looking for a fastball, and he just hung a changeup and I hit it pretty good.

"And once we tied 'em, I thought we pretty much had 'em after that. It seemed that was their chance. They were rolling, cruising along, and Leiter really couldn't pitch any better than he was.

"Looie's hit was huge. He got that hit, Jorge scored. In our minds, 'Bring in Mo. It's over.' Doesn't always happen, but that's our mindset.

"I had just told Mo before Piazza came out, I went to the mound and I said, 'Well, you know what he's trying to do, so don't just groove it in there.' And then when he hit that ball, I thought for a minute it was gone. But it's pretty deep out there. I mean, you look at Bernie, I knew we had won."

*** *** ***

"You fans should really enjoy watching this team," Jeter told the crowd at the Yankees' celebratory parade, "because you're not going to see many like it."

He was right. The three-time defending champs (and four out of five)— who survived extra rounds of playoffs and won as both the underdog and the juggernaut—were the greatest team baseball's seen. It was an aging team full of questions on who would return the next year in 2001.

O'Neill, slumping and slow by the end of the year, grabbed Torre in the on-field celebration at Shea and said, "Don't you ever pinch hit for me again."

In 2001, Tino Martinez would hear season-long rumors about being replaced by Jason Giambi earning one more forever cheer before it did happen the next year.

Piece by piece, the Yankees dynasty was disassembled, recreated to make more playoff runs.

There's a few constants left, but none with the presence of Jeter.

There's elegance one minute, when his pinstriped No. 2 centers a ballplayer's body perfectly skinny and strong, each step statelier than the next, and you picture Jeter in black and white, a classic snapshot of DiMaggio or the Mick.

There's energy the next moment, when you see him darting out of the clubhouse in designer sweats, ready for mischief, but not quite as quickly as he'll dive into the stands to emerge bloody, but holding onto the ball.

All these years later, Jeter's still that kid on the couch competing with his dad, proving he can be as stubborn as his parents taught him to be.

All these years later, if you ask him if he says the word "can't," you'll see a glimpse of his mother's sharpness as he snaps:

"Still don't."

"Mr. November" rounds the bases after his home run beat Arizona shortly after midnight on November 1, 2001 in Game 4 of the World Series. If Reggie Jackson didn't already own the October tag, Jeter—the postseason leader in hits—might with a myriad of clutch plays, including his famous "flip" against Oakland. *Jed Jacobson/Getty Images.*

CHAPTER 19

Paul O'Neill:
Good-bye, Paulie

November 1, 2001, World Series Game 5

vs. Arizona
Yankees 3, Diamondbacks 2

The stats:	AB	R	H	RBI	BB
	3	0	0	0	2

PAULLL ... Ohhhh ... NEILLLL
PAULLL ... Ohhhh ... NEILLLL
PAULLL ... Ohhhh ... NEILLLL

The whole place was chanting it now, belting out a good-bye at a time when the city wanted desperately to hang on to the things it had always known.

About 8 miles away, at Ground Zero, the smoke and debris and the indescribable smell created a living hell.

But this was the euphoric escape from it in Yankee Stadium, where 50,000 people could try to pretend their world hadn't changed. The Yankees were in another World Series game and, for a few hours, the fans who packed the Stadium lived life as normally as they could in October.

They watched the Yankees in the playoffs.

Except this wasn't October, it was November, the September 11 terrorist attacks bumping Major League Baseball into a new month.

And the Yankees had provided the only miracle the city would see, a baseball one, rallying in the ninth the night before in Game 4 of the World Series.

For once, Paul O'Neill grimaced on a baseball field for something other than a bad at-bat. As he absorbed the thunderous
chants of his name in his last game at Yankee Stadium—all
while the Yankees trailed a World Series game—the Yankees'
"warrior" barely avoided crying. *Jed Jacobson/Getty Images.*

But here the Yankees were, again trailing by two in the ninth to Arizona and, for all their claims of "Mystique and Aura appearing nightly" as one banner read, no one was ready to believe the Yankees could do it again.

So along with absorbing a loss that would put the Yankees one from elimination, the fans had to salute the player they called a "warrior."

They all did now, from the real-life warriors, the cops and firemen, to the Bleacher Creatures directly above O'Neill in right field.

They had first chanted his name as part of that ritualistic "roll call" started in '98, a marriage of fans and team designed to celebrate glory days.

The most passionate fans in sports would chant a greeting to everyone from "DER-EK JET-ER" to "PAUL-*IE!*" and refuse to stop until they were acknowledged with a wave of the glove.

The chants had taken them through their favorite times, the fans and team growing together, enjoying the frivolity of summer, enduring the fall crispness because it meant the cusp of another parade to celebrate a championship.

But now the fans were screaming to avoid crying, so grateful for the time away from reality. Not all the fans could escape so easily.

Donald Simpson, the Bleacher Creature who had gleefully taunted Mets fans outside the Stadium a year before, was in Tennessee, his girlfriend thinking he needed to get away from New York after fleeing the Twin Towers.

It was a mistake. He was miserable. He would have felt safe, comforted, among his friends in the bleachers nearly two months after escaping Tower 2.

"Nothing matters; winning, losing," he had said, bordering on tears after Game 2 of the division series against Oakland. "But every little bit helps."

For some, such as Kathleen Santora—who mourned her firefighter brother Chris Santora's death and could care less about the World Series— baseball couldn't help even for a few hours.

But the fans it did help held up a gigantic flag during the seventh-inning stretch. Hiding beneath all the reverence of Ronan Tynan's regal rendition of "God Bless America"—and under the giant star-spangled banner unfurled in the bleachers—was New York's real resilience.

"Hey, Palumbo!" one fan yelled to another. "Hold the flag up with your nose. I always knew that big shnozz would be good for something."

"Hey, hold the flag straight!"

"Hey, sing 'God Bless America' right!"

"Can we sit down yet?!"

And after all that, Debbie Meshejian, a nurse volunteering at Ground Zero, would take the train all the way downtown. There she'd talk about the game with the rescue workers in the respite room.

Then it was back into the reality.

"It's like you get away for a few minutes," a cop who listened to games in his car before returning to the debris said, "then you remember you're in a war zone."

So they'd do anything to avoid returning to that, anything to remember for a few hours that the Yankees could make them feel invincible whenever they stepped inside the Stadium the last few years.

And no one made them feel as tough as O'Neill, the helmet-flinging, bat-tossing hardass who wouldn't stop pumping those old arms and elbows around the bases if he thought there was an extra one to take.

He was theirs for one more inning at least and, loss or no loss, they weren't going to let him go without a proper good-bye.

"PAULLL Ohhhh NEILLLL

"PAULLL Ohhhh NEILLLL

"PAULLL Ohhhh NEILLL"

And after the jubilation ... after Scott Brosius shocked the crowd, his arm shooting up as soon as the ball shot out to left ... his game-tying, two-out, two-run homer coming 24 hours after one by Tino Martinez ... after all the fans leapt up and down, up and down, up and down, just like the pair of delirious cops in right, hugging, hopping, SCREAMING in gleeful disbelief—"THEY DID IT AGAIN! THEY DID IT AGAIN!" ... after all that ...

O'Neill raced back out to right, his eyes no longer swollen from fighting tears, his grimace now its usual game face rather than a response to the fan's salute.

"PAUL-IE!" the fans chanted, grateful for extra innings, another chance to win a game, another glimpse of their guy. "PAUL-IE!"

Later, the Yankees pulled off the unbelievable for the second straight night. And after they won their second straight miracle game—with the tattered American flag from Ground Zero flapping atop the Stadium under a full moon—to send themselves soaring toward Arizona and what seemed a sure championship, O'Neill stood in front of his locker.

His pinstriped uniform was as dirty as could be, just the way it should be. The circle of reporters surrounded him as they had through three straight World Series championships, one of which came right after the death of his father. It was his dad who told O'Neill his midwest background wouldn't matter, that playing in New York would be the best thing for him so many years before when he had been traded from Cincinnati. Eventually, O'Neill realized just how right his father was as he became a core component of the Yankees' greatest dynasty.

And, as he stood at his Yankee Stadium locker in pinstripes for the last time, in a scene that seemed so familiar, O'Neill had no way of knowing the Diamondbacks were about to stun the Yankees in Arizona.

No way to imagine fate would prove the Yankees were no more invincible than their city that year, Mariano Rivera shockingly giving up the Series-winning hit.

So as O'Neill slowly removed his dirt-stained pinstripes, he thanked the fans for their salute. Then he said the kind of words that made them offer one.

"To say goodbye right," he said, "is to say goodbye at a parade."

*** *** ***

"I don't care about that!" Bob Herzog remembers O'Neill yelling at him after he asked about a hitting stat one day. O'Neill threw his T-shirt to the ground, frustrated. "Don't you guys understand? I care about winning!"

Herzog, a reporter for *Newsday*, backed away and scrapped the interview.

O'Neill doesn't remember the story. Or maybe, a few years after retirement, without the game to drive him into the mode he now becomes sheepish talking about, he'd rather not.

"The wheels got turning too quick when I was talking about what was on the field," O'Neill said. "It was easier to talk about how are we playing. ... The important thing is whether the Yankees win or lose."

And O'Neill drove himself incessantly to win. Derek Jeter exhibted that unending drive, but with a cool detachment from at-bat to at-bat, game to game. It was inside, bubbling toward the surface but causing no more than a ripple.

O'Neill?

He didn't allow himself a moment's forgiveness, preaching to Jeter not to give away an at-bat, a pitch, then slamming his helmet in frustration when he himself had.

The seemingly endless tantrums defined O'Neill, even if the definition was often misinterpreted.

When Joe Torre arrived as the Yankees' manager in 1996, he heard O'Neill was selfish. Soon, Torre realized, "The only way he was selfish is he wants a hit every time up."

And if he didn't get one, didn't help the ballclub, O'Neill would stretch his face in an assortment of grimaces and groans, an angry man's Jim Carrey. He would strike out or fly out and the helmet would go flying almost immediately, a howl coming from his mouth, the helmet bouncing violently off the ground and over his head.

In his final season, with the Stadium filled for the rival Red Sox, O'Neill flipped his bat in disgust after getting under a ball in the bottom of the 10th. Which would have been fine except for one small fact. He had tied the game with a home run.

"It's almost embarrassing to react that way after hitting a home run," he said after the Yankees won the game.

It was in that same game when O'Neill—knowing he'd retire after playing in pain his last couple of seasons—listened to the crowd's usual vicious banter between Yankee and Red Sox fans and realized something.

"Man," he thought, "this is gonna be weird not hearing this any more."

Now that he doesn't hear it any more, he looks back on all those bat-flinging, helmet-throwing days as the weird time.

He'll admit it.

He cringes sometimes watching the old tapes.

"There's no doubt; now, when you look back, 'What was I thinking?'" O'Neill said. "If I *was* thinking. At the time, that at-bat, that pitch, that game, that's your whole world. That's your whole life. Obviously some people deal with their emotions differently and there were times I wished I would have."

But the fans didn't. They loved him for it, because the guy *cared*. O'Neill's work day was as hard as the one they had come out to forget. The one that left the Bleacher Creatures above him in right so desperate to build a sanctuary they'd taunt anyone who brought the office with them into the Stadium.

"Lose the tie!" they'd chant at a late-coming arrival who hadn't changed after work. "Buy! Sell!" they'd taunt, making it clear this was a place where formality was out, profanity was in, and you were commanded to commit your focus to the game.

"Let's go, Yank-ees!" a set of Bleacher "virgins" once chanted while an opponent was at bat.

"Where we goin', ya morons? Cleveland's up," Bleacher vet Larry Palumbo sneered, disgusted. "It sounds stupid when you say it like that."

And when O'Neill would lose his temper the way they would over a blown deal or a misplaced memo, they'd love him all the more. Even if opponents called his act whiny, called him a crybaby. They'd learn, too, over the years to understand O'Neill.

When he was with Cincinnati, before the trade for Roberto Kelly in 1993, O'Neill had run-ins with former Yankee and then-Reds manager Lou Piniella.

While the Reds suffocated O'Neill's opposite-field hitting style by trying to force him to pull the ball, Piniella also got tired of O'Neill's ranting routine.

There was a good reason. One easily recognized by any Yankee fan who remembered how popular Sweet "Louuuuu" was from his days of throwing water coolers.

"He reminded me a lot of myself when I was a player," Piniella said during the 2001 American League Championship Series, when he was managing Seattle. "He won a world championship over there with us in Cincinnati, and he's come over here and put some marvelous years together for the Yankees and helped them win four world championships. I'm proud of him. I really am. Paul, at times, probably thinks I don't like him, but I have a tremendous amount of like for him, and also respect."

There was so much to respect.

Not just all those all-star seasons he would have in New York. Or the six straight years he hit .300 or better. Not even that .359 bauble of a batting average in the strike year of '94, when he won the short season's batting title.

Piniella could hit, too. But O'Neill had a lot more similarities than that. Like Piniella, he would suddenly be found—anywhere, any time—practicing his batting swing. And, like Piniella, in the moments when O'Neill wasn't in his intense-filled mode, all the passion turned to compassion, sensitivity.

Which is why one of the most touching portraits of the Yankees' era came in 1999, when the last out of the World Series was recorded. Tragedy refused to yield to triumph that year. And vice versa.

In spring training, the Yankees learned their manager, their leader, had cancer. It would get worse, even after Torre reappeared later in the year. Second baseman Chuck Knoblauch's father had Alzheimer's. Third baseman Scott Brosius would lose his father late in the season. Popular reserve Luis Sojo's father died during the postseason, forcing Sojo to miss a World Series game to bury his dad in Venezuela. And then, with the Yankees up three games to none and poised for their second straight World Series sweep, O'Neill got the call at 3 a.m. His father, Charles, the man everyone called "Chick," had died of heart complications at Lenox Hill Hospital in Manhattan.

"Paulie, he's been carrying a heavy heart for a while; his dad's been suffering," Torre said before Game 4, knowing Chick had been too ill to watch his son play. "There's no sitting and talking to anyone about the meaning of this whole thing. It's just something you have to accept and move on."

It's what the Yankees did better than anyone in the late '90s, overcoming everything that came their way. They had to, they'd tell you. They hated losing. And O'Neill hated it as much as any of them. Because that's how his dad taught him to be. So he'd play that night. He had no choice. His father wouldn't have accepted anything else. It had been like that since Chick, the former minor leaguer, taught his five boys to play back home in Ohio. And taught them to win.

"That was his life," O'Neill said of his father, who coached his 11- and 12-year-old little league teams. "It just made for a perfect summer for me, very competitive little league baseball team. We traveled. Played under the lights. At the time, those games were very important.

"There's nobody in my family that would lose and just walk away with it. Our family bred competitiveness."

So there was another game to win now, another World Series to claim.

You want to know why the Yankees won so much during their latest dynasty? Losing frightened the hell out of them.

Some remembered the sick feeling of '95, when Seattle's Ken Griffey Jr. ran right by them and into the next round. Others remembered '97, the last scene of O'Neill digging, digging, digging, diving for the second-base bag with the desperation of a life guard. He had put the tying run in scoring position but the Yankees fell short of defending their World Series title against Cleveland in the first round.

It hurt.

Burned.

Scarred.

So, sure the Yankees might have looked like one big party with their cover-boy shortstop and comical commercials featuring players like "El Duque" Hernandez emulating his high-leg kick pitching style on the dance floor.

"Coney," he'd say in his Cuban accent, "why don't *you* have a dance?"

But by October, the laughs were gone.

Just the thought of losing ...

"I think we wanted to win more than a lot of other teams," O'Neill said. "In the end, I felt like we should win. After we won in '96, the heartbreak of '97, I think for those next three years we were afraid to lose."

So, O'Neill walked around before Game 4 in '99, a whole different hurt leaving his eyes glassy, along with his other mourning teammates.

Maybe it would be hard to play after hearing the news of his dad's death, but it was his father who convinced him he could play even one day in New York. He didn't think he belonged here after the trade, but his father had told him it would work out. O'Neill couldn't see how then, a Columbus, Ohio, kid living the dream of playing for the home-state Reds only to watch it get interrupted. And for what?

A trip to the biggest city in the country, a world away from what O'Neill had always known? He didn't even know where the Empire State Building was, for cryin' out loud. How would he find his way around and fit in there?

But he would, right from the start with four hits in his first game as a Yankee and, all this time later, he couldn't imagine playing anywhere else.

He loved playing right field here, where he couldn't help but think of covering the same ground Babe Ruth did. Just the way another young boy from Ohio did 50 years before him, when Tommy Henrich roamed right, his mind racing to thoughts of Ruth.

Now Henrich was back home, a retired ballplayer checking in on his old team once in a while.

"That Paul O'Neill," Henrich said once, "is a heckuva ballplayer."

His father had made him that. He would want him to play. So O'Neill did his best to put on a brave face, a game face, amid the surreal pregame Series atmosphere on the field that became routine for the Yankees.

He spotted Biff Henderson, David Letterman's comical interviewer, one of the entertainment reporters who blend in with the celebrities and regular baseball media to fill almost every inch of space around the batting cage.

"Biff," O'Neill said, forcing a grin as he jogged out to shag flies in right, "give me a hug."

A few feet away, Sojo summed up what his grieving teammates were thinking.

"It's gonna be very emotional if we win tonight," he said. "I think the best reward we can get is to win the World Series and just be strong mentally."

The last out was recorded and O'Neill dropped to his knees in right. He jogged in, wiping his eyes, joining the celebration he usually raced to leap atop.

This time, in the middle of a celebration that contained as many tears as it did howling high-fives, O'Neill found his manager.

And when he did, the Yankees' warrior rested his head on the older man's shoulder and sobbed.

"Your dad," Torre whispered, "got to watch this one."

*** *** ***

A year later, O'Neill was sobbing and pulling Torre close again during a championship celebration, but this time, he did the talking.

"Don't you ever pinch hit for me again," he told his manager before giving him a hug after the Yankees won their third straight World Series, over the Mets.

Age and nagging injuries had started to slow O'Neill, leading to speculation it could be his last season in 2000. But he had come back strong again in October, hitting .474 in the World Series against the Mets.

And the Yankees had come back again, too, after struggling down the stretch. And losing the first game of the division series to Oakland.

Of the Yankees' dynasty in the '70s, ace Ron Guidry said "It was like we always were coming back for something. Always came back to prove who we were."

That's what the late '90s/early 21st century Yankees did, too.

But there would be one more comeback story to tell, one last gasp from a dynasty too stubborn to bow to age or the law of averages.

*** *** ***

I t had been another smooth season for the Yankees in 2001, if not for O'Neill.

Assorted injuries knocked him around for most of the year. But now he had a cast on his foot for a stress fracture and couldn't play.

He had missed the last three games against the Red Sox, though the usual Stadium frenzy wasn't the same anyway.

The Yankees had pulled away, giving themselves a 13-game lead in September. On this day, O'Neill wasn't with the team; he was in the city.

Eventual Cy Young winner Roger Clemens was going for his fifth 20-win season against his old club.

One problem. Rain. Lots of it. Wouldn't stop.

The fans raced all over the soaked stands. Singing, screaming, laughing in the rain, not a care in the world.

Finally, news came the game would be canceled. Clemens would have to wait for his 20th win. Maybe he'd pitch tomorrow, at Chicago.

On September 11.

*** *** ***

O 'Neill was working out with his wife and watching TV when the report came on.

And the world changed.

And everything from Clemens's 20th win to the stress fracture on O'Neill's foot became irrelevant.

Because the New York people saw immediately after the planes took down the Twin Towers was one not easily recognized.

One in which your mind became preoccupied with thoughts of absolute strangers rather than the daily routine that keeps your mind occupied with where you have to be and what you have to do.

Everything would change. For good. We were sure of it.

The column that ran on September 12 in the *New York Daily News* by Michael Daly, one of the best at capturing the city, told you that.

In it, he described the scene downtown, where a hundred-thousand dollar check amid the debris seemed insignificant. He couldn't take his eyes off a piece of a shattered picture frame containing a man's family. Everything would change.

The column by Pete Hamill, one of the best writers New York has ever seen, told you that. In it, he suggested athletes and entertainers all take huge pay cuts to help during a difficult economy. For that one week, if never again, the idea sounded nothing like a pipe dream.

In that week, the sight of a kid playing with a tennis ball against the stoop in a New York city neighborhood or the sound of an ice cream truck were the most beautiful images your mind could have imagined.

Because with jets flying overhead and neverending thoughts of smoke and debris and debris and debris and debris and ... death ... your mind couldn't easily picture other thoughts any more.

"By that time, most of the people had played in New York a number of years; we had won championships together and you felt like you were a part of New York," O'Neill said. "That's why it was so hard. I saw that city change. I saw people in that World Series talking to each other and hugging each other. It was brought about by a horrific event, but it changed the personality of New York. It became this close-knit community."

They were smart enough to cancel the games for a week.

O'Neill was asked to visit the rescue workers at Ground Zero so he went, no idea what he could do to provide solace as friends dug through misery for friends.

"We went the next day," he said. "It was crazy. It looked like a movie set. Things like that don't even look like that in real life."

There was the indescribable smell.

The mangled mess that was Tower 7, once a building, now what looked to be a suspended junkyard.

And there was the hole in the skyline that will never be replaced, regardless of what fills the space.

"First thing I remember is, I used to drive down to Westchester from Yankee Stadium every day," O'Neill said. "Soon as you came down the Deegan, you could see the skyline. We had a practice a couple days later; I could see the smoke. It hit you; my God, that's where this happened. Everything you saw on TV was there."

But you didn't see inside, past the smoke, in the pit. Not where volunteer nurses like Eileen Dugan were.

"You know what's bad, you don't get the whole picture," Eileen said, clutching her coffee cup, after a 12-hour shift the week of the attacks. "You see those guys, they're digging with their own hands, there's glass, there's asbestos. They hit a weak spot, they fall through."

So, O'Neill didn't know how he was supposed to help by shaking hands at that kind of a scene. He started to figure it out.

"I didn't have a role," he said. "You see kids smile just for an instant beause they were Yankee fans. It gets them away from what they're doing. I didn't expect to go down there and make anything better because I played major league baseball, but when you have a kid with missing parents, they want to come up and talk baseball for a second.

"It was just a tough time of life, whether you're playing baseball or a writer or an accountant or whatever. Every day you take the field it reminds you of what you've lost."

The Yankees had gone through that back in 1999.

Now the whole city would, too—in a way no one had known. And from day to day, sometimes minute to minute, the impact the Yankees could have on any of it changed.

Nothing mattered. Winning. Losing. But every little bit helped.

*** *** ***

The first real glimpse of baseball as possessing any kind of healing power came in Oakland.

That's when Jeter made his famous flip play and yanked people back into a Yankees' postseason that seemed ready to end as soon as it began.

It was such an amazing baseball play, the kind that made you feel like a kid who could imagine anything, it was impossible to turn away.

And it would propel the Yankees into the kind of run that left people talking about them inspiring the city.

Though not everyone was ready to think of it that way.

"It was sports again; that's what it did," Yankees announcer Michael Kay said. "What an unbelievable baseball game; baseball play, not what is it doing for the world? I never bought into that. I would have been fine if they canceled the World Series."

With each step, the fans started making the Stadium shake as it always had.

With each step, you wondered if that was what the city needed.

"I almost hope they lose," a cop standing guard amid smoking towers at Ground Zero said that October. "I'm afraid it's going to give people a false sense of security."

Maybe a little too much normalcy? In October, New York gets riveted by the Yankees, such an escape from the routine that you can't think about anything else.

When the Yankees won Game 5 of the American League Division Series, rallying all the way back to steal the series from Oakland, the Stadium celebrated as loudly as ever.

"New York, New York" blared with extra meaning. Mayor Rudy Giuliani, an American hero during the time, offered one of his big, toothy grins, accepting Torre's arm around his shoulder as he walked on the field.

Confetti flew and fans knew they could enjoy it all as if nothing was wrong.

Then the next day, you'd be there before a game, another report of Anthrax on the TV or another missing victim of the tower declared dead and you'd be back to that first week after the attacks when all the daily things you had considered important seemed insignificant.

"What are we doing here?" then-*New York Post* columnist Wally Matthews would say, before another mindless news conference of robotic answers on how to win a game.

But you did what you could, which was what you were used to doing. So the Yankees played ball. The reporters wrote about it. And sometimes you'd get lost in such a great game that it felt as important as ever, wrong or right.

Like Game 4 of the American League Championship Series against Seattle. The Yankees, the aging champs, withstood the Mariners' juggernaut to take a three games-to-one lead.

Seattle had won 116 games in the regular season, breaking the Yankees' 1998 mark of 114.

Piniella thought he could finally beat his old team. But after the Yankees looked like their old, invincible selves with two straight wins in Seattle, Piniella was in a panic, desperately vowing the teams would return for a Game 6.

The Yankees, no such promises needed, simply said they had to keep playing hard. That was their way. Pounce on one moment, then prepare to do the same the next. Nothing was taken for granted.

Especially after the Mariners won Game 3 in a rout, threatening to get back in the series.

They would not. Just when it looked like they had.

Seattle's Bret Boone had homered to make it 1-0, Mariners, in the top of the eighth and he laughed because he thought they finally had them.

Then Bernie Williams smacked the thoughts out of Boone's head and the ball over the wall. Tie game.

"Yeah!" police officer Freddy Morales said.

"Yankees, baby!" fire department Capt. Freddy Lafemina said.

They high-fived. The Stadium was rocking and they were celebrating along with everyone else, right behind the railing of the auxiliary press box.

To their left, Yankees owner George Steinbrenner nervously rattled his rings along the rail. To their right, GM Brian Cashman played with a small, blue and green rubber ball, the world in his hands.

"This is therapy," Morales said. "For a few hours."

They had both lost friends. Lafemina spent most of his days looking for them down at Ground Zero, knowing he couldn't expect to like what he found. Even worse, he was worried about the after-effects, the time when all the cheering for rescue workers didn't match the ones coming for ballplayers.

He had talked to workers from the Oklahoma City bombing. Heard a story about a worker who had tirelessly given his time and been thought of as a hero. After the spotlight faded, the man killed himself.

So Lafemina hoped people would remember this time.

Remember to cheer the people he knew folks would think were complaining years later when the trauma lasted, but the initial outpouring of support did not. But for this moment he couldn't help throwing himself into the same frenzy he always had in October.

And when Alfonso Soriano sent the ball over the wall to put the Yankees one win from another World Series, Lafemina was just another starstruck fan reveling in the one celebration his city could offer.

"The Yankees, baby!" Morales shouted as the camera caught Boone in the dugout, shaking his head with a resigned smirk. "The Yankees!"

"New York, New York" came on. The crowed cheered.

"It's great, man," Lafemina said, smiling. "I love this song."

The next night, the Yankees stormed into the Series and O'Neill helped as much as ever. He had started slow in the Oakland series, still adjusting after missing half of the last month. He managed just one hit in five games.

But by the ALCS, O'Neill, like most of his teammates, was his usual clutch postseason self, hitting .417 with two homers and three RBIs.

And he got the Yankees off to good starts in both the series-opener and series-clincher, homering early in each game to give the Yankees a healthy lead.

In the series-clinching fifth game, he blasted a homer in a four-run fourth. Picked up another hit, too, as the Yankees went on to their 38th World Series with a 12-3 win.

When it was over, even Piniella couldn't hold back his affection for his old town.

The Yankees would drub his team again, make his guarantee as useless as the Mariners' 116 regular-season wins would be.

But as Piniella sat in the Mariners' dugout amid a Stadium cheering the way it had for his kind of team back in the '70s, when he saw the Yankees come back the way the city would need to in real life ... well, he couldn't help but admit he'd always remain part-New Yorker.

"... The one thought that did come to my mind strangely enough is, 'Boy, this city suffered a lot and tonight they let out a lot of emotions,'" Piniella said after the game.

"And I felt good for them in that way ... And that's a strange thought to come from a manager who is getting his ass kicked."

*** *** ***

"When you use the words, 'mystique' and 'aura,'" Arizona ace Curt Schilling said at the first World Series press conference, "those are dancers in a night club."

And everyone laughed.

It was the beginning of the World Series, the end of a month-long grind through postseason baseball. And while the group laughed along with Schilling, there was little doubt the Yankees' most feared twosome would not be limited to table dancing.

They had come all the way back from 0-2 to Oakland. They had knocked off the 116-win team.

This was the last stage for so many of the Yankees' dynasty that had captivated the city and controlled baseball the past few years.

O'Neill would retire. Tino Martinez was all but gone, scheduled to be replaced by free agent Jason Giambi. Chuck Knoblauch would go, too.

This was it.

They were going to win one more World Series.

But they'd have to start off doing it without O'Neill.

Torre told O'Neill a little while before Game 1. He was going to start David Justice, who had better numbers against Schilling. With Arizona co-ace and tough lefty Randy Johnson going in Game 2, O'Neill would be out until at least Game 3.

Five years earlier, in their first World Series together, Torre called Paulie in to sit him. Then he changed his mind and O'Neill went out and made a game-ending catch.

But now it was their last World Series together, Torre knowing his right fielder would retire when the last out was recorded. And he wasn't going to change his mind.

"It took me a long time to do it," Torre said when he announced the decision. "Very tough. Very tough."

A few moments later, O'Neill appeared on the interview podium, a place he likes almost as much as the bench.

"I mean, everybody is disappointed," O'Neill said. "You look forward to going in and playing in the World Series. ... To say I'm not disappointed, I'd be lying sure. But if we win the World Series, that's what's the important thing."

No one fared well against Schilling. He beat them 9-1.

And when Johnson followed the next day with a dominating three-hitter for a 4-0 win, the Yankees were suddenly wondering when Mystique and Aura were going to show up.

Apparently, they just don't travel.

*** *** ***

The lines outside the Stadium didn't seem to end.

The president was there to show the nation he wasn't afraid, that he could throw out the first pitch in prime view, undaunted.

And maybe some of the fans would even get to see it after getting triple-checked on their way in. The extra security was nothing like the Stadium had seen before, even by its strict standards. No one was spared the procedure, down to Torre, Steinbrenner and the players. But it was worth it.

When the president threw a first-pitch strike, the crowd roared. On the scoreboard screen, the Honeymooners' scene played on as it did seemingly annually.

"The World Series, Alice! I'm going to the World Series!" Ralph Kramden screamed to his wife.

This was the World Series in New York, at Yankee Stadium and it was a world away from the kiddie pool the Diamondbacks offered at their sun-filled baby Bank One Ballpark.

Outside, fans walked along River Avenue and 161st Street, past all the shops selling jerseys for everyone from "O'NEILL" "JETER" "MARTINEZ" to "GUIDRY" "MATTINGLY" and all the way back to "RUTH."

They gathered together in Stan's Sports Bar, pressed one against the other in a pre-game giddy mess. Or down the block at the Yankee Tavern, ready for the latest magic from a team that never seemed to run out.

Roger Clemens was on the mound and, despite his Cy Young season and 15-strikeout game to beat Seattle in the playoffs the previous year, there were doubts.

The season was squarely on the shoulders of the Rocket and he had yet to perform well enough in that kind of pressure-filled spot.

But he would. He'd throw seven innings of three-hit ball and the Yankees would hold on for a 2-1 win.

O'Neill, finally starting in right, would contribute two hits.

The Yankees were in the Series. Mystique and Aura weren't far behind.

*** *** ***

Schilling was gone by the time it happened.

He didn't want to be, either, because he's the kind of pitcher who will come at you until his arm's dangling to the ground, like that of an orangatang.

The kind of pitcher who loved listening to all that nasty filth coming from the bleachers, the chants where they had their basic formula, sparked by Milton Ousland, the keeper of the cowbell.

Milton would throw his arm out, like a wizard unearthing a hex, banging the cowbell in rhythmic beat between a cacophony of chanting cheers and jeers.

"Hoaaaaaaaa! (dun-dun-dun-dun) Hoaaaaaaa! (dun-dun-dun-dun) Hoaaaaaaaa! (dun-dun-dun-dun)

"Yankees baseball!

"Mets suck!

"Arizona sucks!

"Box seats suck!

"Everybody sucks!"

"The fans of New York are, without a doubt, the most passionate, obsessive, obnoxious, loyal, demeaning, vulgar, loving fans on the face of the earth," Schilling had said before the World Series. "They make it fun to play there, they really do."

But it wasn't as fun when D'backs manager Bob Brenly took Schilling out with a 3-1 lead in the eighth. The pitcher who loved throwing well over 100 pitches tried fighting to stay in after throwing just 88, but Brenly resisted.

He had brought Schilling back on three days' rest and wanted six outs from his closer.

So, after seven three-hit innings in which the Yankees had barely touched Schilling, in came Byung-Hyun Kim.

You might recall the name.

Kim cruised through the eighth, retiring the side in order.

Down to three outs.

Jeter tried bunting his way on.

No go.

One out.

Up came O'Neill, knowing this was his last World Series. Knowing not even the Yankees had much of a shot to win that World Series if they went down three games to one, with two left in Arizona and Johnson waiting.

Torre had moved O'Neill up to second, Jeter up to first on yet another hunch.

O'Neill slapped a single to left. The crowd roared. Then quieted after Bernie Williams made the second out. One more to go.

"Here's Martinez," Kay announced to his radio listeners as Tino Martinez stepped up. "Looking for his first World Series hit this year. He's 0 for 9 in the Series."

Great.

All across the city, fans moaned at the comment. In the Stadium, where they couldn't hear it, the fans braced themselves. They had seen the Yankees come back from so many seemingly sure losses. They had seen Martinez right in the middle of those rallies.

One more time? Please?

"Fly ball center field ... it is way back ... home run! home run! Tino Martinez!" Kay announced. "Oh, but what a moment for Tino Martinez!"

And they were tied. And they were the Yankees again.

The Stadium-shaking, mind-numbing, don't-you-dare-say-they're-done Yankees. The fans screamed out every passionate, obsessive, obnoxious, loyal, demeaning, vulgar thing they could think of as they pounded each other on the shoulders.

And coming around third, O'Neill was one of them again, jumping in the air, thrusting his fist, running.

Jumping, thrusting, running.

One whole mess of a trot for the home run that made him feel like he was back playing ball with his dad under the lights in Ohio, a little kid unable to believe what he'd seen.

Tie game. But it was theirs. Maybe it would be Scott Brosius, who faced Kim to lead off the bottom of the 10th.

Nope. Flied to right.

Alfonso Soriano flied to left.

And up came Jeter. He fouled off pitch after pitch, running the count to 3-2.

In the stands, a fan held a sign up.

"Mr. November."

The clock had just run past midnight, turning Halloween to November 1; the first time major league baseball had been played in November.

Jeter lived for these moments. This stage.

He'd own it.

"Three-two pitch swung on and drilled to right field," Kay announced. "Going back Sanders, on the track ... at the wall ... See ya! See ya! See ya! A home run by Derek Jeter!"

Jeter raced around the bases, his arm forever shooting into the night in victory as he rounded first. He came around third, took a few steps home, then one ... two ... and a leap onto home plate, grinning like a little kid as he disappeared under a pounding, pinstriped wall of teammates.

Yankees 4, Diamondbacks 3.

"Surprising things happen, and yet when you really think about it," Torre said after, "it doesn't surprise you because this ballclub never quits."

*** *** ***

"I know everyone's waiting for that kind of ending, but it's kind of unfair to expect that again," Kay told his listeners at the beginning of Game 5. "That happens every 50 years, I think."

There became less chance of it happening as the night went on.

Stymied by Schilling and blown away by Johnson, the Yankees' anemic offense was now fading against ... Miguel Batista?

A pair of home runs for Arizona off of Mike Mussina had given the Diamondbacks a 2-0 lead and Batista had shut the Yankees out for 7 2/3 innings of five-hit ball.

None of which stopped Milton, the cowbell man, from defiantly telling fans leaving in the seventh—"See you for the comeback. It's gonna be Soriano."

Taped to the blue wall of the upper deck was one more sign of hope.

"Mystique and Aura," the banner read, "appearing nightly."

But it didn't look like it would appear in the ninth, so the chant started. The farewell to O'Neill, coming with the Yankees down 2-0.

"PAULLLL Ohhhh NEILLL

"PAULLLL Ohhhh NEILLL

While O'Neill forever appreciates the fans' farewell that night, he thought he'd have another chance to say goodbye—at a parade celebrating the Yankees' World Series title. Instead, the Diamondbacks rallied to beat the Yankees in Arizona. *Ezra Shaw/Getty Images.*

"PAULLLL Ohhhh NEILLL"

He thought he could never play here all those years ago when his dad told him he would and would play well. But he felt a part of the city now, and the people suffering were reaching out to say good-bye to him and ...

And he looked around and took it all in and did his very best not to cry. Finally, as he made his way off the field, he offered an almost reluctant recognition, a thank you with a thrust of his cap toward the crowd, head down, embarrassed to accept the cheers.

Then the game was over. Again.

Then it was not. Again.

Two outs and two runs down again when Brosius came up with one on.

"Now, remember, Brosius almost hit the ball out last night ..." Kay told his audience.

One pitch later ...

"That one hit in the air to left fielddddd ... "announcer Thom Brennaman said. "Do you believe it?! Good-bye, home run! They have done it again! This game is tied!"

And the stadium shook. And the Yankees showed there was no point in trying to say good-bye.

They didn't know how.

"PAUL-IE!" the fans chanted, welcoming O'Neill back for the 10th.

They'd win it in the 12th. On a single by ... Soriano.

"I told you!" Milton screamed deliriously in the bleachers. "I told you!"

In the Yankees' giddy locker room, O'Neill walked in for the last time in pinstripes. He walked past a smiling Soriano, the Yankees' kid of the team, who was told about the fan's prediction.

"Si?" said Soriano, who didn't yet speak english, his eyes widening. "In-cre-bile."

Past the howling, screaming Yankees, including Brosius, who still may not have wiped the smile off his face. Then he walked over to his locker, taking all the questions that preceded a late-night flight back to Arizona, the Yankees now in command of the Series, 3-2.

"This is my last game at the stadium," he said, removing any doubt.

*** *** ***

Game of My Life
Paul O'Neill

"What I remember about that is just feeling the emotional draining of Game 4 when you started for the park that day and getting back in the Series. Then you start that game, get down. Thinking, 'We're gonna have to go to Arizona, all the way out there and win two.' Then all of a sudden (after Brosius hits the home run) it's, 'Here we go again.'

"[Thoughts of being his last game at the Stadium?] If it was a regular-season game, I would have thought about it more. When you're trying to win the World Series, it's different.

"You can't help but see everybody that helped you. Start thinking about all the things that have happened and the championships and World Series and the flashbacks of the people you've played with. It all goes so quickly.

"[Fans chanting:] I remember hearing something. You think to yourself, 'It's getting louder and louder; what are they saying?' Then all of a sudden ... 'They're saying my name.' My wife and kids were there and talked about how cool that was. Anybody dreams of playing in a World Series game and have them chanting your name.

"That game; we came back again, it almost became a comical thing. That doesn't happen. It happens in card games and fantasy baseball. It doesn't happen in real life. Especially with what had happened in our lives the month before.

"Those are the games I remember from that Series—Game 4 and Game 5. Usually I remember the last one, but when I think of 2001, I don't think of Game 7.

"You start hearing the fans, then you wonder what they're saying. Then all of a sudden, you say, 'Hey, they're chanting my name.' You start thinking about all the things that have happened and the championships and World Series and the flashbacks of the people you've played with. It all goes so quickly."

*** *** ***

After the Game 7 loss, the stunner in which Arizona beat Rivera, O'Neill stood and stared, cross-armed, seemingly forever, in the Yankees' dugout. The flashbacks were ending now along with his career.

Before Game 7, Torre had said you want a team to take it from you, and that's just what the Diamondbacks did, outlasting the Yankees like no one had.

Then O'Neill returned home to a stadium and home clubhouse as quiet as it had been loud a few days before. He cleaned out his locker with his little boy clawing through his stuff, a sign the chants for Paulie would soon be replaced by the calls for Daddy.

New York had meant more to him than he could have ever imagined and he knew he'd never forget it.

Outside, in the chill of a November wind pointing toward winter, O'Neil met with his manager for the last time as a player.

And the pair who had been through benchings and victories and tears, the pair who showed how you could be human enough to mourn, tough enough to win, shared another hug. Then O'Neill offered one more whisper of a wish to Torre, the man with whom he helped build the Yankees' greatest dynasty.

"Stay in touch."

CHAPTER 20

Mariano Rivera:
Thank You, God

October 16, 2003, ALCS Game 7

vs. Boston
Yankees 6, Red Sox 5

The stats:	IP	H	R	ER	BB	SO
	3	2	0	0	0	3

Mariano Rivera hugged the mound at Yankee Stadium, the spot from which he'd leapt in victory countless times now driving him to his knees. He ignored his teammates' celebration, his face kissing dirt, his mouth whispering the same words over and over again.

Thank you.
Thank you.
Thank you.

Rivera would not move, gripping the dirt as tightly, fanatically as his team's greatest rival had clung to the Yankees. Just like the Red Sox, Rivera would not let go, no matter how forcefully the Yankees pushed and pulled, as desperate for him to join their celebration as they had been to earn it.

They were going to the World Series again, their tradition safe, Boston finally bowing to heartbreak despite pushing back harder than it ever had.

Eighty-five years of frustration be damned, the Red Sox refused to easily yield to the so-called Curse of the Bambino, forcing the 2003 Yankees to prove their present could match the past if that undented tradition was going to last. It had taken "everything, everything" for the Yankees to hold off their greatest rivals, as Rivera said later, going to the last pitch of the last game of a season in which the bitter foes traded as many wins, losses, barbs and blows as they ever had.

So many October nights ended with him at the top of this celebration, leaping, arms extended, unbeaten again, on top of the world after winning another World Series.

But this time Rivera, having pitched three scoreless innings, hadn't ended a game. He ensured it would continue until someone else could. And his greatest victory left him too humbled to jump skyhigh. He just sprinted out to the mound he owned and lurched himself into the same steady stream he couldn't stop.

Rocking.

Sobbing.

Praying.

Thank you.

Thank you.

Thank you.

All around him, the fans packing the House that Ruth Built bellowed a roar louder than any that had come before, its tradition trumping itself again.

A loss would have forever changed the baseball world as they knew it.

"You don't want to be the team that lets the Red Sox (win) the World Series," Yankees captain Derek Jeter would say later.

That truth would burn into the Yankees the very next year, when the Red Sox would storm back from a 3-0 deficit in the American League Championship Series and go on to win the World Series, to finally break the curse. Rivera would show he was human in that series in one of the few times he faltered, then graciously accept the Red Sox fans' applause the next season on Opening Day at Fenway Park, showing that while he hated to lose, he could do so with dignity.

But in spring training 2004, when Rivera thought of his greatest game, he had not yet been humbled along with his teammates by the next chapter of the rivalry. Or so many of the chapters that were to come in his own career, from closing out the old Yankee Stadium to setting the all-time saves record and winning another World Series title in 2009, as well as his latest challenge, to come back from the season-ending injury he sustained in 2012.

So, back in spring training 2004, Rivera reflected on the classic ALCS from 2003, when the teams staged one of the best battles of their long, storied history.

Both teams' identities depended on each pitch of Game 7 of the American League Championship Series. The Yankees trying to prove they could live up to their tradition, not betray it. The Sox defiantly vowing they would change theirs; they would break the so-called Curse of the Bambino in the house of the person who supposedly created it.

Never had the stakes been so high between the rivals separated by a four-hour stretch on I-95 and a four-generation string that decreed Yankees win, Red Sox lose.

And now what had been the greatest game of the greatest series of the greatest season of the greatest rivalry in sports had come down to what everyone thought it would—the last pitch.

"It took everything, it took everything," Mariano Rivera said of the Yankees' exhausting, 11-inning win over Boston in Game 7 of the 2003 ALCS. The classic series featured brawls and a back-and-forth fight that commanded the Yankees to live up to every last bit of their tradition and keep the "Curse of the Bambino" alive for one more year. *Al Bello/Getty Images.*

Somehow the Yankees had at that point again survived, the "19-18" chant preserved along with an untainted memory of every Boston beating since the Sox sold Babe Ruth to the Yankees in 1920.

They could see it all slipping away throughout the night, a glimpse of misery coming from Boston's mastery of Roger Clemens.

But then it was gone. The Yankees had come back. They won.

So Aaron Boone, the modern-day Bucky Dent, stood on the field amid the screams, a TV camera pointed at his stunned face.

"I-I-I-I ... I can't even talk," Boone said, his heart seemingly thumping through his chest, moments after his 11th-inning home run ended the game.

And still Rivera would not rise from the mound.

The Yankees piled on one another. Jeter offered another forever fist-pump, leaping into a teammate's arms a few innings after whispering to Boone, "Don't worry; the ghosts will show up eventually."

In the visiting dugout—to which Boston ace Pedro Martinez had retreated just a few innings before, the Stadium raining down taunting chants of "Peddddroooo, Peddddroooo" on him the way he had reigned over Yankees hitters for seven innings—the Red Sox lay defeated.

Disbelieving. Numb.

As they always had.

And still Rivera would not rise from the mound.

David Wells and Roger Clemens grabbed pitching coach Mel Stottlemyre and raced out to Monument Park, a quest to a crypt, a thank-you for the continuation of a curse on their biggest rivals.

All day, Yankees and Red Sox fans had made their own pilgrimages with pleas for the Babe, visiting his grave 20 miles north of the Stadium in Hawthorne, New York.

"Please," Boston fans begged. "Remove this curse."

"Don't listen to them, Babe," Yankee fans sneered. "You're ours."

It had been the theme of the series, the Babe's so-called curse as mythical and comical as his called shot. But now it felt as real as ever.

"He's smiling," Clemens said, pointing to the Babe's picture on the plaque. "He's smiling."

In the tunnel under the Stadium, the Yankees' clubhouse kids sprinted from the Yankees' locker to the visiting clubhouse, laughing as they hopped over mourning Red Sox sprawled on the floor. The players were too devastated to move, the kids too giddy to care.

They had champagne to retrieve.

It belonged to the Yankees once more.

On the mound, Rivera had finally responded to the grabs from his teammates, the shove onto their shoulders. The rest of the Yankees wanted to salute the man who guards their tradition as fiercely as the Bambino's curse ever could.

Slowly, Rivera rose, his lip quivering, his legs shaking.

The fans filling the stands and the bars all over the city couldn't stop cheering, because they had been so afraid Boston finally would force them to do just that.

They couldn't lose. Not to the Red Sox. They had to win. *Had* to win.

Especially after that punk Pedro had thrown down good, old Zim, Don Zimmer's 72-year-old body flung to the ground in that Game 3 brawl.

And especially with the Babe's legacy on the line, a bunch of Bostonians trying to buck the curse with that silly "Cowboy Up" slogan.

But none of that is what reduced Rivera to his knees. It wasn't about beating Pedro. Or keeping a curse alive. Or proving he or his teammates could live up to the unending standards of folks who needed some part of their lives to remain invincible.

This was about him. About his team.

About a man reaching for something he wanted as desperately as anything else in his life and claiming it—all while someone tried to take it away.

And when he found it—when Rivera, the key to the Yankees' latest dynasty because he intimidates opponents with his living, breathing presence—watched the Yankees survive their closest call of a victory, he did not worry about ghosts or hexes.

For Rivera, this was not a curse.

It was a blessing.

"It was personal to me. It was personal with me and the Lord," Rivera said. "Because He made me understand that He's there. ... All day, I was praying to give me strength, to give my teammates strength—and, yes, I prayed to win the game.

"Everyone was exhausted. Everyone was exhausted. But you have so much adrenaline in the game, you forget about it. Everyone was exhausted, everyone was tired. We fight.

"To me, it was just the way we won. Here are two teams leaving everything they've got out there. The best they've got for the winner."

Had to win that game.

Had to win.

*** *** ***

Larry Lucchino was pissed.

It was January 2003 and the Red Sox CEO had all but set up a blockade around Cuban free agent pitcher Jose Contreras.

The Sox wanted him. Didn't get him. Somehow, the Yankees still did.

One more blow for the "Evil Empire," Lucchino growled to the press.

Yankees owner George Steinbrenner heard about the label.

And got ticked. And it was that simple.

Sports' greatest rivalry was raised up a notch so high, no one is sure when it will come down again.

The 2003 plot would play out with a wide cast of characters careening toward a collision course in which the so-called Curse of the Bambino would be buried or grow stronger.

The 1978 season was wild, with the comeback and a one-game playoff. This was more. This was a season full of tit-for-tat battles on the field and off.

Of 10 Yankees wins to the Sox' nine in the regular season. Of Lucchino's griping. Of Steinbrenner's statements, one more entertainingly surreal than the last.

He blubbered like a baby after a win ... in *July* and the collision course kept coming, the Red Sox Cowboy upping their way through the season.

It was a new Red Sox team, one so convinced it could break a curse it conned a Northeastern city into adopting a wild west slogan.

"Cowboy up," Red Sox characters like newcomer Kevin Millar said.

Suck it up. We're not going to lose. Forget the curse.

So many characters.

Millar, the newcomer too goofy to bow to nerves, danced his way across the Sox' scoreboard screen, begging fans to relax. Pedro Martinez, Boston's last hope of a baseball hero strong enough to beat the Yankees. The pitcher who had soothed the sting of losing Clemens and vowed to take aim at all the pain caused by the so-called curse.

"Wake up the Bambino," Martinez had said a few years before. "I'll drill him in the ass."

So what if he went winless the rest of the year?

There was Nomar Garciaparra desperately craving at least one ring to Jeter's four.

Red Sox general manager Theo Epstein, the 27-year-old whiz kid who grew up with his father teaching him to hate the Yankees as any good New Englander would.

In New York, Steinbrenner's blood pressure bubbled to new heights and the barbs between him and Yankees manager Joe Torre finally increased. Outside the press gate at Yankee Stadium, the Steinbrenner Stakeout became a routine form of reporting, a line of writers following the Boss to see if he'd rant even after waving them off 20 times. Usually, the 21st was the trick, Steinbrenner unleashing gems such as this one after a regular-season loss to the Sox.

"We'll be back tomorrow; you mark my words," he said. "One acorn does not a fall make."

And the Yankees' newcomers had something to prove after a disappointing first-round loss to Anaheim in 2002, even Jeter pointing out his teammates hadn't been through the postseason battles their predecessors had.

So you had a Yankees team with stars like Jason Giambi and Japanese import Hideki Matsui trying to make their mark and a starving Sox team ready to taint it.

All season the Yankees and Red Sox gave you memories, all with a nod toward a past they couldn't possibly surpass.

"I don't think they hate each other as much as we did," former Yankees ace Ron Guidry said on old-timer's day and it sure seemed right.

But there were glimpses. Pedro would plunk Jeter and Alfonso Soriano. Clemens would hit Millar. And there were words and dares and stares and things started stewing. The Yankees edged Boston for the division, winning the final showdown.

The Sox sneaked in as the wild card, but had no problems with it, carefree Millar leading the charge into a Boston bar, hopping over the counter in uniform, pouring drinks, pounding away at nearly a century's worth of pain.

No shame in the wildcard. Just cowboy up to the bar and let's take another poke at all that tradition in the playoffs.

And they would.

As hard a shot as they ever had at that point.

But along with a large cast of loudmouths going back and forth, there was one more thing standing between the Red Sox and their quest to finally upend the Yankees.

The quietest part of the rivalry, whose fires burned as hot as any of them. Mariano Rivera.

Nobody got through that guy.

*** *** ***

Growing up in Panama, he didn't know he'd be a pitcher. Or a baseball player.

Rivera—whose fingers grip the baseball to produce the most baffling, seemingly unhittable cut-fastball baseball's ever seen—wanted to play a sport that prohibited him from touching the ball with his hand.

Soccer.

"In my country, you play baseball or soccer," Rivera said. "I played both. Soccer, I was getting hurt a lot. Knees. Ankle.

"I decided for baseball, because once I was playing soccer and I got a cut in my eye and then the other eye. That was tough. I was 17. I said, 'That's it. I can't keep playing this.'"

That was it. That's how baseball's most dominant relief pitcher was born. On rocky dirt fields with cardboard gloves and balls made of tape.

No one knew how great he could become. Even when he signed a contract with the Yankees in 1990, he had no idea where it would take him, other than America.

And, he hoped, Yankee Stadium, the place he had marveled at, growing up a Yankee fan because, well, those were the games they showed back home.

But he was just a quiet kid in a new country, his skinny frame drawing skeptics in the organization, wondering how he'd hold up. It was the same deception his smooth style offered hitters, a lullaby of a delivery disguising a cut-fastball whose alarm jolted hitters awake a moment too late.

But Rivera didn't worry yet about his fate.

"I was just happy to play ball," he said. "There were people telling me to keep going. 'Keep going, keep working at it.'"

So he did. In the meantime, he found his faith.

Ask Rivera why he's developed into the game's most dominating relief pitcher, and he'll shrug as far as his own talent. But he'll thank the Lord and acknowledge, "That's my guide; that's my power source."

And Rivera has been the Yankees' power source through their dynasty of the late '90s and early 21st century.

"It's over," said Jeter, asked what he thinks when Rivera is brought into a game.

He became their set-up man in '96, effectively reducing the game to six innings, Torre laughing at the relative ease his job now entailed—give the ball to Rivera, then closer John Wetteland. Rivera was so dominant as a setup man—striking out 130 in 107 2/3 innings—he finished third in the Cy Young balloting.

Rivera and Wetteland cruised through the postseason, handing the Yankees their first World Series title in 18 years.

But the Yankees weren't ready to hand the ball to Wetteland the next year. This kid, Rivera, they thought; he's a closer.

It had all happened so quickly. Only a few years before, Rivera struggled as a starter in the big leagues, too dependent on a fastball that topped out at 91 m.p.h. But, like a kid with a sudden growth spurt in college, his ball bolted to 95 suddenly, inexplicably.

Then he showed the robotically cool rhythm he's become famous for, unfazed in the '95 playoffs against Seattle, a rookie making vets wonder who he was as he threw 5 1/3 scoreless.

And now, just two years later, he would be their closer.

He blew three out of his first four saves in '97, but settled with 27 on the plus side by the all-star break. He saved the all-star game, too, finished the year with 43 and was just a few outs from pitching the Yankees past Cleveland and into the American League Championship Series.

Except, he didn't.

Sandy Alomar Jr. smacked a home run to right to tie a game and keep the Indians alive, and soon the Yankees were out. Done. Defeated.

"It was tough," Rivera said. "It was tough to lose the series. I learned, whatever you're doing, give your best. I was comfortable with it. Joe was there and he said, 'You know what? Keep working. Play the way you are. Move on.

"And that's what I did."

And then some.

He saved 36 games in '98, barely breathing heavy as the Yankees won 114 regular-season games.

In the postseason, he was nearly unhittable.

And stayed that way for four years.

From '98 to 2001, Rivera didn't yield a run in the postseason, a string of 33 1/3 scoreless that broke Yankees legend Whitey Ford's mark.

He was absurdly overwhelming, even sparking the Atlanta Braves to laughter—while losing a World Series—when he broke three straight bats in '99.

But Rivera remained as cooly detached as ever.

"It was kind of funny seeing those guys laughing at their own player," he said later. "But to me, it wasn't funny. I was trying get the inning over and win the World Series."

It was his domination of the Padres in the '98 Series and the showcase San Diego closer Trever Hoffman provided which produced Rivera's now-famous anthem.

As they heard Hoffman enter the game to AC/DC's "Hell's Bells" in the ninth, some Yankees scoreboard workers realized something.

Mo needed a theme song.

One of the sound guys, Mike Luzzi, came in and popped in a Metallica tape.

The bass started banging a foreboding screech, drums thumping, pulse quickening as the band's ode to hellish nightmares began.

"Enter Sandman" has now become as comforting to Yankee fans as its lyrics—detailing the demons that attack in your sleep—are frightening.

When it plays, the Yankees know Rivera's on his way in, flipping the switch on any thoughts of an opponents' comeback.

When Rivera hears the first beats on his way from the bullpen and the anticipatory roar of a response from the fans, he surely can't help but feel his heartbeat quicken since the song ...

"Doesn't mean anything to me," Rivera said. "Just, 'time to go in.' It's good for the fans."

What would he pick if he had the choice?

"I listen to Christian music," he said.

*** *** ***

It's his Christian faith, Rivera said in 2004, that helped him through his toughest loss. The Yankees had inspired the city with more of their seemingly endless comebacks in the 2001 postseason, just a month after the September 11 terrorist attacks. They would go to the bottom of the ninth inning of World Series Game 7 at Arizona with a lead.

It's over, they thought. And it was.

Just not the way they were used to it ending.

There was a throwing error by Rivera. And a hit batsman. And the hits that never seem to come against him in the postseason, the last a soft blooper from Luis Gonzalez arching over Jeter's head at short and into history.

The Diamondbacks had beaten Rivera to win the World Series and end the Yankees' run of three straight titles.

"To me, it was disappointing," Rivera said. "It was hard."

In the next week, a flight headed for the Dominican Republic—one teammate Enrique Wilson would have been on if the Yankees stayed around to celebrate a world championship—crashed, killing the passengers.

"Enrique would have been on the plane," Rivera said. "God has ways to do things we don't see. At the time, I couldn't understand why we lost this game ..."

So that's how he made his peace. He hated losing, but maybe this had a purpose.

But he wasn't prepared to see any such purpose in 2003. It had been a long season. The Yankees had fought. He started the year hurt, endured the questions of a few blown saves, people thinking he was a machine.

He wanted that, too, wanted the highest expectations because he had them.

Had to win this game.

Had to win.

*** *** ***

"It seemed like it was headed this way," Jeter said as the Yankees prepared for the ALCS against the Sox. "We've probably been the two most consistent teams in the league. Why would you want to face an easier team? If you want to be the best, you have to beat the best."

They had squared off for a trip to the World Series in '99, but the Yankees made it a mismatch. Now the teams were as evenly matched as ever,

Yankees catcher Jorge Posada calling the Sox "the most confident" he'd seen them during their stretch of six second-place finishes.

The Yankees had survived a season of turmoil and took their first big step toward proving they could match their predecessors. They dropped the opener of the American League Division Series, but rallied to win the next three games and beat Minnesota.

Giambi celebrated his first playoff win, his face covered in champagne and relief in the postgame celebration.

Matsui added a big homer, once again stepping up in the spotlight, having been trained to expect it as the larger-than-life "Godzilla" cult hero in Japan.

He had introduced himself to Yankee fans at the regular-season home opener with a grand slam, the kind of moment everyone at the Stadium started to expect. But the words that followed showed just how well-trained Matsui had been, as he explained what helped him.

"I think it was the fans, being in Yankee Stadium, and I think," Matsui said, "maybe the previous Yankees might have helped, too."

The Sox, having overcome an 0-2 deficit to win three straight games from Oakland, were tired of hearing about all those Yankee spirits supposedly deadset against them.

They had stayed in there all year, the teams obsessively watching each other's every move like overzealous parents competing in their kids' candy bar sales.

At the waiver trading deadline on July 31, the Yankees stunned everyone by acquiring Reds third baseman Aaron Boone for top pitching prospect Brandon Claussen, previously labeled untouchable. The rumor started floating that the deal was made as a defense mechanism, the Yankees keeping Boone from Seattle, who would have then traded ace Freddy Garcia to the Sox in a three-way deal.

*** *** ***

"Do I hate the Boston Red Sox?" Jeter said, repeating a question the day before Game 1 of the ALCS at Yankee Stadium. "Do I hate their players? No."

But he'd grin when asked what Boston fans thought of him.

"Come with me for 30 minutes. You'll see."

They hated him because he was the most recent incarnation of Yankees' evil, the symbol for everything they wanted but couldn't have. Come the postseason, the Yankees always seemed to end the game with another win and a pump of the fist from Jeter.

But this had mostly been a friendly rivalry the last few years—a few beanballs from Martinez and the Sox' disdain for Clemens trek into enemy territory notwithstanding.

You just couldn't expect the games to get anywhere near those brawling days of Thurman Munson and Carlton Fisk, Graig Nettles and Bill Lee.

So the first two games at Yankee Stadium were relatively harmless.

"The Sox are here!" Millar taunted fans on the way in, continuing his unfazed, frathouse feel. "The Sox are here."

It was a loose attitude quickly picked up on by Boston fans, who were surrounded by the same, old Bronx taunts.

"Hey, 1918!" a Yankee fan called to a Sox fan before Game 1.

"Yeah! All right!" the Sox fan responded. "Woo hoo! Bucky Dent! Bill Buckner!"

The Yankee fan, beaten to his own game, slunk away, speechless.

The first bad sign for the Yankees came before the game when Challenger, the eagle that flew in for the pregame ceremony, tried to take out the Captain.

The bird was apparently getting old. Or spooked.

Whatever the case, Challenger did not go straight to his trainer on the mound as he usually did. He veered off toward the Yankees, lined up for intros, all but screeching in Jeter's ear and causing him to duck, teammate Alfonso Soriano laughing the whole time.

That was the last light moment for the Yankees, who watched Tim Wakefield float his knuckleball by them for a 5-2 loss.

"You were there; you saw it," Steinbrenner huffed on his way out. "I wasn't very comfortable."

He'd feel a little better the next night when Andy Pettitte bailed out the Yankees as he had in the divisional series against Minnesota, evening the series.

"The Empire Strikes Back," a banner read.

And it had. Now it was on to Boston for the epic Game 3 matchup.

Clemens vs. Pedro.

The pitcher who gave the Sox their last, best shot at winning a World Series vs. the one they hoped would make them forget how close they had come in '86.

Cy Young vs. Cy Young.

Rival vs. Rival.

"ARM-AGEDDON" the front page of the *New York Post* blared.

*** *** ***

As is usually the case with pitching matchups that are hyped beyond belief, neither starter started all that smoothly.

Clemens gave up a two-run single to Manny Ramirez in the first. The Yankees came back with an RBI single by Karim Garcia and a homer by Derek Jeter to tie the game, 2-2, by the third.

Pedro didn't have it. Not early. And when he didn't have it, he was rumored to throw the same head-high fastballs Clemens had been accused of throughout his career.

In the fourth, after giving up another run, Pedro faced Garcia with runners on second and third and no one out.

First base was open.

Pedro's pitch was a fist, right into the back of Garcia, nearly head-high.

Garcia glared at the pitcher, an expression somewhere between crazed and confused. He muttered to himself. Then he took first, hoping for the chance to get even.

It came when Soriano followed with a double-play ball to short. Garciaparra fielded it and flipped to second baseman Todd Walker ... who was taken out with a hard, spikes-high slide by Garcia ... as he turned the double-play.

And it was on.

Walker and Garcia shoved, spitting nasty words at each other.

The Yankees players were off the bench in the dugout, screaming at Pedro, everyone from David Wells to Jorge Posada and Zimmer, the bench coach.

And Pedro screamed back. And looked at Posada. And pointed at his head.

"He's not saying, 'Use your head; he's saying, 'I'll hit you in the head,'" Fox announcer Tim McCarver said.

Posada, incensed, jumped up and pointed at himself and Pedro, as if to say, "You want me, come and get me."

"YANKEES SUCK! YANKEES SUCK!" the crowd chanted.

Suddenly, the Yankees and Red Sox were showing a flash of the intensity their predecessors had three decades before, tension building to an unhealthy level in the stands.

Then it was gone. Enrique Wilson popped out to second to end the inning. The Yankees led, 4-2. It was a baseball game now. For a few minutes.

Then Manny Ramirez, who so often left people wondering what he was thinking, made people wonder if he even *was* thinking.

When he led off the next inning, Ramirez watched a high fastball sail over the plate and nowhere near his head. But that was enough for him.

Clutching the bat, Ramirez charged Clemens, walking slowly, screaming the whole time. And the benches cleared. And the crowd jeered.

And the rivalry was turning ugly the way it hadn't since the '70s.

In a way no one could have imagined in the '70s.

Darting across the field was Zimmer, the Yankees bench coach. The former Red Sox manager had watched Dent beat him with a home run. The man who had been around baseball for everything from Don Larsen's perfect game to these endless Yankee-Red Sox battles.

No one noticed him as the players pushed and shoved each other because, well, you don't expect to see a 72-year-old man make a beeline for the other team's starting pitcher.

Pedro, too, looked startled at the sight of the bullrush, Zimmer, head down, ready to seek revenge for what the Yankees perceived as head-hunting. The pitcher grabbed the old man by the shoulders, stepping aside, flinging Zimmer to the ground.

When he first saw the big, bald head on the ground, Yankees pitcher Pettitte thought it was his teammate, Wells. So did a lot of Yankees.

Slowly, they realized what happened. And they seethed.

And one of the most bizarre days in Yankees-Red Sox history was born.

Now tension filtered through the tiny, crammed park even higher than the usual Yankees-Red Sox hate. Now the emotions weren't just about winning a ballgame, but the teams defending themselves, a contest of wills that seems to give the series advantage to the winner.

And on the mound for the Yankees was the very man the Sox never could count on to simmer down when he was younger. As a young stud pitcher, Clemens had lost his composure in some big games, once getting thrown out of a playoff game for arguing with the umpire.

Now he had every last emotion churning inside him, from a season's farewell tour, to the 300 wins he had in the bank to his last game at Fenway to the raised blood pressure caused by the rumble.

With all that going on, with Clemens desperate to defend his new team all while opposing the team that raised him in the city that often hated him since he left ... Clemens was the most composed man in the park.

He came back to strike out Ramirez. He retired the next six batters. Then, with everyone's pride on the line along with the game, he induced a double-play ball from Ramirez to end the sixth. Two innings later, Rivera came on for the final six outs, coolly confident as ever, locking up the 4-3 win.

But not before the day reached a new level of chaos. In the ninth, a commotion started in the Yankees bullpen in right field, no one immediately certain what was happening. Yankees reliever Jeff Nelson would later say one of the Boston groundskeepers was taunting the team. He told the guy to leave.

A fight broke out. Garcia hopped the fence in right. Posada, in full catcher's gear, raced out from the Yankees' dugout.

In the Yankees' clubhouse, team president Randy Levine was incensed. "There is an attitude of lawlessness permeating everything that's going on here," Levine said. "It needs to get corrected quickly."

The correction the Red Sox made was to assert blame on the part of the Yankees' Nelson and Garcia.

"The Red Sox are terribly distressed about the attack on our employee," Red Sox spokesman Charles Steinberg said. Paul Williams, a part-time groundskeeper and schoolteacher, was cheering for the Sox when the Yankees attacked, the Red Sox claimed.

Nelson said he told the guy to cheer somewhere else and Williams responded he could do what he wanted.

By the end of the day, the Boston Police Department investigated the players.

The rivalry was, to say the least, at a new level.

"I think we've escalated it from a battle to a war," Sox manager Grady Little said.

*** *** ***

When Torre took his spot on the podium for the customary pregame press conference the next day, Zimmer was with him—a clear bandage on his nose, a reddened expression on his face.

He had been in baseball seemingly forever and was, as Torre would so often say, an emotional guy.

The past day he had been held up as some kind of AARP-aged icon, a folk hero for taking on the pitcher. Fortunately, after a lifetime in the game, Zimmer knew better. Knew he was as wrong for rushing Martinez as any of the pitcher's actions that inspired him to do so.

"I'm embarrassed of what happened yesterday," Zimmer said. His chip-munk cheeks started to quiver, his lip following, his voice breaking. Torre rubbed his back, consoling him. "I'm embarrassed for the Yankees, the Red Sox, the fans, the umpires and my family. That's all I have to say. I'm sorry."

And with that, Zim was up and off the podium.

But there was more embarrassment to come.

Call it comic relief.

There was no Game 4 to be played just yet; rain had canceled it. Advantage Red Sox, who could start Wakefield the next day.

So they'd play games inside instead.

The commissioner's office had asked the teams to refrain from talking about the previous game's events so ...

The Red Sox management held a press conference. MLB officials scold-ed the Red Sox, who didn't exactly meet the request of trying to settle things down.

"Who?" Lucchino snapped when asked if he had spoken with Steinbrenner. "You can bet I haven't."

Upon discovering the Red Sox had spoken despite the commissioner's requests, Levine, again enraged, wrote up a statement in response.

It said:

"After we learned that the Red Sox violated the commissioner's order, we called the commissioner's office and received permission to issue the following statement: Both I and the Yankees stand by our statements of yesterday."

Big businessmen, remember. Million-dollar-deal-making men, remem-ber.

Men handling the complex, combustible circumstances with the delicate and deft manner of a seven-year-old sticking his tongue out.

Welcome to the greatest rivalry in sports.

*** *** ***

Wakefield was on again, just as he had been in Game 1. The Yankees couldn't touch him.

Ruben Sierra hit a ninth-inning homer to make it look good, but the 3-2 defeat evened the series and did something else.

It put Wakefield in the Yankees' heads. Worse, the pitcher said the exer-tion-free pitch left him ready to pitch in relief ... by the next day, if needed.

The Sox never got to him in Game 5. The Yankees burst out early, tak-ing a 3-0 lead in the second when Torre's latest hunch—Garcia—came through with a two-out, two-run single.

All while the fans chanted "jailbird," hoping police would charge Garcia for his role in the bullpen incident.

None of that would help them though, as Wells pitched another solid, big game and Rivera came on for another two-inning save. The Yankees had a 4-2 win.

More importantly, as they returned to New York, they were just one win from the Series.

The Red Sox were reeling. Garciaparra was slumping so badly there were suggestions of benching him. Later that night, in the popular Cask 'N Flagon, down the block from the park, the diehard Red Sox fans diluted their troubles and rooted for their cursed cousins in Chicago.

The surprising Cubs were just five outs from bucking their own curse, of the Billy Goat, and reaching the World Series.

Fly ball to left. Curving foul. Moises Alou has a play on it. ... And a fan snagged it. A fan named Steve Bartman, who unknowingly was about to enter baseball infamy.

The Marlins rallied. Won. This couldn't be a good sign, the Sox fans thought as they returned to their beers. But the Sox weren't big on signs in 2003.

So when they arrived at Yankee Stadium, forced to beat the red-hot Pettitte or else go home, they were as loose as if it was spring training.

They jumped on him for four runs in the third, catcher Jason Varitek homering, Yankee-killer David Ortiz and Millar scoring runs with singles. And the Sox led 4-1.

But the Yankees came back, took a 6-4 lead in the sixth. That's it. The Sox were done. Just like always.

Except they weren't.

Garciaparra finally came through, tripling to left-center, scoring when Matsui's wind-blown ball sailed toward the third-base stands. The Sox kept rallying, disrupted the Yankees' fragile mid-inning bullpen.

When it was over, Boston had a 9-6 win. It had the momentum.

It had the Yankees down to one game when the Yankees seemed in control most of the series.

Tomorrow would be Game 7. Clemens vs. Pedro.

Again.

With the Yankee Stadium fans all but calling for blood. With all the tradition on the line.

Had to win this game.

Had to win.

*** *** ***

The Yankees' clubhouse guys were on the phone with different players. Take this way. Don't take that way.

Unbelievable.

The biggest game of the year—of who-knows-how-many-years—and there was no telling if all the players could even get to the ballpark on time.

A water main break had sent the city into chaos, traffic rerouted and stranded, bumper to bumper.

Rivera didn't make it on time, arriving a little past the scheduled hour, a few hours before the game. Jason Giambi sat in traffic before a cop finally recognized him and offered a police escort. He didn't arrive until 5:40 p.m. and by that time Torre had already made out the lineup.

The one that dropped Giambi to seventh.

"I just sense that he's taken on more than any one person needs to take on, and I just thought I'd drop him in the lineup," Torre said.

"It's not about me; it's about the team," Giambi said, echoing so many of Torre's players from the past few years. "Skip talked to me. I'm fine."

At least he was in the lineup.

With Aaron Boone struggling through the postseason and Enrique Wilson known as a Pedro-killer, Torre sat his midsummer addition in favor of the reserve.

It was one more tough spot for Boone, who had received a pep talk from his big brother, Bret, a few days before. Bret, the Seattle second baseman who once thought he had put the Yankees away with a playoff home run, was a guest in the Fox broadcast booth.

He knew all about this place. Tried to coach his little brother as much as he could.

"I remember hitting a home run to put us up in 2001," Bret said of the ALCS that year. "I said 'We're gonna win this son of a. ... Then the wind started swirling. It was blowing. I said, 'Here come the ghosts.' Bernie Williams hit a home run. ...

"It's fun if you let it be," Bret had told his little brother. As nervous as he was for him, Bret wasn't overly concerned. "You play with people, you play against people. Some guys run and hide. He doesn't."

*** *** ***

They gathered in the Yankees' clubhouse before the game, the team coming together once more.

No big speeches. Torre just looked at Posada as he always did. Asked him how many more wins the Yankees needed as became their tradition.

"One," Posada said. He pumped his fist. "Grind it."

There was another player who wanted to speak.

Matsui had acclimated himself to his new country, new team. So he motioned when Torre asked if anyone else had anything to say.

Then, through a translator, the reserved Japanese star gave his team a message. "Today, we're gonna play hard and we're gonna win," Matsui's translator repeated, solemnly. "And we're gonna pop the bottles ... somebody find the (girls) and start the party."

The players couldn't stop laughing.

They were ready to play.

*** *** ***

It was as loud and as quiet as Yankee Stadium has ever sounded.

So loud the rest of the place overran the Bleacher Creatures' roll call in right, roaring right over it.

The boos for Pedro Martinez were as vicious as any, the Yankee fans unleashing their resentment over Zimmer along with their respect for a dangerous opponent.

But then it grew quiet.

Still. As silent as a place full of 56,000 people can be.

Three straight ropes in the second against Roger Clemens, the pitcher who had finally proved himself in pinstripes.

A single by David Ortiz. Another by the Cowboy Up poster child, Millar. Then a drive into the night by Trot Nixon, a 3-0 lead for the Sox silencing the Stadium.

The Sox chased him in the fourth. A homer by Millar giving them a 4-0 lead; a walk to Nixon and a single by Bill Mueller taking most of the Yankees' hope.

Torre went out to take the ball from Clemens one more time, and the fans, crushed by the prospect of a loss they couldn't imagine, still responded. They thanked Clemens with a standing ovation, remembering the past few years—the big games he finally won, the 300th victory he claimed in front of them earlier in the year. He was a Yankee after all.

To most.

"My brother's on the phone," then-*Connecticut Post* writer Mike Puma said, laughing, in the auxiliary press seats. "He said, 'I always knew Clemens was a Red Sox at heart!'"

There wasn't much for the Yankee crowd to chuckle about, though.

Mike Mussina came in from the bullpen, the first time in his career he would come on in relief. Pitching coach Mel Stottlemyre had promised him he wouldn't bring him in during a tense situation, but, Stottlemyre would say later, "I lied."

Runners at first and third and no one out. One of the best pitchers in baseball ready to come back out for the rest of the game for Boston.

Only thing I can do, Mussina thought, is give them the run at third and get out of here down five.

He was wrong.

He struck out Jason Varitek.

Then the speedy Johnny Damon grounded to Jeter at short. Got one. Got two.

Double-play.

The crowd roared in relief, showing the smallest spurt of life. Still 4-0. Still have to face Pedro.

*** *** ***

It was as dark a scenario as the Yankees could have pictured. Pedro was near-ly perfect, retiring 10 of the last 11 he faced entering the bottom of the fifth.

In the bullpen, Rivera's teammates saw the look on his face, frustration, annoyance. He wanted to will them to win. He couldn't understand how they could lose. Not this game.

Giambi, who had struck out in the third, stepped up in the fifth. He had yet to fully adjust to New York in his second full season. He'd shown flashes, that dramatic walk-off grand slam in the rain welcoming him to the Bronx in 2002. But he was still stuck in the shadow of Tino Martinez. Especially after another postseason slump that dropped him from the cleanup spot.

So when Giambi jerked the ball out to center field, he jolted the fans to life.

Red Sox 4, Yankees 1.

One of the least likely players to give the Yankees hope just had. Maybe there was more than they thought. Nope. Not much.

Pedro retired the next seven batters, taking a 4-1 lead two outs into the seventh.

Again, Giambi stepped up. Again, he was on it. He smacked Pedro's pitch right back over the center-field wall and now the Yankees fans sprung from their seats. They had been seven outs from the unthinkable, but now it was just a two-run game, 4-2. It was a ballgame.

One that started to look more like one attended by the Bambino when Wilson, the Pedro-killer, bounced a ball toward first that hit the bag. ... No. It just hopped before it, bouncing fair, then foul, Millar chasing it and tripping on what seemed to be an invisible wire.

Blindsided by the Babe?

Now the Stadium stirred, ready to reclaim its arrogance. Pedro was tiring. They could get to him. They were the Yankees. These were the Red Sox.

Garcia singled to right. Roars. This was it. Up came Soriano. He was due.

Garciaparra went to the mound to settle Martinez. Said a couple of things. Pedro nodded. Drill the Bambino in the ass. He struck Soriano out.

Six outs to go.

In the dugout, Garciaparra hugged his teammate. They had survived the threat.

And Ortiz increased the one aimed at the Yankees, greeting David Wells with a moonshot home run for a 5-2 lead in the top of the eighth.

That was it.

The MLB officials started barking at the Yankees' clubhouse workers. Move the champagne to the Sox clubhouse. Set up the platform.

The painted World Series logo on the grass behind home at Fenway now seemed part of a premonition, not a premature decision.

The Sox were going to do it.

"Hey, you've finally got it," a Yankees fan conceded to a Red Sox fan.

With a rigidly ashen face, the Sox fan replied through gritted teeth "*It's not over yet.*"

*** *** ***

The murmuring started on the Yankees' bench. It extended to the bullpen. Pedro was getting tired. When was Grady Little going to lift him?

Right-hander reliever Mike Timlin hadn't given up an earned run in nine and two-thirds postseason innings. Lefty Alan Embree threw zeroes for six and two-thirds.

But Pedro was the ace, so Little stuck with him to start the eighth. And he looked fine when Nick Johnson popped out to Garciaparra at short. Five outs to go.

Forever.

Jeter doubled to right. Bernie Williams singled. Jeter scored. Red Sox 5, Yankees 3.

The fans were up again, safe to hope. Little was up, too, off to the mound.

And that was it. Martinez had pitched seven and one-third dominant innings, but was tiring at 115 pitches.

The Yankees waited for Little to tap his left arm for Embree and ...

The manager walked off the mound. Pedro stayed.

"This is the most blatant situation for a second-guess in this series," Tim McCarver told the Fox audience.

Up came Matsui.

They would play hard.

Win. Pop the bottles.

But first he had to do something here. So he did. Double to right. Tying run on second and the stadium was shaking now, loud as ever.

These were no longer the invincible Yankees the fans had known all through the late '90s. The ones that made you *know* they'd come back. But this was a taste of that feeling now and they wanted more, these Yankees knocking on the door of their predecessors.

Up came Posada, no time to think about all that finger-pointing with Pedro the other day. Trying not to think at all.

Just get a good pitch to hit. Get a good pitch to hit.

The count went to 2-2.

Posada got his pitch.

"Posada swings; a bloop ... shallow center ... falling ... *falling* ... basehit!" ESPN's Jon Miller called. "Here comes Williams ... Here comes Matsui ... it's tied up!"

At the plate, Matsui hopped up and down wildly, bouncing from team-mate to teammate, high-five to high-five. At second, Posada pumped both his fists, his body shaking awkwardly, his mouth howling along with the other 56,000 voices.

They had done it. They had come back.

The cheers jolted Rivera, who had been warming up in the bullpen. OK, he thought. We tied it up. We tied it up.

Finally, Pedro was gone, taking the long walk back to the dugout, stunned, stinging chants of "Pedrrroooo! Pedrrroooo!" ringing in his ears.

It had been his game all night. Then it wasn't. Just like that.

The Sox escaped the inning. No matter. Yankee Stadium was as vibrant as ever.

Especially when the strains of "Enter Sandman" started coming over the speaker system in the top of the ninth.

With Rivera in the game, it was only a matter of time before Sinatra sang "New York, New York" through those same speakers, right?

Rivera pitched a scoreless ninth. Shocker.

In the bottom of the inning, clubhouse kid Luigi Castillo ran into Boone, now in the game at third, in the locker room.

"Hey, Squeegie, you nervous?" Boone asked.

"Yeah!" Castillo replied. "Aren't you?"

"Nah," Boone said, smiling. "Don't be nervous. We'll be fine."

*** *** ***

The Yankees couldn't score in the ninth. Or the 10th.

The safety net was running out; Rivera could go one more inning, tops.

Wakefield, who had come on for Timlin in the 10th, started his second inning of work in the 11th.

Boone stepped in, not nervous. He wouldn't hide, his brother Bret had said the other day.

Wakefield threw a knuckler. It didn't dance. Or move. It sat there, waiting for Boone's bat to claim it.

"There's a fly ball deep to left ... it's on its way ... there it goes!" Yankees broadcaster Charley Steiner announced on WCBS radio. "And the Yankees are going to the World Series, for the 39th time in their remarkable history!"

Boone extended his arms immediately, lifting them up with a shrug, half-celebration, half-disbelief.

As he trotted around the bases, Rivera raced for the mound, "New York, New York" starting on that seemingly endless loop, the whole place singing along again.

They had done it.

They had done it. How on earth had they done it?

After he finally rose from the mound and was carried off the field, Rivera joined his teammates in a celebration more emotional than they could recall.

And as he walked under the tunnel, Rivera screamed out in relief to no one in particular.

"Cowboy down!" he said. "We *shot* that cowboy."

*** *** ***

Game of My Life
Mariano Rivera

"This one meant a lot because this one was such a good series.

"(Because of the confrontations with Pedro and near-brawls?) Nah, nah. The game itself. You're gonna feel good to the end. Everyone was exhausted. Everyone was exhausted. But you have so much adrenaline in the game, you forget about it. Everyone was exhausted, everyone was tired. We fight.

"(Did he want to make up for 2001?) No, that was history. I wasn't thinking about it. I really don't care about that because I know who I am. I know what I can do. Blow two games a year and everyone's (worried). I'm human. I'm not a machine. All of a sudden, you lose two games. ...

"It was such a great series. Wanted to win it. I wanted to win it. That was that day, something was broke. The water pipe. ... So I got to the stadium late. There was traffic everywhere. It was amazing. Like, 'Wow, everything.' The biggest game, you're just going late. It was funny. Everything was happening.

"I went to the bullpen in the fifth inning. We were losing. Big trouble. 4-0. Man, I was upset. I was like, 'C'mon, let's do it. C'mon, we've gotta do something here. Didn't come all the way here to lose this kind of game like this.'

When they see Rivera on the mound, the Yankees usually think "It's over" as captain Derek Jeter said of baseball's all-time saves leader, famous for closing out one postseason win after the other. But Rivera would come through against the Red Sox in a different role, ensuring the game would continue for three innings until Aaron Boone won it with his historic home run. *Doug Pensinger/Getty Images.*

"Had that conversation with the Lord. It's like, 'C'mon,' you know? I was upset. It's not possible. All of a sudden, everything started changing. Everything started changing.

"Jason hit a home run. Then again. Wow. Think it was 5-3, 5-2. Ortiz hit a home run. ... I was like, 'OK.' Everything started changing.

"I didn't see (Posada's game-tying hit) because I was throwing. I just started hearing the noise, and screaming. And I looked and yeah, we tied the game. 'OK.'

"That was in the eighth inning, but I thought they were gonna pull Pedro in the seventh. And their bullpen was doing good. I mean, their bullpen was doing really good. I was like, 'OK, we've gotta find some way, some how to win this game.' Then they leave him there and I say, 'OK, this is is a sign. This is a sign right here.'

"Jeter. Then Bernie. Then Matsui. Then Jorge gets that little blooper.

"(Entering the ninth in a tie game) Oh, I knew. I knew it was going to be me. I wanted to be there. Ninth inning, game tied, you've gotta go to your closer. Hometown. You've gotta go to your closer.

"One inning at a time, you know, because ... we had chances to win it. Things happen so I keep going back there. I think Ortiz hit a double with two outs. Then I thought, 'I've gotta get this guy out.'

"(Going into the 10th inning) Mel told me, 'You're good for another inning.' 'Yeah, I'm ready.'

"And then we got to the third inning, was 1-2-3. Came back in. I mean, I was ready for the fourth. I was ready for the fourth. But Mel told me, 'No, no, no.'

"I was like 'Oh, c'mon.' Mel told me no. I said, 'No, man, c'mon. You sure?' Mel said, 'No, but we're gonna score one run. We're gonna score right here.'

"All of a sudden, one pitch, home run.

"(When I collapsed on the mound), I was just thankful. Thankful. Thankful to the Lord. Amazing. Amazing how the Lord works. I was just thankful. Exhausted and crying. You know, as a Christian, when things happen like that, it's just a sign, basically. The Lord loves you, you know? That's the beauty of it. That's the beauty of it.

"(If we had lost) No, I wouldn't have been upset with the Lord. I lost in the World Series. Because there's always a reason why things happen.

"(Most emotional game ever) Definitely. Yeah. Because of the way we won. Because of the way the whole series was. And, you know, being there and fighting like a team. That was the thing. And the Lord supporting us right there.

"I've been in big games, don't get me wrong. But this was the best."

*** *** ***

The curse lived.

Rivera's blessing remained.

The ghosts of Yankee Stadium seemingly rose every October during that Yankees' era, at least at Yankee Stadium. Sometimes there seemed to be no other explanation. Or, at least, the unexplainable seemed no less plausible than anything else.

But that's not where the real ghosts come from for the Yankees' teams who are most remembered.

What drives those Yankees each year is born as much of the present and future as it is the past. Born from the haunting feeling of not living up to a tradition that demands your absolute best, the baton passed from one generation to the next.

Those who don't live up to their championship predecessors become ghosts of a different sort, disappearing, fading; their memories obscured by mediocrity on a team that won't tolerate it.

It's been the same since Ruth set the standard, and young players like Tommy Henrich first yearned to live up to it eight decades ago.

You become aware of where you are. Realize you'd better do something if you want to stay there and fit in.

What does it mean to be a Yankee?

What makes the players who follow in Ruth's footsteps able to perform on the biggest stage in sports?

"See that's the way that I won't think about it," Rivera said. "No, no, no. You have 25 heroes here. Twenty-five stars. Every individual has to do their job. That night was, whoever. That doesn't mean he's a hero or superstar, it means that that's the job that he's supposed to do. He did his job. And he gave us an opportunity to win.

"That's that."

CHAPTER 21

CC Sabathia:
"That's What You Come to New York For"

October 16, 2009, ALCS Game 1

Vs. Anaheim
Yankees 4, Angels 1

The stats:

IP	H	R	ER	BB	SO
8	4	1	1	1	7

He didn't try to pretend he had nothing to prove, because there was always something to prove. From the time he was a boy on those Little League mounds, back in Vallejo, Calif., he had been like this.

CC Sabathia would cry because he couldn't get all the hitters out, and his mother, Margie, would have none of that. One time she yanked him right off the mound, told him to go ride his bike home. Her big kid with the given name of Carsten Charles and the frame that would one day reach 6-foot-7 and 290 pounds wasn't allowed much of a response, so he just did what he was told.

But the frustrating blend of emotion and perfectionism that would serve as a blessing and a curse through Sabathia's career would stubbornly persist.

Had to prove himself. Always. Every start.

The difference between the 29-year-old man awarded the richest contract a pitcher had signed, the one about to take the ball for the Yankees in Game 1 of the 2009 American League Championship Series, and that crying 12-year-old?

After striking out Angels pinch hitter Mike Napoli to end the seventh in Game 1 of the 2009 ALCS, CC Sabathia remembered "it being so loud in the stadium and just getting, like, the goosebumps and being really fired up." Sabathia was on his way to two wins and an ALCS MVP award, eventually helping the Yankees claim their first World Series title in nine years.
AP Photo/Kathy Willens

Well, not all that much in some ways, Sabathia would admit. He would no longer cry on the mound, but the emotions could always creep in and take him out of an inning and frustrate him and … And that would not happen against the Angels, he promised himself.

It couldn't.

This is what he had come to New York for, both for himself and the Yankees.

He had something to prove and so did they.

He had helped lead the Cleveland Indians within a game of the World Series in 2007, but the Boston Red Sox beat him up in a potential clincher, and stormed back from a 3-1 deficit in the series to stun the Indians. That came three years after Boston shocked the Yankees, making that baseball-history-shaking comeback from a 3-0 deficit in 2004 to forever change the dynamic of the rivalry and go on to its first World Series victory since 1918.

It had not been nearly that long without a title in the Bronx, but in Yankee years, a nine-year World Series drought and five-year hiatus from at least reaching the ALCS damn near seemed like it at times.

So, after missing the playoffs in 2008, the Yankees stunned the baseball world by denting their hefty bankroll to add another top free agent in Mark Teixeira along with Sabathia and A.J. Burnett, committing nearly half a billion dollars on the three players.

So Sabathia knew how important it was for him to get past his playoff history against the Red Sox and his one bad start for the Brewers in 2008, which came after he exhaustively carried Milwaukee on his back down the stretch to reach the postseason.

He knew it was important for the Yankees to show they could finally get past an Angels team that had twice knocked them out of the postseason in the past seven years.

"The Yankees had had trouble against the Angels in the playoffs and it was a huge series, and I felt like that was the reason why I came to New York, to help them get over the hump," Sabathia said.

So he told himself before the game not to overthrow. To "stay within myself." He tried to settle the nerves that always threatened to derail him, from the time he was a kid to when he was a young star with the Indians left to figure it out on his own when veteran Bartolo Colon was traded.

Back then, Sabathia could lose so much focus when things went wrong, and he once apologized to his teammates and fans for doing so, because he felt like he had given up in a start.

But he was not as young now. He was the guy, the laid-back Californian choosing the frenzy of New York as a free agent in December 2008 because he craved winning more than the comforts of home. And because his wife, Amber, and the kids would be with him and they could make anywhere home as long as they were together.

Together was the vital part. CC knew that as well as anyone. Knew it because he missed that as a kid, when one day the dad he was named after, who took him to all those baseball and football games and on all those bike rides, disappeared.

The drugs took his father away at a crucial time, but 12-year-old CC's mother never let bitterness take over her heart, so it didn't steal her son's either. Eventually, he would reconcile with his father, embrace him, listen to his dad tell him, "You're going to be playing in New York, you're gonna win a World Series in New York."

CC would smile and all but wave his hand, still a young pitcher for the Indians, one who wanted to play so badly that as a rookie he had his mother finally negotiate his bonus so he could get started when talks stalled through his agent, as she later told Sports Illustrated.

Nah, Dad. That won't happen.

"You watch," his father would tell him. "Steinbrenner's gonna come get you, they want you in New York."

The young pitcher's ego would rise along with his bank balance, and he would begin to party, donning thousands of dollars of jewelry while shedding his relationship with high school sweetheart, Amber, as well as his mother's advice to slow down.

The words did not affect Sabathia, 21 years old and a millionaire, out on his own in 2002 and enjoying the lifestyle that came with sudden success in the big leagues, after going 17-5 the previous year, in his rookie season.

But the gun pointed at the back of his head did.

It was held by former Cleveland State basketball player Damon Stringer, in a downtown Marriott in Cleveland. There, Stringer and former Cleveland State teammate Jamaal Harris would catch sight of Sabathia's expensive jewelry and intercept him and Sabathia's cousin, Jomar Connors, in the elevator. The robbers would go back to Sabathia's room and come away with $44,102 worth of cash and jewelry, according to police, but eventually were caught and convicted.

Sabathia would come away with a clarity that ultimately proved much more valuable.

Suddenly, the budding superstar no longer felt the allure of the fancy jewelry and the wild nights out as much as he did the need for the people who would keep him from requiring such things.

He called his mother, frightened.

He called Amber, remorseful.

Let's get married, he told his then-ex-girlfriend. This wouldn't have happened if you were here.

They all came out. Amber. His mother. His father, who had been weakened by HIV, and would die the next year of stomach cancer at 47. The same year CC married Amber and welcomed Carsten Charles III, his first son, who he would call "Lil C."

"It was a life-changing decision," Sabathia said of the perspective the robbery provided, to propose to Amber and ask his parents to come to Cleveland. "I immediately knew right after, the very next morning. There was no question. Wanting to be committed, make sure I was making the right decisions. I felt like having her there and my mom there and my dad, that was the right choice to make. I think it was 100 percent a fork in the road and being able to have that opportunity ... You know, most people don't get that until it's too late. I felt like that was one of those times where I needed to make a change and I did and it worked out for the best and it was a blessing.

"Being 22 years old, top of the world, you know you're invincible. No one can say anything ... For most people, it ends up being too late. I think I was just blessed enough to be able to come out of my situation and still have my career and still have everything in front of me."

Sabathia would be grateful for the bonding time again with his father, before he lost him. And grateful to his mother for her part in allowing the men to reconnect. The toughness that Margie Sabathia showed in raising her son— even suiting up in catcher's gear to catch CC until his 14-year-old future major-league arm became too much for her to handle—extended way past a baseball field. Thanks in part to her ability to forgive her son's father, CC's memory of him includes a reconciliation along with the disappointment.

"We went through some tough times, and he definitely could have been there a little more than he was," Sabathia said of his father. "He was dealing with some drug problems. He could have definitely been there a little more.

"But I have to give my mom a lot of credit that she never bad-mouthed him, she never once said anything that would make me be upset with him. It felt like I owed her ... to be able to kind of pick up our relationship where it left off when they split. I'm definitely grateful to her for that, him being passed now and to be able to have him around those extra years in my late teens and early 20s really made a huge difference."

The difference was especially huge in 2003, when the cancer had weakened the elder Sabathia, known to friends and family as Corky. He had moved back to California, where Margie took care of the man she never divorced. Doctors told him he shouldn't travel, even when Lil C was born. But the man who couldn't show up in Sabathia's early teens would find a way to be there to see his boy have one of his own sons.

"He was really sick when he passed away, the doctors and everybody said he kind of hung on to see my son," Sabathia said. "He flew to Cleveland, the doctors said he shouldn't have done that, because he was in California. He was able to be there when he was born.

"So it was good to be able to have that, after my Dad left, to be able to be around him and to forgive him and all that stuff."

*** *** ***

Alex Rodriguez would often say he couldn't have handled New York or the Yankees when he was younger, that he needed to mature. Sabathia would likely agree regarding himself.

"It's something that when I was in Cleveland early in my career, I had a big problem with," Sabathia said of controlling his focus on the mound. "My emotions, you get too high, you get too low. ... It was tough. ... I had a lot of people who helped me work it out.

In Cleveland, his progress culminated with him winning the Cy Young Award in 2007, when he went 19-7 with a 3.21 ERA and 209 strikeouts in 241 innings.

But then came that stunning postseason loss to the Red Sox. Injuries decimated the Indians the next season, turning what should have been a perennial playoff contender, with Sabathia and 2008 Cy Young Award winner Cliff Lee as a potent 1-2 combination, into a yard sale.

Traded to the Brewers in July, Sabathia quickly dismissed his disappointment at the lost opportunity in Cleveland and created one in Milwaukee. He went 11-2 with a 1.65 ERA, completing seven of his 17 starts, including a controversial one-hitter, in which the Brewers attempted vainly to have an infield single changed to an error for Sabathia. Most importantly, Sabathia threw on three days' rest repeatedly down the stretch to help the Brewers reach the playoffs for the first time in 25 years.

Exhausted, he would cough up five runs in 3 2/3 innings in a playoff loss to the Phillies, who would go on to win the World Series.

"Us playing basically playoff games for the last 10 days, I think it took a toll on us," Sabathia would say as he prepared for his first playoff run with the Yankees the next year. "We kind of ran out of gas during the playoffs."

But, he added, "I think those experiences that I've had the last couple of years in the playoffs will make me a lot better."

*** *** ***

He started his Yankees career dangerously close to serving as another example of disappointment and opulence, the high-paid pitcher getting shelled in his first two starts for his new team. The second came in the $1.5 billion palace of a ballpark known as the new Yankee Stadium. The place infamous, when it opened, for the "moat" that would cut off blue-collar fans from the new Legends Suites designed to target the type of corporate fans more apt to wear out their voices making pitches to clients than cheering.

Sabathia could have appeared to fit a cynical portrait of the 2009 Yankees, constructed from oodles of cash, such as the seven-year, $161-million deal the lefty signed, a record number for a pitcher. Or the Yankees' overall gaudy spending spree designed to christen their new home in style and end their World Series drought a year after they missed the playoffs for the first time in 14 years.

But, upon closer inspection, Sabathia did not fit the profile of some big-money mercenary, mostly because he had earned that cash by being exactly the opposite.

One of the reasons the Yankees couldn't help but lure Sabathia with everything from an open checkbook to general manager Brian Cashman's recruiting trip to California was because he had showed the previous year just what he was willing to do to earn that money.

Sabathia couldn't stop pitching on short rest, regardless of his agent's fears that he could be damaging his arm and, by extension, his value as he headed into his big free-agency pay day.

He had to take the ball.

"I think I love to play," Sabathia said of his penchant for pitching on short rest in an era when it's often discouraged. "Most of the time in Milwaukee everyone talks about, 'What made you pitch on three days' rest?' I didn't want the season to be over.

"And we had some guys hurt and guys go down, and I felt like if this is the best opportunity we have to win, then I'll take the ball. It comes from not wanting to lose and wanting to play."

After so many failed attempts to get past the first round—and failed would-be pitching saviors— this was the guy.

But Sabathia loved living in California, where he would eventually start his PitCCh In Foundation to help his neighborhood of Vallejo, where drugs sometimes loomed as a threat to the potential of kids like young CC, who dodged the trap.

It took him weeks to mull the Yankees' initial offer, which came in at six years, $140 million, and reports indicated Sabathia preferred to pitch in his home state of California, for the Dodgers or Giants. It took a visit from Cashman—who left the baseball winter meetings in Las Vegas and flew to California—to seal the deal. Along with an extra year, $21 million more, and an opt-out clause after three years, protection in case Sabathia got homesick.

Finally, Sabathia made his decision.

"Ten minutes after he left my house, I looked at my wife and said, 'I'm going to be a Yankee,'" Sabathia said at his first Yankees press conference. "I still get chills saying that."

Once Sabathia made his decision, he committed all the way, quelling concerns he didn't want to pitch in New York. He bought a house in Alpine, N.J., to set up roots. Three years later, he signed a contract extension instead of opting out, despite heavy speculation he would again enter free agency.

"Well, I mean, obviously everyone wants to have a chance to play at home," he said, reflecting on his thought process. "And that's what I had to kick around. But do I want to be home or do I want to have a chance to win every year? Amber and I, we always talk about wherever it's just us together and the kids, we can be wherever, and we'll make that home."

The chills Sabathia described would hit him throughout his first year.

He met the Boss a few times in spring training, George Steinbrenner humbled by age and weakness in his last year of life. But the Boss still had enough of a presence to intimidate Sabathia—and to put him at ease.

"I was nervous. I was scared to death," Sabathia said. "Really nervous. Trying to think of something to talk about. But he was really cool. He was laid back. He knew who I was, he knew all my stats. We talked about baseball. I think it helped a little bit that Reggie [Jackson] was there. Made it a little more comfortable for me. It was good."

Despite weeks of spring training as a Yankee, Sabathia suddenly felt the magnitude of his status as he prepared to take the ball on Opening Day in Baltimore.

"It's something that I didn't really realize until I got here, that it's baseball history," he said. "It's fun to be a part of it and put on the pinstripes. I always tell the story that I didn't realize how—and this is gonna sound cliché, or kind of phony—but I remember sitting in the locker room [when] I started the first game against Baltimore, Opening Day.

"... To actually put on—and it wasn't even the pinstripes, it was the away uniforms, it said 'New York' across the front. It kind of gave me goosebumps. 'I'm pitching for the Yankees.'"

He would not pitch well for the Yankees that day, Sabathia humbled as he gave up six runs in 4 1/3 innings, in a 10-5 loss.

Things would not get much better at the new Yankee Stadium opener against the Indians, when the fanfare of the new ballpark, with its high-class restaurants and Grand Hall, would draw praise for its amenities and criticism for a palatial feel and extravagantly-priced seats..

The famed Yankee Stadium "ghosts" were gone now, along with the latest dynasty's aura of invincibility. Sabathia and his fellow big-name newcomers were brought in to put this team over the top, not blend in. They had something to prove. As did Alex Rodriguez, who would attempt to rewrite his own failed championship bids in an especially difficult way, embarrassed in spring training by his admission that he had used performance-enhancing drugs years before and humbled by a hip surgery that would keep him out the season's first month.

"The park still looks kind of like the old stadium," Sabathia told reporters after the game. "But it's a weird feeling, too. Going out ... it being a clean slate, a new era of Yankee baseball."

Sabathia would pitch a lot better, though his control hurt him a bit, as he gave up one run, but walked five and left after 5 2/3 innings against his old team and old pal, starter Cliff Lee. The Yankees would lose 10-2 and get off to a slow start.

Looking back, Sabathia said all the fanfare of those first two games, as well as his first time pitching against the Red Sox, is exactly what he would eventually need.

*** *** ***

The Yankees' star-studded juggernaut soon righted itself. Rodriguez returned and homered in his first at-bat, setting the tone for what would be a redemptive season for him on the field, even if his performance could not clear the taint of his admitted PED use.

The rest of the newcomers helped Sabathia fit in and he would do the same, his jovial personality quickly helping to mend fences in what had been a clubhouse with some fractures. Mark Teixeira took the pressure off Sabathia and vice versa. A.J. Burnett brought fun with his famed cream pie celebrations as the Yankees energized the new stadium with one walk-off win after the other. And Nick Swisher? The dude full of energy and fun chipped away at the Yankees' old businesslike approach.

It just all clicked.

Sabathia was as big a reason as any, going 19-8 with a 3.37 ERA and taking on his famed workhorse role by throwing 230 innings. But this time he didn't have to exhaust himself down the stretch as he did the year before.

As the postseason began, Sabathia was ready to take the ball as often as possible to do what he came to New York to do—to finally get that 27th World Series the Yankees sought, as evidenced by the uniform number on manager Joe Girardi's back.

*** *** ***

Sabathia pitched the Yankees past the Minnesota Twins in Game 1 of the American League Division Series, picking up a 7-2 victory behind a pair of two-run homers, from Derek Jeter and Hideki Matsui.

The Yankees swept the Twins and advanced to their first ALCS since the infamous series against the Red Sox in 2004.

But as much as Sabathia appreciated that win, for himself, and his team, he knew it was only a step.

It was World Series or bust, and that journey continued with him getting the ball in Game 1 of the ALCS.

The Angels had a lineup loaded with pesky hitters who could be nuisances on the bases. They pestered the Yankees throughout a pair of playoff series earlier in the decade, both times humbling a supposed Yankees' juggernaut.

This was no time for Sabathia to fall victim to the emotion that could make him unravel, because the Angels would prey on such behavior.

On a frigid night with vicious winds that prompted the teams to dress for winter during warmups, Sabathia tried to shrug off the cold, since he pitched so often in Cleveland. But later even he acknowledged "it was about as cold as it gets" and dubbed the weather "pretty nasty."

So was Sabathia.

The Yankees quickly put him up 2-0 in the first when they took advantage of a rare Angels error and Alex Rodriguez drove in a run with a sacrifice fly and Hideki Matsui singled in another one.

Sabathia took it from there, mixing his fastball with his changeup and off-speed pitches, to dominate the Angels.

The Angels reached him for a run in the fourth, when Vladimir Guerrero doubled and Kendrys Morales singled him in with two outs, to make it 2-1.

But Sabathia would not unravel. Not feel anything like that little kid who was sent home on his bike. He secured the last out of that inning, and retired the next eight batters, even pouncing off the mound to snag a bunt by Torii Hunter and throw him out at first.

The Yankees added to the lead, Matsui doubling in another run to make it 3-1 in the fifth, before the Angels had another rare miscue in the sixth that led to an unearned run to make it 4-1.

With one out in the seventh, Sabathia, prone to wildness in previous postseasons, walked his first batter of the game, also his first of the '09 play-offs. With two outs, and the runner on second, Sabathia geared up to face pinch hitter Mike Napoli.

The new Yankee Stadium crowd began a chant it had not yet roared:

"CC! CC! CC!" the fans screamed.

The adrenaline surged through Sabathia, whose emotions might inwardly wreck havoc, but who rarely showed them on the mound.

Until he struck out Napoli to end the seventh and caused the fans to unleash their glee.

Sabathia howled right along with them, pumping his valuable left arm and pointing to the Yankees' dugout as he walked off the mound, not yet knowing he would come back for one more scoreless inning.

"That was a great feeling to have the stadium rocking and to be chanting my name, and to be able to get a strikeout," Sabathia said after the game. "I was pretty pumped up. I don't really show a lot of emotion a lot of times, but it came out of me there."

It was one game, but it sent exactly the message Sabathia wanted to deliver. To the Angels. To his teammates. To the fans, who had entered the new Yankee Stadium and the new era wondering if it would be different from the last few years.

He could do this. He could beat the Angels, and so could the Yankees. They could finally end the World Series drought.

*** *** ***

Game of My Life
CC Sabathia

"The game, probably, pitching in the ALCS, that first year in 2009, starting Game 1 at Yankee Stadium, was the most memorable for me.

"I just think at that point it was probably the biggest game I had pitched in my career, being able to pitch in the ALCS for the Yankees—obviously we won the World Series that year. At that point, that just sticks out to me the most, Game 1 in the Bronx, new stadium. That game sticks out more so than any one.

"It was amazing, and you know the whole year, I pitched Opening Day that year, I pitched the first game in the new stadium, first game I started against Boston, being a Yankee, I think all those games prepared me for being ready for that atmosphere and for that Game 1. It was great from the start; I walked out of the dugout, people were cheering, the stadium was loud. It just had that New York feel; that's what you come to New York for.

"Throughout the year, I had gotten really close to Andy [Pettitte], getting a chance to talk to him and be a close friend of his, have him talk about all the stories, the World Series, and all these different strategies he had to go through, and I think it really helped me, him more so than any other guy my whole time I've been in New York, especially my first year.

"I think that I was pretty hyped up for the game, but my emotions were under control and I was just pedal to the metal. I remember telling myself, 'Go out and [try not] to overthrow and try to stay within myself,' which is a big thing for me. I remember throwing the first fastball and it was 93, 94, and usually I have to hype up to get 93, 94 now, so having the ball come out that easy, it felt like I had a lot of power, felt like I was in command, felt like it was going to be a good night. I just remember telling myself in between pitches, in between innings, you know, 'Just keep your foot on their throat and don't let 'em come up for air or give them any kind of momentum.' Especially being Game 1 and being in New York, I kind of wanted to make a statement, and we did that that first game.

"... [When the Yankees scored two in the first] that kind of helped me settle in. I just remember that being a really tough lineup and not wanting to give them any momentum. Them scoring those two runs right off the bat helped a lot.

"I didn't know if I was finished or not, but I just remember walking off [to finish the seventh]. ... I just remember it being so loud in the stadium and just getting, like, the goosebumps and being really fired up. I've had some big moments, obviously winning the World Series a couple weeks later, but that was probably the one that'll stick out the most, so far."

*** *** ***

Sabathia did it again three days later, again taking the ball on short rest. He allowed one run in eight innings in a 10-1 victory that put the Yankees up 3-1 in the series. That allowed them to step on the Angels' throats, with a pair of performances that earned Sabathia the ALCS MVP.

"He's a horse. He's a monster," Alex Rodriguez, who had three hits and a home run amid his own monstrous playoff run, said after the game.

They won the series in six games, Sabathia's buddy, Pettitte, clinching a trip to the World Series, part of a unique trifecta in which the perennial post-season star won the deciding game of each playoff series. Finally, the Yankees returned to baseball's grandest stage.

Sabathia again faced his old teammate, Cliff Lee, in the World Series opener against the Phillies, and Lee out-dueled him in Philadelphia's Game 1 win. Sabathia gave up only a pair of solo homers to red-hot Chase Utley, but the bullpen imploded in a 6-1 loss.

But Lee would not do what Sabathia had, when he so desperately want-ed to ensure his team's season would continue. Sabathia once more took the ball on short rest in Game 4, while the Phillies opted not to bring back their ace for another showdown, despite trailing the Series 2-1.

Sabathia gave the Yankees 6 2/3 innings of three-run ball and left with a 4-3 lead. He would not get the victory, but the Yankees would, 7-4, stunning the Phillies with a two-out rally for three runs in the ninth. Johnny Damon famously stole two bases on one play, and Rodriguez again came through with a clutch hit, doubling him in before Jorge Posada singled in two more runs.

All the familiar faces had blended in with the new ones and by the Series-clinching game, Hideki Matsui, once the high-profile free agent signee, finally helped ensure all of them would get what they had sought when they joined the Yankees.

Matsui tied a World Series record with six RBI in the 7-3 win in Game 6, tagging old rival Pedro Martinez for a home run in the second, among his three hits, and leading the Yankees to that coveted 27th World Series.

They celebrated throughout the new Yankee Stadium, from the Core Four of Derek Jeter, Mariano Rivera, Pettitte and Posada, to long-awaited champion Rodriguez, to the new gang of Sabathia, Mark Teixeira, A.J. Burnett and Nick Swisher.

"That was unbelievable," Sabathia said. "It being the first year for the new stadium, a bunch of guys coming in—Tex, A.J., Swish, being able to pull it all together … it felt like the whole year we were gonna win, and be able go out and put it together, put together a championship season."

Above it all, the giant stadium scoreboard screen displayed a simple mes-sage.

"Boss, this one's for you!"

George Steinbrenner was not well enough to be at the ballpark. He would die the next year, the new Yankee Stadium turning as somber in memo-riam as it was loud on this night. But the Yankees saluted him as they cele-brated their title.

"This is for him," Hal Steinbrenner, who had been in charge of the cur-rent Yankees, told reporters of his father. "The entire postseason, this whole team has felt that way."

Sabathia appreciated the opportunity to bring the Boss one more ring, and the chance to claim a piece of that Yankees' aura he had felt in awe of months earlier.

"I think that's just being a part of Yankee history, to hear Jete talk about the Boss and hear 'Sado and Mo and Andy, and be a part of something special, especially with those guys, it feels good," Sabathia said.

He celebrated with his family, Amber next to him in the bedlam of the clubhouse and six-year-old Lil C up on his shoulders, later telling his Dad how he had fended off Phillies fans who critiqued his Yankees gear during the series.

Even years later, the first of Sabathia's four children would watch the World Series DVD and tell all the stories, from the clubhouse to the parade. And his father, who would be sure to take him to plenty of other sporting events, would smile.

"Me and my son have the exact same relationship as me and my dad," Sabathia said. "We're really close, we're really tight."

As Sabathia called his mother amid the celebration, the woman who used to scold him right off the mound congratulated him. And she reminded him of the prediction his father had made.

"Your dad called it," she told him, reminding Sabathia how his father had always said he would go to New York and win a World Series.

"And it kind of brought me back and remembered, and he did," Sabathia said. "He always believed that, but for it to happen the very first year I get here is pretty crazy."

In that moment, Sabathia had nothing to prove. Instead, he said, "It was just pure joy."

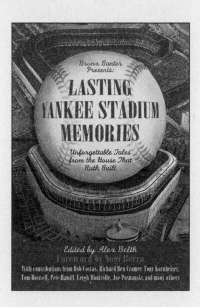

Lasting Yankee Stadium Memories

Unforgettable Tales from the House That Ruth Built

Edited by Alex Belth
Foreword by Yogi Berra

In *Lasting Yankee Stadium Memories*, editor Alex Belth of BronxBanterBlog.com collects personal essays by some of the most well-known and respected voices in sportswriting and entertainment today. In these revealing, sometimes hilarious, oft-touching essays, the contributors recount their favorite moments inside the most famed of all American stadiums. The book also includes a special chapter on the new Yankee Stadium.

Contributors include: Bob Costas (NBC, HBO) • Richard Ben Cramer • Pete Hamill • Tony Kornheiser (ESPN) • Tom Boswell (*Washington Post*) • Dave Kindred (*Washington Post*) • Leigh Montville (*Sports Illustrated*) • William Nack (*Sports Illustrated*) • Joe Posnanski (*Sports Illustrated*) • Jane Leavy • Pat Jordan • Maury Allen (*New York Post*) • Bob Klapisch (*Bergen Record*) • Tyler Kepner (*New York Times*) • Allen Barra (*Wall Street Journal*) • Marty Appel • Jeff Pearlman • Alan Schwarz (*New York Times*) • Charles Pierce (*Boston Globe*) • Steve Rushin (*Sports Illustrated*) • Nathan Ward • Mike Vaccaro (*New York Post*) • Rob Neyer (ESPN.com) • Ken Rosenthal (ESPN) • Scott Raab (*Esquire*) • Luis Guzman

$14.95 Paperback • ISBN: 978-1-60239-979-2

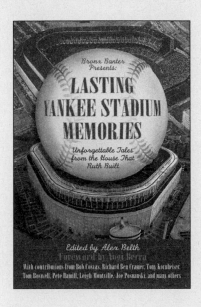

Lasting Yankee Stadium Memories

Unforgettable Tales from the House That Ruth Built

Edited by Alex Belth
Foreword by Yogi Berra

In *Lasting Yankee Stadium Memories*, editor Alex Belth of BronxBanterBlog. com collects personal essays by some of the most well-known and respected voices in sportswriting and entertainment today. In these revealing, sometimes hilarious, oft-touching essays, the contributors recount their favorite moments inside the most famed of all American stadiums. The book also includes a special chapter on the new Yankee Stadium.

Contributors include: Bob Costas • Richard Ben Cramer • Pete Hamill • Tony Kornheiser • Tom Boswell • Dave Kindred • Leigh Montville • William Nack • Joe Posnanski • Jane Leavy • Pat Jordan • Maury Allen • Bob Klapisch • Tyler Kepner • Allen Barra • Marty Appel • Jeff Pearlman • Alan Schwarz • Charles Pierce • Steve Rushin • Nathan Ward • Mike Vaccaro • Rob Neyer • Ken Rosenthal • Scott Raab • Luis Guzman

$14.95 Paperback • ISBN: 978-1-61321-237-0

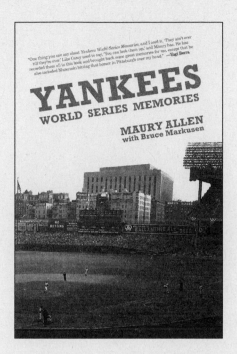

Yankees World Series Memories

by Maury Allen with Bruce Markusen

No two phrases in American baseball go together better than "World Series Champions" and "New York Yankees." The most iconic franchise in American sports, the Yankees have taken home 27 World Series titles. Out of the thousands of games and millions of memories that have come to define this epic team, Maury Allen has distilled the greatest championship moments in this newly revised edition of *Yankees World Series Memories*. The name says it all—within these pages readers can relive all the glory, passion, and excitement of Yankees domination. Critical reading for any baseball fan, *Yankees World Series Memories* is a nail-biting compendium of athleticism and skill. Readers young and old will relish tales of baseball's golden age and the thrill of modern victories. From Yogi Berra to Derek Jeter, Maury Allen highlights the absolute best of Yankees baseball.

$16.95 Hardcover • ISBN: 978-1-61321-095-6